The EVERYTHING
Get-a-Job Book

Dear Reader,

When I first started working in the career-planning arena in the early 1990s, the job market was difficult. I saw how looking for work added a huge amount of stress to people's lives. Whether it was the financial implications of being unemployed that kept them up at night or the fear of rejection that loomed large in front of them, this was one of the most difficult situations many of my clients had faced. I, myself, was not a stranger to the job search, and knew how grueling it could be.

Fortunately there are ways to turn the odds in your favor when it comes to looking for work, and I am pleased to present them to you. Remember that, for the most part, you are in control of this situation. Sure, the job market may not always be favorable, but there is a lot you can do to improve your chances of finding a job. The most important thing you can do, though, is to remain positive. A positive attitude is just as important as a good resume.

Best of Luck!

Dawn Rosenberg McKay

The EVERYTHING® Series

Editorial

Publisher	Gary M. Krebs
Director of Product Development	Paula Munier
Managing Editor	Laura M. Daly
Associate Copy Chief	Sheila Zwiebel
Acquisitions Editor	Lisa Laing
Development Editor	Katie McDonough
Associate Production Editor	Casey Ebert

Production

Director of Manufacturing	Susan Beale
Associate Director of Production	Michelle Roy Kelly
Prepress	Erick DaCosta Matt LeBlanc
Design and Layout	Heather Barrett Brewster Brownville Colleen Cunningham Jennifer Oliveira
Series Cover Artist	Barry Littmann

Visit the entire Everything® Series at *www.everything.com*

THE
EVERYTHING®
GET-A-JOB
BOOK

2nd Edition

The tools and strategies you need to
land the job of your dreams

Dawn Rosenberg McKay

Adams Media
Avon, Massachusetts

This book is dedicated to my family.
Your support and patience mean so much.

An Everything® Series Book.
Everything® and everything.com® are registered trademarks of F+W Publications, Inc.

Published by Adams Media, an F+W Publications Company
57 Littlefield Street, Avon, MA 02322 U.S.A.
www.adamsmedia.com

ISBN 10: 1-59869-159-7
ISBN 13: 978-1-59869-159-7

Printed in the United States of America.

J I H G F E D C B A

Library of Congress Cataloging-in-Publication Data
is available from the publisher.

This book is available at quantity discounts for bulk purchases.
For information, please call 1-800-289-0963.

Contents

Other Letters / 113

Looking for a Job Online / 123

Employment Services / 135

Researching Companies / 145

Interviewing / 157

New and Recent Graduates / 239

The Mature Job Candidate / 249

Top Ten Reasons to Get a New Job

1. Your boss is driving you crazy.

2. Your coworkers are driving you crazy.

3. You have climbed as high as you can up the corporate ladder.

4. Your boss has asked you to put your job ahead of your family.

5. Your boss has taken away many of your responsibilities.

6. Your job saps you of energy and motivation.

7. Your employer wants you to do something illegal or unethical.

8. You think you should earn more money and your boss has refused to give you a raise.

9. You want more responsibility.

10. You lost your job.

cknowledgments

Thank you to my friend and business partner Michele Lipson.
Your research skills are beyond compare.

Introduction

▶ THE JOB SEARCH. If the mere words scare you, you'd better get used to them. You will be engaged in this process at least once, but almost definitely more than that, in your lifetime. It is not a pleasant activity, nor is it easy, but it is a reality. It is in your best interests to become as skilled at the job search as you are skilled at anything else you do. You never know when you will have to embark on this journey.

You can have the greatest set of skills and experience, yet finding a job may elude you. Your success is dependent on many factors, some of which are under your control and others not. For example, a bad economy may slow down hiring, making it take longer to find a job. You may be considered too young or too old. There's nothing you can do to change those things, but you can work around them. Employers may frown upon the fact that you are returning from an extended absence from the job market. Again, there's nothing you can do to change that, but you can make the best of it. Regardless of your circumstances, there are things you can do to make yourself as competitive as possible.

First of all, you must make sure you are looking for the right job for you. If the job you get isn't the right one for you, before too long you'll find yourself back where you started. You must treat your job search like a job in and of itself. You must plan your job-search campaign and stay focused and organized.

Since your resume introduces you to potential employers, it is important that it makes a good—no make that a great—first impression. Your resume should entice employers to call you in for an interview. Make sure it conveys why you are qualified for the job.

As an astute job seeker, you must utilize all the tools that are available. It is impossible to look for work today without using the Web. Learn how to get the most out of your online job search. Once an employer contacts you, it is in your best interests to learn as much about the company as possible. The Web is an invaluable tool at this point in the job search as well.

The way you present yourself in a job interview can mean your success or your failure. Your resume got you in the door, but your job interview can garner you an invitation to stay. Be prepared for any question an interviewer might ask you. Learn how to get around sticky situations and inappropriate questions.

You may breathe a sigh of relief when you finally get a job offer. And you should—it means you were successful at the job search. It doesn't mean you have to accept the offer. You should first determine whether the job is right for you. If not, you may just have to keep going until you find one that is.

This book will take you through the entire job-search process. You will discover how to put together a resume that opens doors. You will find out where to look for jobs. You will learn how to perform well on job interviews. Finally, this book will teach you how to determine if a job offer is right for you. Good luck and happy hunting.

Chapter 1

Before You Begin Your Job Search

Before you start looking for a job, ask yourself, "What do I want to do?" and "What am I qualified to do?" Your answers to these questions will help you determine how to conduct your job search, or even whether you are ready to start it. You may find that the type of job you thought you wanted isn't the one that's best for you, or you may find out that you don't have the right skills. You may have to reconsider your plans, even continuing your education and training if necessary.

What Kind of Job Do You Want?

One of the biggest mistakes job seekers make is to start looking for a job before they're really ready—even before they have figured out what career field they want to work in and what job they are qualified for. Before you begin your job search, you must have a clear picture of what you want to do, what you can do, and where you want to do it. You need to define your objectives clearly. Good career planning is essential. Remember, it's not just a job; it's a step in your career.

A Good Match

Time and again, career counselors report that one of the most common problems job seekers run into is that they don't consider whether they're suited for a particular position or career. Keep in mind that, on a daily basis, you'll spend more time on your job than you spend doing anything else. It's important to know that you'll enjoy the work. If you are thinking about becoming an elementary school teacher, be sure you enjoy spending a great deal of time with children. If you want to be an accountant, ask yourself if you're meticulous and if you like detail-oriented work. If you want to work for a daily newspaper, be sure you can handle a fast-paced, high-pressure environment.

A Job and a Lifestyle

When you choose a career, you are also choosing a lifestyle. If you decide, for example, that you want to be a management consultant for an international firm, it is likely you'll be spending a great deal of your time in an airplane. You'd better like to fly!

You also have to think about where you will have to work. Some jobs exist primarily in certain areas. Do you want a career that would require you to live in a large city? Or would you rather live in a less populated, rural area?

Compensation is another important factor you must consider. Do you feel it is more important to make a lot of money or to be fulfilled by your work?

What will your work schedule be? If you want to have a flexible work schedule, you will have to choose a job that allows for one. Are you willing to work the long hours that are common in certain fields? If not, there are some jobs you shouldn't consider, like most jobs in the legal profession.

Think about how fast you want to advance. Some careers offer a much greater chance than others do to advance quickly. In other fields, the opportunities for advancement are virtually nonexistent. When looking for a particular job in your field, you should also be aware that companies do not all offer the same opportunities for advancement.

Career-planning professionals have learned that money does not equal job satisfaction. A person who is not doing work he enjoys will not have job satisfaction even if he is earning a lot of money. That does not mean compensation isn't important. One should earn enough money to have the lifestyle one wants, but should also look for a job that is fulfilling.

Self-Assessment

If you are in the process of choosing a career, a self-assessment is in order. A self-assessment looks at your interests, values, skills, and personality. These factors help determine which careers you will find most satisfying and in which you will be the most successful. Although it's been said that you are what you do, think about this phrase reversed: You do what you are. Your personality, likes, dislikes, and values should determine what you do and where you work, not the other way around. Self-assessment is usually done through vocational or career tests that include interest inventories, values inventories, skill assessments, and personality inventories.

Interest inventories let you home in on your interests by presenting you with a series of statements and then asking you whether you agree or disagree with each one. The premise of interest inventories is that people with similar interests will be successful in the same type of work. Here are some statements you might find on an interest inventory:

- I enjoy playing golf.
- One of my favorite activities is reading.

- I would rather participate in sports than watch sports.
- I would rather watch sports than participate in sports.

A test that focuses on your values will consider the importance to you of different values. Here are some questions you might find on a values inventory:

- Do you enjoy making a difference in people's lives?
- Is having a prestigious job important to you?
- Do you need to have a lot of leisure time to be happy?

FACT

When involved in the self-assessment process, many people elect to work with a career counselor. Many municipalities offer free or low cost career-planning services. Your local employment office can help you locate such services. Career counselors also operate private practices. The National Career Development Association maintains a list of career counselors, arranged by state, on their Web site: *www.ncda.org.*

A test that assesses your skills will not only ask if you have certain skills, it might also ask if you enjoy using them. Although you may not have the skills you need to work in a particular field, it doesn't mean you shouldn't consider that career for the future—after you've obtained them. Here are some questions you might see on a skills assessment:

- Are you good at working with numbers? Do you enjoy working with numbers?
- Do you pay attention to details? Do you like having to pay attention to details?
- Are you good at working with people? Do you enjoy working with people?

Career-planning professionals have discovered that people with certain personality types are well suited for some careers but not for others.

A personality inventory like the Myers-Briggs Type Indicator will look at factors such as traits, motivations, and attitude.

How to Use What You've Learned about Yourself

Now is the time to use what you've learned about yourself to choose a career. The results of your self-assessment will include a list of occupations that are considered suitable based on your personality, values, skills, and interests. Investigate fully each career your self-assessment may have indicated is appropriate for you in order to determine if it is a good match. Once you've done that, your job search will be much more focused and easier; if you try to pursue too many different avenues, you'll only frustrate yourself. Having a well-developed plan based on objectives you've taken time to think about is easier on you—and will make you a stronger candidate.

Your first course of action when researching occupations is to get some basic information such as job descriptions, working conditions, job and industry outlooks, education and training requirements, and earnings. You can use government resources available both in print and on the Internet to accomplish this. Before making your final decision, get a personal perspective by talking to those working in a particular field.

Job Outlook

Once you've figured out what occupations you would enjoy, you need to figure out which one is the best option in terms of the outlook for that occupation over time. Will there be many job opportunities available or are there more applicants than there are jobs? In addition to considering what the competition will be like to get the job, you must also think about what the competition will be like to advance.

Whatever you do, don't jump into a particular field just because it appears on a list of the hottest careers for this decade. You need to choose a career in terms of whether it is suitable for you based on what you've learned about your interests, skills, values, and personality, and whether it will offer good opportunities for you.

Industry Outlook

You should also look at the industry in which you want to work, keeping in mind that your occupation may allow you to work in a variety of industries. For example, an accountant can work in the timber industry or in the health care industry. The government publishes data on both job outlook and industry outlook.

If an industry is flourishing, it could mean many more exciting challenges and better opportunities—but it could also mean that the industry is going to be in flux for a while. You may have to jump from one company to the next throughout your career. Sometimes it's a good idea to consider careers in industries that are slowing down or maturing, because they're more likely to have greater opportunities for advancement than industries that are booming and flooded with applicants. Sometimes an industry may be doing poorly in one geographical area but well in another. This is no reason to give up on that industry, but you may have to consider relocating.

What Can You Offer Employers?

While it's very important to figure out what a job or industry can offer you, it's also important to spend some time thinking about what you can offer an employer. The first thing you bring is a set of skills that are necessary to do the job. You should have considered your skills during your self-assessment. If not, this is the time to do it. What skills do you have? Are your skills up to date? Are you willing to get some additional training if they are not up to date?

For example, suppose you enjoy writing. You've liked writing since you were young, and you always excelled in English and writing courses in high school and college. Now look at the industry you're considering. If you'd like to become a journalist, there are probably some skills you did not pick up from your English courses, such as interviewing and research skills. You might consider taking an adult education course in your local community, or taking some classes at a local college that you could put toward a degree if you wanted to. On a smaller scale, you could speak to the editors of some local newspapers and ask them some questions about what they look for in a journalist. All of these avenues will make you more knowledgeable about the skills you need to enter the field.

Also think about the attributes you have that do not necessarily fall under the "skill category." For example, will your outgoing personality charm clients? Will your ambition and ceaseless energy drive you to work long hours? Once you've compiled a mental list of what you have to offer an employer, you'll be more confident in your abilities and more prepared to present them when the time comes.

Setting Goals

So now you've chosen a career and figured out what you have to offer employers. You must feel relieved. After all, you're on your way to getting a job. Not so fast! Yes, it's true that you have taken a huge step toward getting a job, but your work has only just begun. Getting a job is hard work. The job search is, in fact, a job in itself. As in any job, you must be organized in order to succeed. The first thing you need to do to organize your job search is set goals. A goal is something you want to achieve. There are two kinds of goals: long-term goals and short-term goals.

Long-term Goals

Long-term goals are those that could take three to five years to achieve. Your long-term goals will change over time depending on where you are in your career. If you've chosen to pursue a career for which you must get additional training and education, then a long- term goal might be to get a job in your field after you fulfill those requirements. If you already have all the necessary requirements, a long-term goal may be to advance to a top position in your field.

Short-term Goals

Short-term goals are generally achievable within a few months to a year. Taking the examples from the previous section, if you want to pursue a career for which you need additional training and education, a short-term goal may be finishing that education and training if that can be done relatively quickly, or it may be simply registering for and beginning to take courses. If you already meet the requirements to start working, your short-term goals will include finding a job in your field.

For a goal to be viable it must meet the following criteria: You must be able to verbalize your goal. Your goal must be realistic. You must believe you can achieve your goal. You must be flexible enough to change your goal if you need to.

You can then break the short-term goal of finding a job into smaller pieces. These smaller pieces would include writing your resume, finding job openings, writing cover letters, and applying for jobs.

For Students and Recent Graduates

Students and recent graduates face different challenges when embarking on a job search than do those who have been working for a while. While seasoned job seekers may be faced with some of the same issues, students and recent graduates are dealing with them for the first time.

Choosing a Career

Whether you are choosing a career for the first time or the fourth time, you should go through the steps outlined in the earlier part of this chapter. It can be helpful to focus on what you've been good at and what you've enjoyed doing in the past. Which classes were your favorites? In which ones did you find least cause for complaint? If biology rang your bell, how about working in a hospital lab? Maybe your natural proclivity for English could come in handy as an editor at a publishing company or as a copywriter at an ad agency. You may even decide you loved a particular subject so much that you actually want to be a teacher and pass that love on to others. Keep in mind that some occupations may require that you continue your education and training.

Employers like job candidates who have real interests and a clear direction. They know that if you're interested in a particular industry, company, or job, you're more likely to enjoy the position, perform well, and stay with the company. Employers don't like to hear that you are not at all discriminating and will take whatever job they have available. Stay focused on a particular job function.

What Employers Are Really Looking For

You may be surprised to learn that employers generally are not looking for candidates with the best grade point averages, who were involved in the most clubs, or scored the highest in sports. They want to find employees who are the best fit for the job. Why? Those candidates will stay the longest.

The average college graduate stays with her first employer for only nine months. Employers have concluded that most new young hires are unrealistic about what entry-level jobs entail and will soon leave in search of something "better." They're right.

This costs companies a lot of money, because training new hires is expensive. It's not surprising, then, that most companies—especially those with training programs—will be interested in whether you're likely to remain in that position.

How can you show a company you won't move on too soon? You must display a true interest in the industry, in the job function itself, and particularly in that employer. Intelligently discussing the company, current trends in the industry, and showing that you are genuinely interested in the job are two great ways to communicate to an interviewer that you're a low-risk hire.

You can also demonstrate commitment by stressing only those extracurricular activities that you pursued for an extended period of time. You should also choose to highlight those activities from which you developed the most desirable skills. For example, if you want to demonstrate your leadership skills, talk about the organization in which you sat on the board. This shows that you didn't just participate in many different activities, jumping from one to the next. You picked ones in which you could play an active role. If the activity you highlight is one which you spent a lot of time and energy doing and something you made progress in over the years, it will carry more weight than many activities you were only nominally involved in.

Show the employer you are committed to the firm by making it clear that you know what you want. You should show that you have a realistic feeling for what the job entails, that you understand what the pluses and minuses are in the position you're considering, and that you've decided, after making a realistic assessment of the job, that it's something you'd enjoy doing for a substantial period.

Maturity is another factor that employers weigh heavily. Some students or recent graduates, in one-on-one situations with older adults, may not come across as being mature and confident enough for the professional world. Unfortunately, such judgments are often made based on assumptions, but they are sometimes based on an impression made during a job interview. It is up to you to convince the employer otherwise. When on a job interview, make sure you project yourself as a mature candidate who is ready to enter the business community. Practice a firm handshake and learn how to make good eye contact. You can learn more about how to conduct yourself on a job interview in Chapter 13.

Be Professional

It's always important for a job seeker to display a professional demeanor, but this is critical for students and recent graduates lacking work experience. Just as in college you were in the role of student, in this next phase of your life you will be in the role of employee. You must adhere to the standards of communication, appearance, and conduct expected in the workplace. Professionalism is something you need to prove to employers the very first time you make contact with them.

One way you can communicate your professionalism is by presenting a resume and cover letter that follow an acceptable format, which will be discussed in Chapter 4. Your resume should be printed on paper that is a neutral color and is free of any design. It should be well organized. Your cover letter needs to be well written. It is imperative that both your resume and cover letter be free of grammatical and spelling errors.

ALERT!

Make sure your career plans are realistic. You have to start somewhere. Accept that most entry-level positions are usually lower paying and less than glamorous. It will probably take you a number of years to achieve your career goals and advance to your ideal job. Consider an entry-level job the first step toward attaining your long-term goals.

You also need to be careful when choosing an e-mail address. Your e-mail address may be the first thing an employer learns about you when you initially contact a company. The e-mail address you use for personal e-mail can invoke any sort of image you want it to—fun, silly, sexy, or whatever you would like people to think of you. The one you use for work-related e-mail, however, should project only one bit of information—that you are a professional adult who is serious about your work. Your name, either first and last name or some combination that uses your initials, is your best choice; for example, *johnbrown@gmail*.com or *jbrown@gmail.com*.

Your first "in person" contact with a potential employer will likely be at a job interview. Remember that appearance does matter. The way you look will either convey that you are a professional, or it will convey that you are still a student. You want to project a professional image. You can never go wrong wearing a business suit to a job interview. Be on time for the job interview. Not only is it rude to be late, punctuality shows you are a responsible person. Since you can't account for extra traffic on a particular day, make sure you give yourself more than enough time to get to the interview.

Employers want articulate workers. Speak clearly and use a voice and tone that projects confidence—even if you don't feel very confident yet. Use professional lingo that demonstrates your knowledge of the field. Avoid the slang that is fine to use with your friends. Do not, under any circumstances, use obscenities.

Show that you are someone geared toward growth and open to change. No employer wants to spend time and money training someone for a short-term position. You must assure the employer that you are going to stick around once your training is complete.

For Those Returning to Work

You may have taken a hiatus from the work force because you wanted to stay home with your children or because you needed to take care of a sick relative. Regardless of the reason you left the work force, starting a job search when you decide to return won't be simple.

Same Career or New One

Before you do anything else, you have to decide if you want to continue with the career you had prior to leaving the work force. Did you enjoy the work you did? Will work in this field be compatible with your lifestyle, which may have changed since you last had a full-time job? Has the field changed? Is it a good one to be in right now, or have job and advancement opportunities dried up? Are your skills up to date?

If you are about to take a hiatus from work and plan to re-enter the field later on, stay informed of goings-on in that field during your absence. Read industry journals, keep in touch with former coworkers, and attend conferences if possible. If you are trying to re-enter the field right now and haven't kept on top of things, do some cramming. Go online and search for information. Call your former coworkers.

If you decide to move on to a different field of work, you need to pick one that is suitable for you. The realities of your life—for example, children who need you at home before a certain time—will have an influence on your choices. You may have to find a career that doesn't require late hours in the office or a lot of travel.

Using Your Transferable Skills

An absence from the work force often gives people the opportunity to develop new skills. For example, a parent with children in school may have participated in a parent teacher association. Someone else may have taken the time away from the work force to do volunteer work. Whatever it is you chose to do with your free time, figure out what skills you gained from those experiences. You may be able to use those transferable skills to demonstrate to a potential employer that you have what it takes to work for him.

Perseverance Is Key

Today's job market is competitive. As a job seeker you face many challenges. If you're new to the job market, or returning after a hiatus, things will be especially tough for you. For one thing, technology doesn't wait for anyone. Even a few years of time off is enough time to make you feel out of touch with the latest computer and Internet offerings. This is why you have to throw yourself into the deep end and do whatever it takes to get up to speed. Do research, take classes, build a network of professional contacts, and generally observe what's happening in the field you've chosen.

There will be times when you'll feel overwhelmed, dejected, and unsuccessful. It's likely that you'll suffer at least a few rejections before you get an acceptance, too. But this is all part of the process, and believe it or not, you'll be stronger and more knowledgeable when all is said and done.

If you recognize this fact and keep putting sufficient effort and energy into your job search day after day, you'll greatly increase the number of opportunities open to you and ultimately find the job you deserve. After all, your job search can itself be considered your first full-time assignment. Treat it as such, and you'll reap the rewards.

Chapter 2
Basics of Job Winning

Succeeding in your job search takes more than writing a spiffy resume and knowing the right thing to say on a job interview. It involves more than learning how to evaluate and negotiate the best job offer. It even takes more than having the right skills and experience. To succeed in your job search, you must commit to the process. You must be organized as you search for a job. You must carefully plan your job-search campaign. You must know where to look for a job and how to best utilize all those resources.

Getting Organized

Planning and keeping track of your job-search efforts will pay off in the long run. A few hours of organizing can save you countless days of unnecessary footwork and can make or break your quest to find a rewarding position.

Make a to-do list at the beginning of each day and try to accomplish each of your goals by the end of that day. Keep your desk or work area free of clutter. Use a large appointment book or handheld computer to record all your appointments, names of contacts, and phone numbers. Under each entry, write down all pertinent information. Bring this to each appointment.

Create a chart or similar system that shows where and to whom you've sent your resume. Use it to track whether or not companies have responded and when and if you need to follow up with a phone call.

File away any information about an employer you collect along the way as well as relevant documents like copies of applications, resumes, and cover letters. Hold on to help-wanted ads and copies of job announcements. You never can tell when someone you contacted about a job some time ago will call. While you may have forgotten all about sending an employer a resume a month back, it may have been making the rounds at the office.

Oversized index cards or pages in a binder are another useful way to organize your job search. Keep each contact's name, position, company, address, telephone number, contact method, follow-up date, status, and other important details on individual cards for quick reference. Notes detailing when you called, with whom you spoke, and what responses you received should be included on this card. If you are responding to an advertisement in a newspaper, clip the ad and paste it onto the card, along with the name of the newspaper and the date. If an employer or networking contact gives you her business card, you can staple it to an index card and jot down any other pertinent information. Keep your cards in an index-card box in alphabetical order.

Planning Your Job-Search Campaign

No matter how terrific they may be, your resume and cover letter alone will not land you a job. You need a comprehensive and well-defined plan to job seek effectively. A plan will help you keep up the vigorous pace of the job-search process and keep you from becoming frustrated or unmotivated. It will also enable you to pace yourself and monitor your progress against pre-determined goals. If your plan is not effective, you'll be able to see problems more clearly and tackle them head-on by changing direction or using different techniques.

Your job-search plan should incorporate a number of different job-finding methods, described later in this chapter. Predict how much time you are going to spend pursuing these different avenues and set up a specific weekly schedule for yourself. It's important not to overlook this step; it will help you be more productive and less likely to fall behind.

Do Your Homework

If you're trying to enter a new field, your first order of business is to do a little background research. Find out the current trends in the industry and become familiar with names of the major and up-and-coming players. Your industry's trade journal and informational interviews are two terrific ways to find this kind of "insider" information.

FACT

According to the Bureau of Labor Statistics of the U.S. Department of Labor, the following industries will experience the highest growth through the next several years: Education and Health Services, Professional and Business Services, Information, and Leisure and Hospitality.

If you're a veteran of the field in which you're looking, make sure you keep up with industry trends by talking with your associates, attending your professional association's functions, and reading your industry's trade journals.

Informational Interviews

Consider conducting at least one informational interview, particularly if you're an entry-level job seeker or a career changer. An informational interview is simply a meeting that you arrange in order to talk to someone in a field, industry, or company that interests you. This kind of interview allows you to:

- Examine your compatibility with the company by comparing the realities of the field (skills required, working conditions, schedules, and common traits of people you meet) to your own personal interests.
- Find out how people in a particular business, industry, or job view their roles and the growth opportunities in their business.
- Conduct primary research on companies and industries.
- Gain insight into the kinds of topics your potential interviewers will be concerned about and the methods for interviewing.
- Get feedback on your relative strengths and weaknesses as a potential job candidate.
- Become comfortable talking to people in the industry and learning the industry jargon.
- Build your network, which can lead to further valuable information and opportunities.

To set up an informational appointment, request a meeting, either by phone or by letter, with someone who has at least several years' experience working in your field of interest. Your goal is to learn how that person got into the business, what he likes about it, and what advice someone with experience might pass on to someone interested in entering the field. If you don't know who to contact for an informational interview, ask relatives, teachers, and friends if they know someone.

Tell your contact right away that you'd like to learn more about the industry or company and that you will ask all the questions. Most people won't feel threatened (especially if you assure them you're not asking them for a job) and will usually be willing to help you.

E ALERT!

If you tell a contact that all you want is advice, make sure you mean it. Never approach an informational interview as though it were a job interview; stick to gathering information and leads and see what happens. Also, unless you're specifically requested to do so, sending your resume to someone you'd like to meet for an informational interview will probably give the wrong impression.

Now that you've scheduled an informational interview, make sure you're prepared to take the lead. After all, you're the one doing the interviewing. Prepare a list of ten to twenty questions, such as:

- How did you get started in this business?
- What experience helped you to be prepared and qualified for this job?
- What do you believe is the ideal education and background for a career in this industry?
- What are your primary responsibilities in your current job?
- What do you like most about your job, your company, and your industry?
- What do you dislike most about them? What's been your greatest challenge?
- If you could work with anybody in this field, whom would you want to work with?
- Five years out, what are your career goals?
- What are typical career path options from here?
- If you could change something about your career path, what would you change?
- What are the most valuable skills to have in this field?
- What specific experiences helped you build these skills?
- What opportunities do you see in this business?
- Why did you want this job?
- What would you say are the current career opportunities for someone with my qualifications in the industry?

- If you were in the job market tomorrow, how would you get started? What would you do?
- What are the basic requirements for an entry-level position in the industry?
- What would be on a must-read list in your field?
- Where do you see the industry heading in the near future?
- Is there a trade association that might aid me in my job search?
- What things impress you when you interview candidates for positions in this field?
- What would be turn-offs when you interview candidates?
- What critical questions should I expect to be asked in a job interview?
- What advice would you give to someone looking for a job in the industry?
- Is there anything else I should know about the industry?
- Do you know of anyone who might be looking for someone with my qualifications?

Always end by thanking the person for her time. Also promise to follow up on any important leads she has provided and to let her know how things turn out. You should also send a thank-you note within one or two days of the informational interview.

Follow up periodically with everyone in your network—even after you get a job. Once you develop a network, it's important not to lose those contacts. You want to translate your informational network into a support network and maintain it throughout your career.

Setting Your Schedule

The most important detail of your job search is setting up a schedule. Of course, since job searches aren't something most people do regularly, it may be hard to estimate how long each step will take. Nonetheless, it's important to have a plan so you can monitor your progress.

When outlining your job-search schedule, have a realistic time frame in mind. If you are searching full-time, it could take two months or more to find a job. If you can search only part-time, it will probably take at least four months. This time frame depends on what the market is like at the time.

If you're unemployed, remember that job seeking is tough work, both physically and emotionally. It's also intellectually demanding work that requires you to be at your best. So don't tire yourself out by working on your job campaign around the clock. At the same time, be sure to keep at it. The most logical way to manage your time while looking for a job is to keep your regular work hours.

If you're searching full-time using several different contact methods, try dividing up each week, designating some time for each method. By trying several approaches at once, you can evaluate how promising each seems and alter your schedule accordingly. Keep in mind that the majority of openings are filled without being advertised. (This fact will be discussed in more detail in the following sections.)

The Best and Worst Ways to Find Jobs

You may be surprised to learn that some of the most popular job-search methods are unsuccessful for most of the people who use them. Ideally, you want to use a variety of methods to contact employers. Among the most popular resources and methods are contacting employers directly, finding announcements in classified ads, networking, Internet job search, and employment services. The first two methods are discussed in the following sections. The latter three will be discussed in Chapters 3, 10, and 11, respectively.

Contacting Employers Directly

The most effective way to get a job is to contact employers directly, regardless of whether you know of an opening. Step number one is to make up a checklist for categorizing the types of firms for which you'd like to work. You might categorize them by product line, size, customer type (like industrial or consumer), growth prospects, or geographical location. Your list of criteria might be short. If so, good! The shorter it is, the easier it'll be to locate the company that's right for you.

ESSENTIAL

To get just a bit of information about companies before you contact them (you don't need more than that yet) use directories like Dun & Bradstreet's *Million Dollar Directory* and Standard & Poor's investment guides. They list basic information about companies, including the name of the president and a brief description of the company's products and/or services. These directories, as well as many state manufacturer listings, can be found in your local library.

Aren't the largest, most successful companies the best places to look for a job? Don't they offer the most security? Contrary to what many believe, this is not always the case. In recent years, some of the largest and most successful companies in America have been dramatically downsizing their work forces. These companies are not necessarily secure places to work. Furthermore, these giants are the very companies that are deluged with resumes and job applications. For example, some of the largest banking corporations receive as many as three thousand resumes every day!

A better plan is to contact the many moderate-size companies that are not necessarily as well known. These companies are a much better source of jobs: They're large enough to have a number of job openings at any given time but small enough that they're often overlooked by other job seekers.

Next, try to decide at which of these firms you're most likely to find a job. Try matching your skills with those that a specific job demands. Consider where your skills might be in demand, the degree of competition for employment, and the employment outlook at each firm.

Now you'll want to assemble your list of potential employers. Build up your list to at least one hundred prospects. Then separate your prospect list into three groups. The first tier of around twenty-five firms will be your primary target group; the second tier of another twenty-five firms will be your secondary group; and the remaining names you can keep in reserve.

After you form your prospect list, begin working on your resume. Once your resume is done, start researching your first batch of twenty-five prospective employers. Can you see yourself on the job? Would you be happy working at each of the firms you're researching? You also need to find out enough about each company to sound like you've done your homework. Far too few job seekers—especially recent college graduates—take the time to find out details about the companies to which they apply. Find out what products the company makes, with whom they compete, what their annual revenues are, and any other meaningful information. Use this information during phone conversations and in correspondence with recruiters at the company.

But don't go all out on your research yet! You won't get interviews at every company you contact, so save your big research effort for when you start to arrange interviews. Use one resource at a time and find out what you can about each of the twenty-five firms in the batch, keeping a folder on each firm. If you know anyone at a company on your list, add to your research by contacting that person. See if you can arrange an informational interview.

If you find out something that might disqualify a company from staying on your list—for example, they're about to close their only local office, they've just begun a hiring freeze, or they're being investigated for wrongdoing—cross that firm off your prospect list.

The first step in contacting a company directly is to send out your resume with a personalized cover letter. The letter should be addressed to a specific person; avoid mass mailings of identical letters that say "To whom it may concern" or "To Human Resources."

After sending your letter and allowing sufficient time for the person to receive it, call. The idea is to call that person one or two days after your resume arrives, so they are likely to remember you.

Can you call the company to see if there are any job openings before you send your resume? If you're unusually confident and articulate on the phone, you may have success with this approach. Such calls are especially effective if you're contacting smaller companies, since you're more likely to reach a key decision-maker directly rather than being blocked by a secretary. However, at larger companies, you'll find that simply sending a resume and cover letter is much more effective. Many companies have recorded job information lines to announce their job openings.

After you've sent your resume and cover letter, always follow up with a phone call. What you say on the phone is important, but so is how you say it. You need to speak with an air of confidence. Even though a company may not have a particular job opening, you need not be apologetic for calling. All companies hire at some point, and each has, at least in theory, a responsibility to be courteous when an outsider makes a call inquiring about potential job openings.

Will all your calls be answered courteously? No. Some will be answered brusquely—often you'll be calling someone who is busy. But you must project confidence on the phone.

ALERT!

When you make a follow-up phone call after sending a resume, you'll customarily find yourself speaking with someone from the human resources department. This is common, and often unavoidable. If at all possible, however, try to speak directly with the hiring manager. If you responded to an ad for a job opening and addressed your resume to a particular contact person, you should try to speak with that person. Remember, the human resources department weeds out applicants, but the specific hiring manager is the one doing the hiring!

It's important to be succinct on the phone. One good way to do this is by writing out a short script for yourself. Be sure not to sound as if you're reading this script, but do become familiar with it, so you won't forget what you want to say even if you are nervous.

You need to make three points:

- The reason you are calling
- The kind of position in which you are interested
- Why you would be a strong candidate

You should do this briefly—in twenty seconds or less. At the same time, be sure to speak clearly and slowly enough to be understood.

Classified Ads

Are newspaper ads a good source of opportunities for those entering the job market? Unfortunately, they are not always. Department of Labor statistics show that most people do not get their jobs through newspaper ads. One of the reasons newspapers are not a good source for job opportunities is that once a company advertises a job opening in a newspaper, it is deluged with hundreds of applications. This is often quite disruptive; a company will typically try anything and everything to fill a job opening before resorting to listing it in the classified section. This means that few job openings are listed in the newspaper relative to the number of jobs available at any given time.

There's more bad news. By the time a job is listed in the classified ads, there's a good chance the position has already been filled or is close to being filled. Even if the position is still available by the time the company receives your resume, the competition will be so fierce that your chances of getting an interview are small.

For all these reasons, relying solely on newspaper ads is usually a tough way to get a job. This is not to say that you should ignore promising opportunities you see advertised, but you certainly shouldn't make scanning the want ads your only research activity.

Think of your job search as a military campaign. You have to follow every avenue you can to win, but some avenues are likely to be more productive than others. It's hard to say which approach is going to pan out, so you shouldn't rule out any possibilities. At the same time, you can't afford to spend too much time in any one area that's less likely to be productive.

Instead of responding only to current newspaper ads, try responding to the old ones, too. If you respond to a newspaper ad that's many months old, it's possible the person who was hired to fill the position didn't work out. In a situation like this, there won't be hundreds of other people responding to that ad when you call. Also, a company that had a job opening seven months ago is likely to have a different position opening up now that hasn't been advertised yet. Old help-wanted ads can help you to find companies you'd like to work for, and you can send a resume and cover letter inquiring about possible openings. You should not, of course, mention that you are applying for the specific position listed in the newspaper months earlier.

There is often a fairly long interval between the time a manager first starts thinking about filling a position and the time an opening is publicized. You may find old newspapers almost as useful as newer newspapers for unearthing potential job opportunities.

Getting Ahead of the Competition

The difference between finding a terrific job in a relatively short time and suffering through a prolonged job-seeking campaign can be a little extra effort. Following are some of the ways you can get that "extra edge" and outshine the competition:

Read the Trade Literature

Make a habit of reading the trade literature of the industry you're focusing on; you should also read some background books about the field. Remember, your aim is to sound like an industry insider. You'll need to be familiar with industry-related topics while you're networking and interviewing.

Re-evaluate Your Plan if Necessary

Another key to job searching is staying with the plan you made, even if it doesn't seem to be working at first. Of course, you'll need to re-evaluate every once in a while to make sure your chances of getting the job you want are realistic. If everyone you speak to tells you the industry is in bad shape, that there are layoffs at companies of all sizes, that the outlook for newcomers is bleak, maybe you should look into a different field. If everyone you speak to tells you you're underqualified, perhaps you need to look into firms where the competition for positions is not as fierce—or consider a position where your qualifications are more suitable. You may decide to try another city or even another field.

Get Tips from Other Job Seekers

Meet and talk with other job hunters from time to time. Seek out job hunters who, like you, are creative and innovative in their search. Share leads, insights, and techniques. Doing this on a regular basis will yield fresh ideas and help keep up your morale.

Some job seekers choose to join a club. Members of these job-search clubs can offer support and advice to one another. Career development professionals often help run meetings. Look for announcements in local newspapers. Call your local Department of Labor office to find out if they know of any clubs. You can also see whether your public library offers this service.

Keep Networking

Go back again and call those people you already contacted for leads several months ago. It's important to keep your name fresh in their minds and continuously check in with them. Always be courteous and respectful but also persistent. If you keep getting a contact's voice mail, try sending an e-mail instead. You may be pleasantly surprised to catch her in a more open and generous frame of mind. Or perhaps new leads have arisen since the last time you spoke with your contact, but you haven't heard about them due to her hectic schedule. Whatever information you eventually do receive, always show your gratitude and thank the person for her time and effort. Your goal is to make friends in high places—and keep them.

How Long Should Your Job Search Take?

It is very hard to determine how long a typical job search will take because there are so many factors involved in what is usually a very important life decision. One school of thought suggests that the average job search lasts approximately one week for every $2,000 of income sought. For example, if your goal is a position that pays in the $30,000 range, your search will take approximately fifteen weeks. This is only a rule of thumb; keep in mind that a lot of it is chance, depending on the job market, your personal preferences, and your qualifications and presentation.

If you're like many job seekers, you'll have to contact several hundred companies before you find the right job. If you put tremendous effort into your job search and contact many companies each week, you'll probably get a job much sooner than someone who is only searching casually and sending out one or two resumes a week.

Avoid the trap of letting yourself believe that job searching is easier for everyone else than it is for you. It's all too easy to become frustrated when you aren't seeing immediate results from your hard work. At this stage in the job-search process, it's normal to have self-doubts. Don't let your doubts overwhelm you. Job searching is tough, whether you're a recent college graduate or someone who's been in the workplace for years. Stay with it, work hard, have confidence, and you will get the right job!

Again and again during your job search, you'll face rejection. You'll be rejected when you apply for interviews. You'll be rejected after interviews. For every job offer you finally receive, you'll probably have been rejected many times. Don't let rejections slow you down. Keep reminding yourself that the sooner you apply to companies and get those rejections flowing in, the closer you'll be to obtaining the job you want.

For Students and Recent Graduates

As a rule, the best jobs do not go to the best-qualified individuals—they go to the best job seekers. This is a vitally important point, especially if you are competing for an entry-level position. Even though you may compete with people who have stronger credentials, you can still get the job you want if you're willing to put in the extra effort and energy necessary to outshine the competition.

That brings us to a very important piece of advice: Don't let yourself get caught up in what everyone else is doing! Most college students, regardless of their grades, have all the basic requirements for the typical entry-level job. You must demonstrate that in addition to fulfilling the basic requirements, you stand out from the competition and deserve that extra consideration. If you know that a large number of people are trying to interview with just a few highly sought-after companies, don't spend all of your time doing the same. Instead, try to interview at the companies others may have overlooked. Try something different, and you'll be likely to come across several job openings before your competition does.

Go Get Some Experience

Perhaps the biggest problem college students face is lack of experience. Many schools have internship programs designed to give students exposure to the field of their choice as well as the opportunity to make valuable contacts. Check out your school's career services department to see what internships are available. If your school does not have a formal internship program or if no available internships appeal to you, try contacting local businesses and offering your services. Often, businesses are more than willing to have an extra pair of hands (especially if those hands are unpaid!) for a day or two each week. Or try contacting school alumni to see if you can "shadow" them for a few days and see what their daily duties are like.

FACT

Internships aren't just for students. If you didn't do an internship while still in school, doing one after graduation can still be beneficial and, if you're planning on getting into some of the more competitive fields, practically unavoidable. Advertising, public relations, entertainment, and publishing companies have a history of hiring former interns. Even if your internship doesn't turn into a full-time situation, you'll be well on your way in the field. You'll have made contacts, learned important skills, and added another credential to your resume.

What do you do if, for whatever reason, you weren't able to get experience directly related to your desired career? First, look at your previous jobs and see if you can highlight anything. Did you supervise or train other employees? Did you reorganize the accounting system or boost productivity in some way? Accomplishments like these demonstrate leadership, responsibility, and innovation—qualities that most companies look for in employees. And don't forget volunteer activities and school clubs, which can also showcase these traits.

Taking Action Before Graduation

One important way to get that "extra edge" in your job-hunting campaign is to start as soon as you can. It bears repeating that the beginning of your senior year is an ideal time to begin; by the time graduation comes along, you'll be well into your search and will have several possibilities in mind that you're prepared to take action on.

Companies often send recruiters to interview job candidates at various colleges. The on-campus interview is generally a screening interview, to see if it's worth the company's time to invite you in for a second interview. Do everything possible to make yourself stand out from the crowd.

The first step is to check out any and all information your school's career center has on the company. If the information seems out of date, check out the company on the Internet or call the company's headquarters and ask for any printed information.

QUESTION?

Do most students have jobs secured before they graduate?
No. In fact, most students won't have jobs by the time they graduate. So if you fall into this category, don't panic—you can still take plenty of other steps to distinguish yourself. For example, internships and part-time jobs in your field are not bad ways to gain some experience.

Many companies will host an informational meeting for interviewees, often the evening before interviews are scheduled to take place. Do not miss this meeting. The recruiter will almost certainly ask if you attended. Make an effort to stay after the meeting and talk with the company's representatives. Not only does this give you an opportunity to find out more information about both the company and the position, it also makes you stand out in the recruiter's mind. If you had your heart set on a particular company but weren't able to interview with them, attend the information session anyway. You may be able to persuade the recruiter to squeeze you into the schedule. (Or you may discover that the company really isn't the right fit for you after all.)

Interview Tips

College students are notoriously inexperienced with interviewing. It makes sense; these are people who've been in school virtually their whole lives. Many employers will expect a certain level of inexperience, but that makes this an even better opportunity for you to strut your stuff. Consider the following helpful tips.

- **Try to check out the interview site beforehand.** This includes knowing how to get there—and how long it will take. Having an idea of what to expect will also help you prepare mentally.
- **Arrive at least fifteen minutes early.** The last thing you want to do is undermine your opportunity to make a good first impression by being late.
- **Make sure your communication skills are up to snuff.** If you want to be taken seriously, you need to be able to communicate clearly, intelligently, and professionally. Practice eliminating slang and curses from your vocabulary before the big interview.
- **Never lie about your GPA.** Some employers ask for this information, and others don't. If they do ask, and you lie, the truth may be revealed later anyway (in your transcript, for example). You can, however, explain if there is a reason you don't feel your grades reflect your abilities, and mention any other impressive statistics.

Conducting Your First Job Search

Ideally, for the first few months after graduation, try to look for a job full-time. If you're able to do this, be sure to work from a vigorous, intense job-search plan that allows you to invest about forty hours a week.

Vary your activities a little bit from day to day—otherwise it will quickly become tedious. For example, every Sunday you can look through the classified ads. On Monday, follow up on these ads by sending out your resume and cover letter and making some phone calls. On Tuesday, you might decide to focus on contacting companies directly. On Wednesday, you can do more research to find listings of other companies to contact. Thursday and Friday might be spent networking as you try to set up appointments to meet with people and develop more contacts.

ALERT!

Many graduating students enter the job market thinking that getting a job will be like applying to college. Applying to companies isn't like that at all. Success will not go to the job searcher who invests little effort, becomes discouraged, and takes the first job possibility that comes around. Remember, the time you put into your job search will be time well spent if you make sure all of that effort and energy is going in the right direction.

If you don't have a job secured after a few months, you might also consider finding a part-time position, even if it's not in your field. (Financially, it may be something of a necessity at this point.) With a part-time job, you'll earn some money and gain a valuable sense of personal accomplishment. After some time of tedious searching, you'll probably have dealt with your share of stress; a part-time job will break up your routine and keep you motivated and enthusiastic about your job search. Working part-time also displays initiative and a good work ethic, which is something recruiters like to see.

For Those Returning to Work

Things move very rapidly and you may find, when you begin your job search, that things have changed some since you last worked. If nothing has changed in your field, the process of getting a job probably has. Take your resume, for example. The last time you looked for a job, you may have used a typewriter to compose your resume. You may have written one resume and sent that out to everyone. Since it's so easy to use most word processing programs now, you can quickly put together separate resumes to target each job for which you are applying.

ESSENTIAL

If you don't have access to a computer that can be used for job-hunting purposes, find one. There are several businesses that rent out computer work stations by the hour. Most offer high-speed Internet connections. You may spend more than you bargained for if you are there for an extended period of time, though. You may opt to sign up to use a computer at a public library. Many libraries have a number of computers set aside for public use (including some that have Internet access). Call ahead of time to find out the library's policies.

If you've been unemployed for a long time, computers may not have been a big part of your life at work. If your hiatus from work has been short, it's likely that computers were part of your life when you were employed. Even so, technology changes and you may not be familiar with some of the newer software out there. You may not be as familiar with using the Internet as you could be. If you're not computer literate at all, consider yourself substantially disadvantaged. To be adequately prepared for today's work force, take an introductory computer course. For a nominal fee, community colleges in your area can help you master most commonly used programs, like WordPerfect and Microsoft Word. If you're low on funds, ask your friends for help. There's a PC owner in every bunch, and you're bound to run into one who'll agree to show you the ropes.

Chapter 3
Networking

Networking is a much-used buzzword in the business arena, yet it is often misunderstood. Networking simply means utilizing your connections to enhance your career and to help others who want to enhance their careers. Networking is something you should always be engaged in. If you already have a network in place, it will be much easier to access it when you need it—like when you are job hunting.

Why You Should Network

Some people falsely believe that you don't need to begin to network until you are looking for a job. That would be akin to starting to take better care of your body after you have been diagnosed with heart disease. At that point, the damage has already been done. It's a much better idea to try to stay healthy in the first place with regular exercise and a balanced diet. Think of networking the same way; it's something you can do to keep your career healthy.

There are many ways in which being part of a professional network can benefit your career. Of course, the first thing that comes to mind is the job search. Some career counselors feel that the best route to a better job is through somebody you already know or to whom you can be introduced. People like former coworkers, friends of friends, neighbors, and even former classmates can turn out to be very helpful in your job search.

There are other reasons to network, too. Members of your network can offer you advice on work-related matters, provide information, hook you up with potential clients, and even help you find potential employees when you need to hire someone. The larger your network, the more opportunities you'll find to get help achieving your goals.

Building Your Network

Building a network can seem like an overwhelming task, especially if you think you are starting without any contacts at all. Well, guess what? You already have contacts—unless, of course, you've been living in a cave for the last fifteen years. It's likely you have relatives, friends, and acquaintances. Sure, not all of them can personally help you with your career—they probably don't even work in the same field you do—but they haven't been living in caves, either. They have friends and acquaintances they can introduce you to who may be able to help.

Begin your network with as many people whom you know personally as you can. Dig into your personal phone book and your holiday greeting card list and locate old classmates from school. Be sure to approach people who perform your personal business, like your accountant or insurance agent. By the nature of their professions, these people develop a broad contact base.

While you may meet a great contact at your cousin's wedding or your sister's birthday party, these aren't always the best places to trade business cards. Luckily, there are events that provide perfect opportunities for networking, such as business seminars, community events, business conferences, fundraisers, and industry trade shows

Career development experts recommend you build your contact base beyond your current acquaintances by asking each one to introduce you, or refer you, to people in your field of interest. You start off with a few people, and then grow your network from there. If you have fifteen personal contacts and each one introduces you to three additional people, you will now have forty-five contacts. Each one of those contacts can introduce you to others. Before you know it, you'll have over a hundred contacts in your network. Some will be valuable, and some won't be—at least not at the present time. Keep these contacts, though. They may come in handy in the future.

How to Develop Contact Lists

Since the first people you'll draft for your network are probably going to be friends and family members, you don't have to do anything too formal. Generally, you can give them a call or send an e-mail, telling them a little about your career plans, if they don't already know what they are, and asking if they know anyone in your field. It is when you have to begin contacting the friends of friends and family that you must get more formal.

Communicating with a Contact by E-mail

The easiest way to develop a contact list is to send a networking letter by e-mail. You can clearly spell out what your needs are and give the person the opportunity to reply on his own schedule.

If you don't know the contact personally or he isn't someone with whom you are familiar, word your correspondence in a businesslike manner. In other words, don't use your addressee's first name (unless you're already on a first name basis with him) or an overly casual writing style. If you've been in touch with him recently, remind him of this—for example, "It was great seeing you at the Chicago Writers' Convention last month" or "It's been several months since we bumped into each other on that flight to London. How are you?"

Often you'll send a networking e-mail to an addressee to whom you have been referred by a mutual acquaintance. In this case, immediately state the name of the person who referred you, such as "Jean Rawlins suggested I contact you." Ask your new contact for advice about your field, information, or the names of other contacts. Do not ask for a job at this point. Chances are, if your e-mail is politely persuasive, people will be interested in talking with you.

Here's a sample networking e-mail:

Dear Ms. Wilson:

Peter Price suggested I contact you. I am studying to be an accountant, and Mr. Price mentioned that you have worked in this field for the past few years. He thought you would be a good person for me to talk with. I would like to know a bit about the ins and outs of the accounting field. I will be graduating shortly and I'm not sure what area I want to specialize in. If possible, I would like to meet with you to get your advice. In addition, if you know of anyone else with whom I should speak, please let me know.

You can get in touch with me by replying to this e-mail or calling me at (303) 555-5555. Thank you for your time. I look forward to hearing from you in the near future.

Sincerely,

Michael Picard

Communicating with a Contact by Phone

Reaching out to a contact by telephone usually offers something e-mail doesn't—immediacy. You won't have to wait for a reply, and if you don't get one, you won't have to wonder if the recipient is ignoring you or if he didn't receive your message. You may also get the information you are looking for right away, whether that comes in the form of a date for a meeting with this person or the name of another person to add to your list. On the other hand, you may be calling at a bad time, possibly interrupting your contact in the middle of something important. The person on the other end of the line may also feel put on the spot. If you do choose to use the telephone, be polite, be brief, and make your intentions clear.

A good introduction is imperative to getting your networking relationship off to a good start. Aim for a balance of brevity and completeness. Don't simply call someone and say, "Hi, Mr. Pitt. This is George. Linda told me you do quite a business in the stock market. Do you mind telling me about it?" Write out a short statement, including not only what you want but also who you are. If you waste someone's time, his opinion of you will take a nose-dive. So practice your delivery before giving the pitch, and make sure to tailor each one to the situation at hand.

Many people are, at first, a little uncomfortable calling people they don't know and asking for contact names and interviews. You'll be nervous the first few times, but with practice you'll feel much more comfortable and confident making calls. The key is to think about what you're going to say in advance, pick up that phone, and just do it. No one else can network for you. Once you gain some confidence, you'll find that your calls will make a big difference in your job-search campaign.

Communicating with a Contact in Person

Strike up conversations with people you meet at social and business events. While it may be awkward to ask someone what she does for a living, mention what you do, and she may tell you. Lo and behold, the opportunity to add someone to your network may appear out of the blue. The person you're talking to may happen to work in your field, or may know someone who does. While you may find it difficult to ask for help from someone in person, this isn't an opportunity you should pass up. You can ask for help right on the spot, but if this is a social event, you should instead ask for a meeting at a later date. Ask if it would be okay to contact her later and make sure you get an e-mail address or phone number, asking which one she prefers you use.

FACT

Business cards, if you keep them simple, are relatively inexpensive to have printed up. They are a great way to get your name and contact information circulating. When you meet someone you want to have in your network, instead of scrambling around for a scrap of paper and a pen, hand them a professional-looking business card. Remember to ask for theirs, too.

Developing Your Network Online

The Web is a fertile ground for establishing connections for your network. For several years, people have been communicating online with others who share their professional interests by taking part in discussion groups. Online networking services allow you to develop contacts through the Web. Some people find participating in message boards or forums on trade association Web sites to be very helpful.

Online Discussion Groups

There are many online discussion groups on a variety of topics, including those that are career-related. These groups are available through services such as Google Groups (*http://groups.google.com*) and Yahoo! Groups (*http://groups.yahoo.com*). Search for groups in your interest areas, which might include anything from job hunting to current computer technology to the industries you're considering for employment. You will have to register for the group or groups you want to join.

When you join a discussion group, there are several rules you must follow. You might even receive a list of these rules from the group's administrator. You may be told that all discussions must stay on topic. You will likely be reminded that "flaming," or being hostile to another group member, is not allowed. You may be asked not to post "spam" on a message board. This means you shouldn't advertise services or business opportunities. In the same vein, you should be wary of any business opportunities you see posted on a message board. Most of them are scams.

Online Networking Services

Online networking services began as a way for people to establish social networks but are increasingly being used by many to establish business networks. Two business-oriented online networking services are LinkedIn (*www.linkedin.com*) and Ryze (*www.ryze.com*). Here's a general step-by-step look at how online networking services work:

1. You join an online networking service, either on your own or through an invitation from an existing member.
2. You create a personal profile.
3. You invite your contacts, including colleagues and friends, to join your network.
4. Your contacts invite their contacts to join the network.
5. The network grows and grows.

While online networking services can be a great tool, you take a risk anytime you put information about yourself out there on the Web. You should exercise extreme caution whenever you reveal anything about yourself online. Most services won't post contact information without your permission, but read each service's privacy policy to make sure. Remember that what you post on the Web is out there for public consumption—if you can see something online, so can your current employer or a prospective one.

Trade Association Forums

A great way to network with others in your field or industry is through trade association forums or message boards. Most associations require that you be a member before you are allowed to access the forum. Membership brings you other benefits as well, so it may be well worth the cost. When you post on a forum be sure to follow all the rules, like being polite to other members and respecting people's points of view.

Maintaining Your Network

Now that you have your network assembled, you may think that you can take a break. Not so fast! Building your network is only half the battle. Now you have to monitor and maintain it to be sure that all your hard work does not go to waste. And, of course, your newly arranged network will not be any help to you unless you use it!

Think of your network as an organic being. It will change over time—you will lose contacts and you will gain contacts. Like any living thing, it must be nurtured and maintained. Nurture your network by letting your contacts know you appreciate their help. Send a thank-you note if someone has helped you in any way, including simply giving advice. Not only is this courteous, but that person may be an important business contact for years to come—especially if the individual is active in your industry. Don't let your network sit stagnant. E-mail or call your contacts periodically just to check in with them. If you let your network sit idle, it won't be available to you when you need it.

In addition to thanking contacts for any assistance they have provided, you should also offer to help them out whenever possible. You may feel like you're the only one who needs help (and you may not think you have anything to offer), but this is far from the truth. Even though your aunt Cindy in the fashion industry is not helpful to you in your ambitions to be a lawyer, one of your contacts might be desperately searching for a fashion-merchandising job. Put those two together, and you'll have a solid contact for life.

For Students and Recent Graduates

As someone just starting your career, you may think the goal of networking is to find a job. Wipe that thought from your mind for now. Your goal is to make connections with people who are working in your field so that you may learn from their experience. Through these connections you may ultimately meet someone who can help you get a job. For now though, focus on asking for advice about the field you are entering.

QUESTION?

What should I do if I know that a contact has a suitable opening available?

Even if you saw the ad in the classifieds and you know you'd be perfect for the job, you shouldn't mention it. Remember, you earned this contact through networking, not by reading a classified ad. (Of course, if the person asks whether you saw the ad, don't lie, but point out that you're calling as a result of speaking to so-and-so.) You want to position yourself as an industry insider who is networking around, not as just another person responding to an ad.

The Key to Networking

One of the secrets of networking is to know what you want—or at least appearing to know what you want. If, when you are making networking calls, you tell your contacts you're interested in the industry they work in and if you sound even somewhat knowledgeable about that industry, that makes you more or less an industry insider.

How do you start? Keep up to date with the industry. Read the trade publications. These are specialized journals and magazines that address the concerns of professionals in a given industry. Virtually every type of business has at least one.

It's Who You Know

Coming out of school, there's a good chance you have a very large social network. "Yeah, a lot of good that'll do me," you may be thinking. "How can my freshman roommate help me with my career?" Your friends probably can't help you with your career directly—after all, they have no more experience than you do. But their parents or other relatives might be in a position to help you. Asking close pals to contact their relatives on your behalf is a most effective way of building a network. Be ready to reciprocate the favor.

ESSENTIAL

Many colleges try to foster relationships between their alumni and their current students. Alumni often look to their alma maters to find qualified candidates to fill positions for which they need to hire. Fraternities and sororities often have gatherings where alumni and current students can get together for the purpose of networking.

Professors can also be a valuable resource when it comes to expanding your network. They probably come into contact with experts from their respective fields regularly and some, particularly adjunct faculty members, may have full-time jobs in their respective fields in addition to teaching. Ask them about their associates. This will help you add to your network.

A Sample Networking Conversation

When talking to a new contact, be sure to drop names that will be meaningful to the person to whom you're speaking. Always let your contact know who gave you his name—for example, "Ally Kendreck suggested I call you." If you've been in contact with a well-known person in the field, make that known, too. As you continue networking, you'll find yourself dropping names of other people in your network. Don't be uncomfortable with this; this is the way it's done.

Here's a sample of what your networking conversations should sound like:

You: Hi, Uncle Ted! It's Emily. As you might have heard, I just graduated from college, and I want to pursue a career in banking. Is there anyone you can think of who might be willing to talk to me about the banking industry and fill me in on some background information?

Relative: I really can't think of anyone in the banking industry—but why don't you call up my attorney, Don Silva. He's not a real close friend, but I deal with him every month or so. He knows a lot of business people, not necessarily in the banking industry, but you never know. Why don't you call him and see if he can be of any help. His number is 555-1234.

You: Thanks, Uncle Ted!

You then call the attorney, immediately identifying who referred you:

You: Mr. Silva, my name is Emily Sampson. My uncle, Ted Giemza, suggested I call you. I'm interested in a career in banking, and I wondered if you might know anyone in that field who might be able to talk to me briefly about the industry.

Attorney: Well, I'm not really sure. Let me think about it a little and I'll get back to you.

Keep the momentum on your side by offering to follow up yourself:

You: That's fine. If you want, I can call you back. If there's someone in the industry you can refer me to or someone who might know somebody else in the industry, I'd really appreciate it.

If a networking contact seems reluctant, you could redirect the conversation in this way:

Attorney: Gee, I do know a few people in the industry, but they're probably not hiring now. . . .

You: That's fine. I just want to talk to someone briefly to find out what's going on in the industry. If you'd like, I can stop by for a few minutes at your convenience so we can meet, and in the meantime maybe you could think of some other names you'd feel comfortable referring me to.

If your contact is hesitant to give any names out without seeing in person that you're a polished, professional individual, you may be able to overcome some of that reluctance by setting up a face-to-face meeting. This technique also gives your contact the opportunity to think of some more names of people he can refer you to.

Career Fairs

Career fairs are another great, often overlooked, job-hunting resource. These organized gatherings of representatives and hiring managers from various companies afford you the opportunity to introduce yourself and often interview on the spot. Since putting a face and personality to a resume is a crucial part of decision-making in the hiring process, going to a career fair is a proactive way to get your foot in the door.

FACT

At career fairs you are given the chance to exhibit your skills, enthusiasm, and experience to many companies all in one day at one location. Some of these companies will have specific openings to fill. In addition, a job fair can save you time and money that would have been spent sending out multiple resumes by mail or waiting for advertised openings.

Many career fairs are industry-specific. For instance, you can find fairs that specialize in the high-tech, sales and marketing, or health care fields. Others are simply labeled "professional," and consist of representatives from a wide variety of industries.

Upcoming career fairs are often advertised in newspapers and online through job-hunting Web sites.

Here are tips to help you maximize your success at a career fair:

- **Dress the part:** Dress as you would for a formal job interview.
- **Bring your resume:** Make sure you have plenty of copies to pass out to potential employers.
- **Act like a professional:** Shake hands with those you meet, stand tall, and speak clearly.
- **Go solo:** Traveling with a pack of your friends may distract you from making as many new connections as you can.

For Those Returning to Work

When you take time away from the workplace, you should keep your network alive. Sometimes life gets in the way and it isn't possible to do that. There are children to care for if that is the reason you left. There is a business to run if you left to pursue that avenue. There are papers to write and tests to study for if you left work to attend school. You may have had too much to do and networking wasn't something that was high on your list of priorities. There's nothing you can do about it now. What's done is done. All you can do is rebuild your network or build a new one.

Re-establishing Your Network

You can try to re-establish connections with those who were on your network before you left work. Many of your old contacts may be interested in hearing you are returning to work. Send e-mails if you have addresses, or phone your contacts. Remember that some of them may no longer be at the same jobs they were at previously. You can try to track them down by asking other members of your network acquainted with those contacts if they know how to reach them.

You can also try using a search engine, like Google, to look for your long-lost contacts. In addition to helping you locate them, you may be able to learn what they are doing now. You can use what you learn about an individual as an icebreaker when you make your phone call—for example, "I heard you were just elected to the executive board of the AMA. Congratulations!"

Making New Connections

You may have to build your network from scratch entirely, or at least make some new connections to bulk it up a bit. Spending time away from the workplace probably means you were spending your days elsewhere. If you took time away from work to be a stay-at-home parent, your personal network may now include people you met on the playground, other parents at your child's school, or those with whom you worked on volunteer projects. If you were a student during your time away from work, look to your professors for contacts, as was discussed earlier in this chapter. If you left the workplace to start your own business, your customers may now be candidates for your network.

Chapter 4
Resumes

The very first thing a potential employer will learn about you comes from what she sees on your resume. This is why it is essential that you put a great deal of effort into creating a document that not only highlights all your skills and experience but also presents them extraordinarily well. You can think of your resume as an advertisement that will entice an employer to want to know more about the product you are selling—which just happens to be you.

4

Types of Resumes

There are three basic resume types: chronological, functional, and a combination of those two types. Which one you should use depends on your situation and where you are in your career. Generally speaking, chronological resumes are the most popular, listing your job experience in reverse chronological order; functional resumes focus on skills; and combination resumes include both your job experience and skills.

Chronological Resumes

Most job seekers use a chronological resume. It follows a very simple format. It lists each job you have had, in reverse chronological order. In writing one, you would start with the most recent job and work your way backward. While chronological resumes are the most popular, they aren't the best choice for everyone.

Someone who can demonstrate a solid history in a particular field of work can use a chronological resume. In order to use this type of resume, which highlights your work history, you must have been employed in the same field for a substantial period of time. In addition, you must be able to show that your career has grown during that time—your work responsibilities have increased, for example. This is particularly important if you are seeking a position that is a step above the most recent one on your resume.

QUESTION?

What kind of paper should I use for my resume?
Choose a neutral color like white, off-white, cream, or light gray. Use a solid color—no dots, lines, or watermark that will detract from the content of your resume. It's not necessary to use very expensive paper, but don't use anything too thin or flimsy.

A chronological resume is not a good option for someone who does not have a solid work history. If you have moved from job to job, or if you haven't had a job in a while, don't use a chronological resume. If you do not have experience in the field in which you are looking for work, this resume type isn't a good option either. For example, if you are a career changer or a recent graduate, you should consider using a functional or a combination resume.

Functional Resumes

Unlike a chronological resume, which emphasizes your experience, a functional resume focuses on your skills. If you use this type of resume, you will list your skills or groups of skills that are pertinent to the job for which you are applying. You will follow each one with a list of accomplishments that demonstrate a proficiency with that skill.

A functional resume can benefit a job seeker who doesn't have a solid work history. It is a great tool for someone who is entering a new field or returning to work after an absence. If you picked up skills through experiences other than paid employment, for example from volunteer work, you can play up those skills on a functional resume. Even if your work history is spotty, it is possible that you learned some skills on the jobs you had. Ask yourself, "Do I have skills that are relevant to the job I want?" If you have the skills that an employer is seeking and you can demonstrate your proficiency in them, you can use a functional resume.

A functional resume is not a wish list of skills that you think you have, you want to have, or you think an employer desires. If you don't have relevant skills, you shouldn't use this type of resume. You must be able to show proof of ownership of the skills you are claiming to have. If you can't prove, by listing accomplishments that demonstrate them, that you have these skills, you will have to choose another type of resume. You may even realize that you have to develop these skills or perhaps look for a job that is more suitable for you.

Combination Resumes

A combination resume takes pieces from both the chronological resume and the functional resume. It emphasizes your skills while also highlighting your job history. On a combination resume, you will list your relevant skills, along with accomplishments that demonstrate each one. You will follow that with your work history, listing jobs beginning with the current or most recent and working backwards in time. You will not include a description of each one.

A combination resume gives you the opportunity to play up your skills while also proving that you have a solid work history. You may ask, "Why would I use this type of resume instead of a chronological resume?" Let's say your job titles do not adequately describe the work you did or the skills you used to do it. A combination resume could help the person who reviews your resume focus on the relevant skills you can bring to the job rather than the irrelevant job titles you had.

ALERT!

You may have had a job at some point that was totally unrelated to your career. It may have been something you took on to make ends meet while you continued to look for more suitable work. You may consider leaving this job off your resume. If you do, though, make sure you title your "Work History" section "Relevant Work History."

Just as you wouldn't use a chronological resume if you didn't have a solid work history, you shouldn't use a combination resume in those circumstances, either. Use a functional resume instead. If you can't demonstrate you have skills pertinent to the job for which you are applying, you're best off using a chronological format; neither functional nor combination is the right resume choice for you.

Structure of a Resume

When writing a resume you will have to follow some basic guidelines, depending on the type of resume you use. Your resume should reflect who you are, so you get to decide on the physical layout and design. Remember that the more conservative your field, the less leeway you have here. You will find sample resumes in Chapter 5. Those samples will help illustrate the instructions given in this section.

When setting up your resume, here is the standard format you should use. Your contact information always goes at the top. Whether you are writing a chronological resume, a functional resume, or a combination resume, you will need to start with your contact information. This will include your name, address, telephone number, and e-mail address. You will put each of these items on a separate line, and will either center or left-justify this information on the page. Your name should be in bold type.

While you have little control over your name, address, and telephone number, you do have control over your e-mail address. Your e-mail address says a lot about you since you are the one who chooses it. Use a professional-sounding address. Your name—first and last, your first initial followed by your last name, or your last name followed by your first initial are some good choices. Don't use anything suggestive or playful, or an address that reveals something that you would not want a prospective employer to know about you. You should use a personal e-mail address and not your work e-mail address.

FACT

By many accounts, the time an employer spends reviewing a resume is less than a minute. Your resume should be fairly short—no more than one page long. Your descriptions should be brief, and you should get to your point quickly. Write them as sentence fragments, not as complete sentences.

The next item you will put on your resume is your objective. This item is a must. Your objective should clearly state the position you are seeking. You can, and should, target it to the job for which you are applying. Go ahead and use the description of the job opening you want to fill to compose your objective.

Your objective will be followed by a summary of qualifications, which serves as a synopsis of your entire resume. Your summary of qualifications will tell a potential employer what makes you a good fit—no, make that the best fit—for the job. Use a bulleted list containing four or five statements, about one to two lines each. Each one should tell a potential employer about one attribute. This list can include the number of years' experience you have, one of your strengths, relevant credentials, and a skill. Choose things that are most relevant to the position for which you are applying. Remember, your summary of qualifications can be targeted to each potential employer depending on his needs.

Do I have to list every job I've ever had on my resume?
If you have a very lengthy work history, you may want to omit some earlier jobs, especially those unrelated to the position you are seeking. You shouldn't omit a job from your chronological resume if it will make it look like there is a gap in your work history.

Which items follow depend on the type of resume you are using. If you are using a chronological resume, your work experience will go next, but if you are using a functional or combination resume, this is where you would put your relevant skills. On a functional resume or a chronological resume, you would show your education next. On a combination resume, your next item would be your work history, which would then be followed by your education.

Your resume should be no longer than one page. To achieve this, keep your statements short and concise. Use keywords that are pertinent to the job you want. If you can't avoid a two-page resume, don't staple the pages together. Make sure your name and phone number are present on each page of a multi-page resume should they become separated.

Putting Together a Chronological Resume

If you are using a chronological resume, you will list your work history after your summary of qualifications. You can title this section "Work Experience," "Job Experience," "Relevant Work (or Job) Experience and Accomplishments," or anything else you feel makes sense for you. The first job you will list is your current job. If you are not currently employed, you should list your most recent job first. Then go on to list each job you've had.

Dates of Employment and Job Information

At the beginning of each entry indicate the period of time during which you worked at the job. Use years only. You should not use specific dates, which include month, day, and year.

The next part of this entry is your job title. Use your actual job title even if it doesn't adequately describe the work you did. If someone checks your references and is told you had a job title that isn't the one you listed on your resume, you will look dishonest, even if your intentions were innocent. The name of the employer and the city in which you worked should follow this.

The Job Description

Now comes the most important part: writing the job description. This is the part of your resume that will let a prospective employer know what you will bring to her company. Some people think a job description should look like this: "Responsible for supervising five people." This job description does not tell the employer a lot about you.

Anyone who is looking at your resume and considering whether you would be a worthy candidate to interview for a job wants to know if you have the right qualifications. She wants to learn about you and what you can bring to the job.

Describe your job in terms of your accomplishments. By highlighting your accomplishments you will illustrate to an employer what you already accomplished and infer what you can accomplish if you were to work for her. Instead of saying "Responsible for supervising five people," you should say, "Delegated responsibilities to a team of five people according to each member's skills." That gives the employer a more concrete idea of what you did on that job. Continue to list your other accomplishments in a similar fashion.

ALERT! Do not begin statements on your resume with the words "I" or "My," as in "I assisted customers who were having problems with their computers" or "My job was to answer phone calls." Begin each statement instead with a verb. An example of a statement that begins with a verb would be "Developed a system for categorizing customer complaints."

Always start each accomplishment or description with an action word—something that describes the effort you took to accomplish a task. Here are some examples of action words:

- developed
- guided
- scheduled
- organized
- presented
- persuaded
- consulted
- achieved
- succeeded
- established
- designed
- solved
- improved
- delegated

- reduced
- increased
- decreased
- planned
- implemented
- instructed
- taught
- analyzed
- resolved
- created
- trained
- initiated
- assessed

Action words are powerful. When a hiring manager or someone in human resources quickly scans your resume, these words should jump out at her. Action words speak on your behalf, saying "Hey, look at this. This person has what we're looking for."

Putting Together a Functional Resume

When you use a functional resume, the "Relevant Skills and Accomplishments" section follows your summary of qualifications. Alternately, you may call this section "Relevant Experience and Accomplishments." In this section you will list major skills or job functions. Examples of these major skills include management and supervision, teaching, and customer relations.

You should list three to four major skills. Beneath each one, you must list accomplishments that demonstrate that skill, just as you would do when putting together the job description in a chronological resume. You should have a bulleted list of three to five accomplishments. Remember to use action words.

Your resume doesn't have to be printed on a laser printer, but make sure the printer you use produces clear copies. Don't photocopy your resume. If you don't want to print out each one individually, you should have the work done by a professional print shop. Do not hand address your envelopes even though that may seem easier than running them through your printer individually. Even if you have very neat handwriting, it looks unprofessional.

Putting Together a Combination Resume

A combination resume brings together characteristics of a chronological resume and a functional resume. The finished product is a document that highlights an applicant's skills and accomplishments while at the same time takes into account her work history. The work history section of a combination resume backs up the skills and accomplishments section.

While this type of resume results from combining aspects of the functional resume and the chronological resume, it more closely resembles the former. It is actually almost identical to a functional resume. The sole difference is that the skills and accomplishment section is followed by a list of jobs listed in reverse chronological order.

As you would do in a functional resume, in a combination resume you would put your "Relevant Skills and Accomplishments" section right after your summary of qualifications. In the relevant skills and accomplishments section, list three to four major skills followed by a bulleted list of accomplishments, just as you would if writing a functional resume. A job history section will follow. Briefly list your current and past jobs from the most recent to the oldest. Do not include job descriptions.

Education, Training, and Credentials

The last section of your resume, regardless of whether you are using a chronological, functional, or combination resume, should list education, training, and credentials. Anyone looking at your resume who wants this information will know, automatically, to look at the bottom of the page. You can alter the title of this section as necessary—for example, you may only have education, not training or credentials.

How far back into your schooling do you need to go? If you have a college degree, you should not include any education prior to that. There is an exception to that rule. If your education prior to college included something that helps qualify you for the position for which you are applying, you should include it on your resume.

For each entry in this section, list your degree—for example, B.B.A. in Marketing—followed by the name of the school, the city in which it is located, and the year the degree was conferred.

FACT

Employers don't have a lot of time to read each resume they receive. They need to be able to scan each one and immediately find the skills that can fill their needs. Make sure you list the skills on your resume so they can be found at a glance.

Training is anything that has prepared you for the job you want, other than formal education, which you will include under education. It can include a continuing education class, a workshop, or another program that does not award a degree.

If you have credentials that allow you to work in your field, list them in this section. If you are applying for a job as a teacher, for example, you have to be certified by the department of education in the state in which you want to work.

Advice For Dealing with Special Situations

At some point, you may find yourself in a situation that will cause you some distress as you put together your resume. Such situations might include being a first-time job seeker with no experience, returning to the work force after a long break (after being a stay-at-home parent, going back to school, etc.), or looking for a new job after being fired from your previous one. The following sections offer advice for dealing with these kinds of situations.

If This Is Your First Job

Since a resume usually contains information related to your work experience, you may worry about writing one if you have never had a full-time job. It is important for you to realize that experience does not come only from paid full-time work. Ask yourself these questions:

- Have I done any volunteer work?
- Have I taken on a leadership role in a club or organization?
- Have I done any internships?
- Have I participated in any extracurricular clubs?
- Was I in a fraternity or sorority?
- Have I ever had a part-time job?
- Have I worked on particularly challenging projects in school?

Do not consider any of these activities trivial. Each one brings with it valuable experience. For example, a group project you did in school taught you to work as part of a team. Your leadership position in an extracurricular club helped you learn how to delegate jobs to others. Since you don't have extensive job experience, a functional resume will be your best choice. Go through each of these activities and pick out a few accomplishments related to the job you are pursuing.

If You Have Gaps in Your Work History

You may have gaps in your work history if you took time off to raise a family or to attend school. You should use a functional resume, which, as discussed earlier in this chapter, will accentuate your skills rather than your employment background.

You cannot, and should not try to, hide the fact that you took time away from the workplace or make excuses for it. Discover, instead, the transferable skills you gained while you were not getting paid for your work. For help figuring out what your transferable skills are, ask yourself the questions listed in the previous section, "If This Is Your First Job."

If You Were Fired

If you were fired from a prior job, you should still list it on your resume. Omitting it will leave a gap in your work history, which you will need to somehow explain. Remember, also, that even if you were fired from a job, you probably gained valuable experience while you were there. You may have to explain why you were fired when you go on a job interview, but you do not have to worry about that until later. You will find out what to do when you get to Chapter 13.

If you do choose to leave a job off your resume because it isn't relevant to your current career path, then you can title the section that lists your employment background "Relevant Work History" in order to let whoever looks at your resume know that this is not your complete work history. If you are asked to complete a job application, you will need to include all jobs, though, so you may have to explain why you didn't include a job on your resume.

If You Are Changing Careers

Dealing with a career change is similar to having to write a resume when you don't have any work experience. The difference is that you do have work experience, though it may seem to you as if the experience you have is unrelated to your new career. You should write a functional resume if you are pursuing a career in a new field of work. When selecting the skills or functions to highlight in your resume, you might have to dig deep to find things you did in your previous career that will help you in your new one.

Lying on Your Resume: Don't Do It!

You want to apply for a job, but you fall a bit short in terms of your experience or education. Or perhaps you don't have a particular skill that a potential employer wants a job candidate to have. You may think to yourself, "Why not just make something up?" After all, it would only be a little white lie. What if you said you had a bachelor's degree when you are only twelve credits short of graduating? No one would ever know—or would they?

A small lie on your resume, one that makes you appear more qualified for the job, might get you a job interview. You may even get a job offer without anyone finding out about it. Then you might have to consent to a background check or pre-employment screening. Oops. Easy come, easy go.

FACT

An increasing number of companies are doing background checks, or pre-employment screening, on job candidates before hiring them. In addition to being honest when discussing your experience and education, you must make sure any credentials you list on your resume are up to date.

Let's say the employer doesn't do a background check. After all, they are expensive to do. So, the employer hires you. You start working for her. A few months later the truth comes out, as truth often does. Will your new boss look at you and say, "You know what, Bob? We love you anyway. We want you to stay. You've proven yourself to be a great employee, even without those twelve credits"? It is highly unlikely that would happen because what is at issue here is not the lie you told, but rather the fact that you lied. Your boss's trust in you will be broken.

If you think you are qualified for a job in spite of being slightly short of meeting all the requirements that an employer has laid out, then be honest about it. Send a cover letter that clearly explains why you think you are qualified for the job regardless of not meeting that one qualification. Play up qualifications you do have, and downplay that one you do not have. You may not get hired—or you may. Even if you do not get the job, you'll still have your integrity.

Chapter 5
Resume Samples

In the last chapter you learned different ways to format your resume. Choose a format based upon your particular situation. Remember, no two job hunters are exactly alike and neither are any two resumes. Your resume should give an employer a snapshot of who you are at this moment in time. On one page, it concisely tells the story of where you've come from, where you are now, and where you plan to go. Use the sample resumes given in this chapter to guide you in putting together your resume.

5

Last-Minute Resume Tips

Do you remember all you've learned about putting together your resume? There is certainly a lot to keep in mind, but a basic rule of thumb is to let common sense prevail. Professionalism and clarity are of great importance in a resume, as is relevance to the position you're applying for. You don't want the person reviewing your resume to be confused about your objective or any of your prior experience. A resume should be clean-looking, immediately understandable, and informative. The following are some other helpful tips to keep in mind when creating your resume:

- Use a professional-sounding e-mail address.
- Use bold print for section titles of your resume.
- Use an action word to begin each statement on your resume.
- Use bullet points to list items on a resume.
- Statements on a resume are not complete sentences and therefore you should not use a period to end them.
- Use bold print to emphasize job titles.
- Use a simple, easy-to-read font like Arial or Times New Roman.
- Proofread your resume carefully and thoroughly—it should be free of spelling and grammatical errors and typos.

There's no guarantee that a well-organized, clean resume will get you the job you want; after all, it's the content of the resume that truly counts. But a professional approach can certainly weigh heavily in your favor. The following pages offer some sample resumes for you to consider as you put together your own resume.

SAMPLE CHRONOLOGICAL RESUME   Jeffrey Shaefer is looking for a job as a bank teller. Since he already has experience in the field, he can use a chronological resume to present his work history. His prior two jobs were in other fields, but Jeffrey was able to highlight some skills needed for his current field when writing descriptions of those jobs.

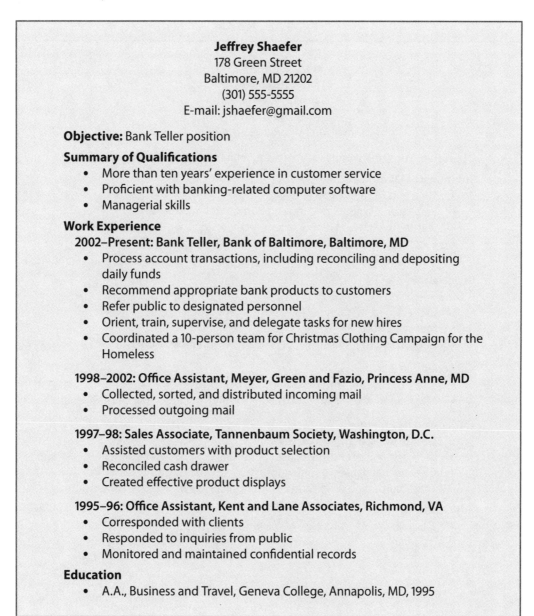

Jeffrey Shaefer
178 Green Street
Baltimore, MD 21202
(301) 555-5555
E-mail: jshaefer@gmail.com

Objective: Bank Teller position

Summary of Qualifications
- More than ten years' experience in customer service
- Proficient with banking-related computer software
- Managerial skills

Work Experience
2002–Present: Bank Teller, Bank of Baltimore, Baltimore, MD
- Process account transactions, including reconciling and depositing daily funds
- Recommend appropriate bank products to customers
- Refer public to designated personnel
- Orient, train, supervise, and delegate tasks for new hires
- Coordinated a 10-person team for Christmas Clothing Campaign for the Homeless

1998–2002: Office Assistant, Meyer, Green and Fazio, Princess Anne, MD
- Collected, sorted, and distributed incoming mail
- Processed outgoing mail

1997–98: Sales Associate, Tannenbaum Society, Washington, D.C.
- Assisted customers with product selection
- Reconciled cash drawer
- Created effective product displays

1995–96: Office Assistant, Kent and Lane Associates, Richmond, VA
- Corresponded with clients
- Responded to inquiries from public
- Monitored and maintained confidential records

Education
- A.A., Business and Travel, Geneva College, Annapolis, MD, 1995

SAMPLE FUNCTIONAL RESUME   Mary Connors has been employed as a sales representative for a clothing manufacturer for ten years. She is an avid gardener and shares her expertise with others by volunteering for local organizations. She is now trying to combine her vocation with her hobby by finding a job selling landscaping supplies. Mary is using a functional resume to highlight her sales skills as well as her gardening expertise.

Mary Connors
14 Silver Bell Street
Garden, MI 49835
(906) 555-5555
E-mail: mconnors@verizon.net

Objective: Position as a sales representative in landscaping supplies industry

Summary of Qualifications
- Ten years of sales experience
- Very strong skills in landscaping and garden maintenance
- Self-motivated and highly organized
- Excellent communication skills
- Demonstrated ability to exceed sales goals

Experience
Sales
- Exceeded sales goals for five most recent years
- Met sales goals for five prior years
- Responded to requests for price quotes within two hours

Relationship Building
- Successfully built and expanded sales territory
- Maintained relationships with over 45 retail buyers or purchasing agents

Landscaping Expertise
- Designed gardens for two parks
- Won first place for three consecutive years in the Delta County Gardening Club annual garden design contest
- Teach gardening workshops for the University of Michigan Extension

Education
- B.S., Marketing, University of Michigan, 1996

SAMPLE COMBINATION RESUME While Joseph Mannion is looking for a job in his current field, he wants one that is a promotion from the one he has now. Since he has relevant skills, he has chosen to use a combination resume. This format will allow Joseph to emphasize those skills and show off his work history.

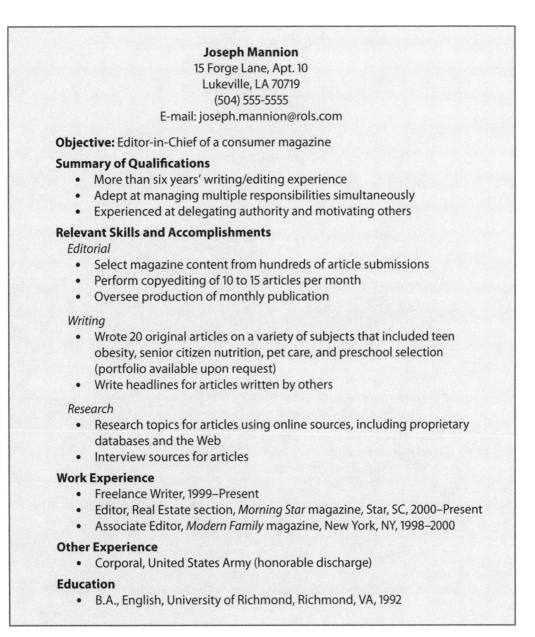

Joseph Mannion
15 Forge Lane, Apt. 10
Lukeville, LA 70719
(504) 555-5555
E-mail: joseph.mannion@rols.com

Objective: Editor-in-Chief of a consumer magazine

Summary of Qualifications
- More than six years' writing/editing experience
- Adept at managing multiple responsibilities simultaneously
- Experienced at delegating authority and motivating others

Relevant Skills and Accomplishments
Editorial
- Select magazine content from hundreds of article submissions
- Perform copyediting of 10 to 15 articles per month
- Oversee production of monthly publication

Writing
- Wrote 20 original articles on a variety of subjects that included teen obesity, senior citizen nutrition, pet care, and preschool selection (portfolio available upon request)
- Write headlines for articles written by others

Research
- Research topics for articles using online sources, including proprietary databases and the Web
- Interview sources for articles

Work Experience
- Freelance Writer, 1999–Present
- Editor, Real Estate section, *Morning Star* magazine, Star, SC, 2000–Present
- Associate Editor, *Modern Family* magazine, New York, NY, 1998–2000

Other Experience
- Corporal, United States Army (honorable discharge)

Education
- B.A., English, University of Richmond, Richmond, VA, 1992

SAMPLE RESUME FOR SOMEONE RETURNING TO WORK   Scott Ville is returning to work after being a stay-at-home parent for almost twelve years. Shortly after Scott left the workplace, the Web took off. He became interested in the field and learned how to design Web pages. Although he never received formal education in Web design, he did take some online courses to further his skills. He honed his craft by volunteering to design Web sites for local groups. Now he wants to become employed in this field. Scott is using a combination resume to highlight his strong skill set.

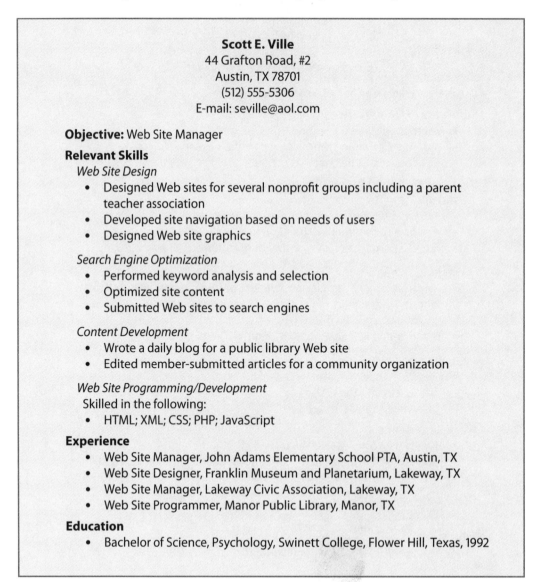

Scott E. Ville
44 Grafton Road, #2
Austin, TX 78701
(512) 555-5306
E-mail: seville@aol.com

Objective: Web Site Manager

Relevant Skills

Web Site Design
- Designed Web sites for several nonprofit groups including a parent teacher association
- Developed site navigation based on needs of users
- Designed Web site graphics

Search Engine Optimization
- Performed keyword analysis and selection
- Optimized site content
- Submitted Web sites to search engines

Content Development
- Wrote a daily blog for a public library Web site
- Edited member-submitted articles for a community organization

Web Site Programming/Development
Skilled in the following:
- HTML; XML; CSS; PHP; JavaScript

Experience
- Web Site Manager, John Adams Elementary School PTA, Austin, TX
- Web Site Designer, Franklin Museum and Planetarium, Lakeway, TX
- Web Site Manager, Lakeway Civic Association, Lakeway, TX
- Web Site Programmer, Manor Public Library, Manor, TX

Education
- Bachelor of Science, Psychology, Swinett College, Flower Hill, Texas, 1992

SAMPLE RESUME FOR FIRST-TIME JOB SEEKER (SOME EXPERIENCE) Carrie Eisenberg is a recent high school graduate looking for an entry-level job. She has part-time work experience in sales and has also worked as a hostess and waitress at a local restaurant. Carrie shows off her related experience in a chronological resume.

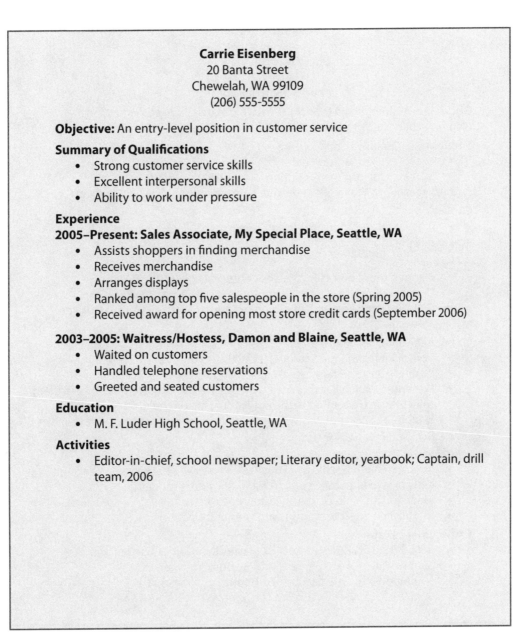

Carrie Eisenberg
20 Banta Street
Chewelah, WA 99109
(206) 555-5555

Objective: An entry-level position in customer service

Summary of Qualifications
- Strong customer service skills
- Excellent interpersonal skills
- Ability to work under pressure

Experience
2005–Present: Sales Associate, My Special Place, Seattle, WA
- Assists shoppers in finding merchandise
- Receives merchandise
- Arranges displays
- Ranked among top five salespeople in the store (Spring 2005)
- Received award for opening most store credit cards (September 2006)

2003–2005: Waitress/Hostess, Damon and Blaine, Seattle, WA
- Waited on customers
- Handled telephone reservations
- Greeted and seated customers

Education
- M. F. Luder High School, Seattle, WA

Activities
- Editor-in-chief, school newspaper; Literary editor, yearbook; Captain, drill team, 2006

SAMPLE RESUME FOR FIRST-TIME JOB SEEKER (NO RELATED EXPERIENCE)
Alexandria Cryor is a recent college graduate trying to find a job in the field in which she just received a degree. She doesn't have any work experience in this field—tourism—but she does have skills that employers should find desirable.

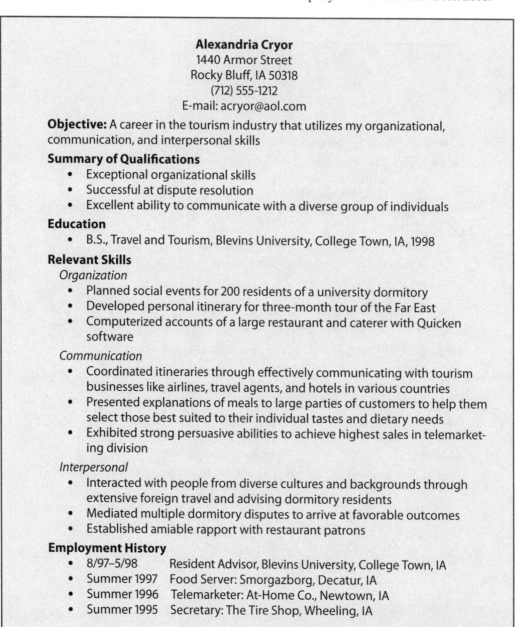

Alexandria Cryor
1440 Armor Street
Rocky Bluff, IA 50318
(712) 555-1212
E-mail: acryor@aol.com

Objective: A career in the tourism industry that utilizes my organizational, communication, and interpersonal skills

Summary of Qualifications
- Exceptional organizational skills
- Successful at dispute resolution
- Excellent ability to communicate with a diverse group of individuals

Education
- B.S., Travel and Tourism, Blevins University, College Town, IA, 1998

Relevant Skills
Organization
- Planned social events for 200 residents of a university dormitory
- Developed personal itinerary for three-month tour of the Far East
- Computerized accounts of a large restaurant and caterer with Quicken software

Communication
- Coordinated itineraries through effectively communicating with tourism businesses like airlines, travel agents, and hotels in various countries
- Presented explanations of meals to large parties of customers to help them select those best suited to their individual tastes and dietary needs
- Exhibited strong persuasive abilities to achieve highest sales in telemarketing division

Interpersonal
- Interacted with people from diverse cultures and backgrounds through extensive foreign travel and advising dormitory residents
- Mediated multiple dormitory disputes to arrive at favorable outcomes
- Established amiable rapport with restaurant patrons

Employment History
- 8/97–5/98   Resident Advisor, Blevins University, College Town, IA
- Summer 1997 Food Server: Smorgazborg, Decatur, IA
- Summer 1996 Telemarketer: At-Home Co., Newtown, IA
- Summer 1995 Secretary: The Tire Shop, Wheeling, IA

SAMPLE RESUME FOR A CAREER CHANGER   Joanne Grant has been a librarian for a while, but now she wants to change careers. She has decided to become an event coordinator. Her skills in that area were acquired during her tenure as a librarian. To demonstrate those skills, she has chosen to write a combination resume.

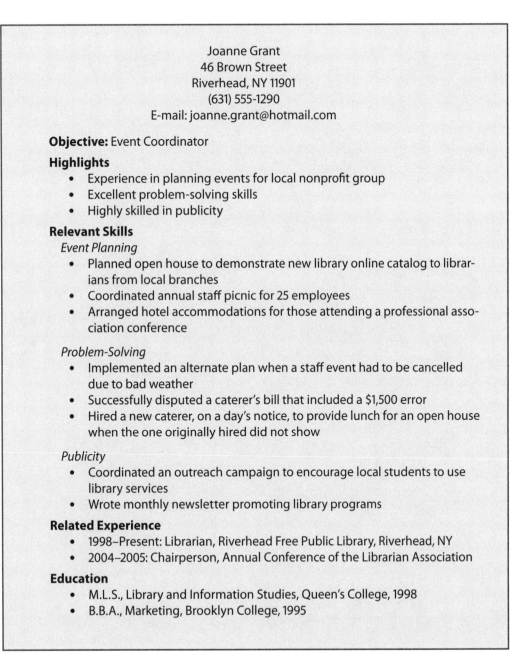

Joanne Grant
46 Brown Street
Riverhead, NY 11901
(631) 555-1290
E-mail: joanne.grant@hotmail.com

Objective: Event Coordinator

Highlights
- Experience in planning events for local nonprofit group
- Excellent problem-solving skills
- Highly skilled in publicity

Relevant Skills

Event Planning
- Planned open house to demonstrate new library online catalog to librarians from local branches
- Coordinated annual staff picnic for 25 employees
- Arranged hotel accommodations for those attending a professional association conference

Problem-Solving
- Implemented an alternate plan when a staff event had to be cancelled due to bad weather
- Successfully disputed a caterer's bill that included a $1,500 error
- Hired a new caterer, on a day's notice, to provide lunch for an open house when the one originally hired did not show

Publicity
- Coordinated an outreach campaign to encourage local students to use library services
- Wrote monthly newsletter promoting library programs

Related Experience
- 1998–Present: Librarian, Riverhead Free Public Library, Riverhead, NY
- 2004–2005: Chairperson, Annual Conference of the Librarian Association

Education
- M.L.S., Library and Information Studies, Queen's College, 1998
- B.B.A., Marketing, Brooklyn College, 1995

Chapter 6
Electronic Resumes

When putting together your resume you will give a lot of thought to its physical appearance, including font, layout, and paper. An increasing number of employers, though, don't want a hard copy of your resume. They will instead ask you to submit an electronic copy of it through an online form or via e-mail. While you will use all the bells and whistles provided by your word processing software to make a paper copy of your resume physically appealing, a copy that you will submit electronically will have to be plain and, yes, somewhat boring.

When Do You Need an Electronic Resume?

You need to have an electronic resume whenever an employer asks you to send your resume by e-mail or submit it through an online form. Many employers will input your resume into a database called an automated applicant-tracking system. This system will scan your resume, along with the hundreds of others the employer receives, for keywords that match keywords in their job descriptions. Those whose resumes have the best fit will move on to the next step of the hiring process.

In order for an automated applicant-tracking system to scan a resume well, it must be in a format it can read. Pasting your conventional resume into an e-mail message or into an online form simply won't do. You must put together a special version of your resume to be used when you are asked to submit it electronically, which will probably be quite often.

Sometimes job seekers choose to utilize a resume bank. The concept is similar to the one described above. Your resume is put into a database and scanned for keywords. Employers looking for candidates to fill open positions will look through this database for resumes that are suitable. As with an automated applicant-tracking system, your resume must be formatted so that a computer can read and decipher it.

Before you go ahead and throw out your old paper resume, be advised that not all companies stay up to speed on the latest technology. Many companies simply don't have the equipment to directly receive e-mailed resumes and to search online databases for job candidates. Having a paper copy of your resume is still a necessity, especially since you'll need to bring it with you to all those job interviews!

Formatting

Whether you're applying to a company that uses automated tracking systems or paying to have your resume loaded onto a resume bank, keep your resume simple. The same elaborate formatting that makes your resume beautiful for the human eye to behold makes it impossible for a computer to understand. Additionally, if you get too complicated with bullet points and subheads, your resume may become impossible to follow.

Font Size and Style

Stick to a basic font—this is no time to express your creativity. Choose a nondecorative font with clear, distinct characters, like Times New Roman or Courier. It's more difficult for a scanner to accurately pick up decorative fonts like script (which you should also avoid on a conventional resume). Usually the results are unintelligible letters and words.

A font size of 12 points is ideal. Don't go below 10 points, as type that's too small may not scan well.

When formatting an electronic resume you should not use italics or underlining. You can generally use boldface type. If you are asked to avoid that as well, use capital letters instead to set off major section headings like "Experience" and "Education."

Layout and Length

Avoid the temptation to use lines and graphics to liven up what is an otherwise visually uninteresting resume. A resume scanner will try to "read" graphics, lines, and shading as text, resulting in computer chaos. Also avoid nontraditional layouts, like two-column formats.

As mentioned previously, you should keep your resume to one page in length. Use concise phrases that include keywords that are pertinent to the job you want. That said, don't try to compress space between letters, words, or lines to fit everything on one page—this makes it more difficult for the computer to read. Leave plenty of space between sections.

Abbreviations

Most resume-scanning systems recognize a few common abbreviations, like BS, MBA, and state names, with or without periods. Widely used acronyms for industry jargon, like A/R and A/P on an accounting resume, are also generally accepted, although it's advisable to spell out most abbreviations. If there's any question about whether an abbreviation is standard, play it safe and spell it out.

Paper and Printing

Sometimes you may be asked to send your resume by snail mail, but are told it will be scanned into an automated system. If you are asked to send a hard copy, don't bother to print it on expensive paper. Use standard, 20-pound, 8½- by-11-inch paper. Because your resume needs to be as sharp and legible as possible, use black ink on white paper. Make sure the result is letter quality. Always send an original, not a photocopy, and mail your resume rather than faxing it.

When sending an electronic resume by e-mail, include a cover letter in the same message, followed by the resume. Use the cover letter to summarize your strongest qualifications. If you're responding to a classified ad, try to use some of the same keywords the ad mentions. Be as attentive to your grammar and spelling as you would be if sending a paper version of a cover letter.

Contents

The information you include in your electronic resume doesn't really differ from a traditional resume—it's simply the manner in which you present it that changes. Traditionally, resumes include action verbs like "managed," "coordinated," or "developed." Now employers are more likely to do keyword searches filled with nouns, like degree held or software you're familiar with. Employers rarely search for personal traits when doing a keyword search, but when they do, traits like "team player," "creative," and "problem solving" are among the most common they look for.

Keywords

Using the right keywords or key phrases in your resume is critical. Keyword searches tend to focus on nouns. Let's say an employer searches an employment database for a sales representative with the following keyword criteria: sales representative, BS/BA, exceeded quota, cold calls, high energy, willing to travel. Even if you have the right qualifications, if you don't use these keywords on your resume, the computer will pass over your application. To complicate matters further, different employers search for different keywords.

Although there is no way to know for sure which keywords employers are most likely to search for, you can make educated guesses. Check help-wanted advertisements for job openings in your field. What terms do employers commonly use to describe their requirements? Job seekers in your field are another source, as are executive recruiters who specialize in your field. You'll want to use as many keywords in your resume as possible, but keep in mind that using the same keyword five times won't increase your chances of getting matched with an employer. Note, however, that if you're posting your resume to a job-hunting Web site, a small number of such sites rank resumes by the number of keywords and their frequency of occurrence.

Contact Information

Your name should appear at the top of the resume, with your address, telephone number, and e-mail address immediately underneath. Rather than centering that information as you did on your conventional resume, it should be left-justified on your electronic resume.

Keyword Summary

This is a compendium of your qualifications, usually written in a series of succinct keyword phrases that immediately follow your name and address. Place the most important words first on the list, since the computer may be limited in the number of words it will read.

Objective

If you are submitting a resume in response to a specific job announcement, you should have an objective on your resume—using the job title being advertised, of course. If you are submitting your resume to a database and multiple employers will have access to it, forgo the objective. Include a few keywords in the objective, to increase your chances of getting matched ("a position as a financial analyst where I can utilize my on-the-job experience and MBA").

ONLINE RESUME   Notice that it doesn't contain bullets and words are not italicized or underlined. All text begins flush left, with spaces between paragraphs and sections. Boldface is usually acceptable when submitting your resume through an online form or if you are mailing a hard copy that will be scanned into a database. If you are sending the resume via e-mail, you should avoid boldface type entirely. You can use uppercase letters instead.

MICHAEL S. DILUZIO
27 Pageant Drive, Apartment 7
Cambridge, MA 02138
(617) 555-5555

KEYWORD SUMMARY
Accounting manager with seven years' experience in general ledger, accounts payable, and financial reporting. MBA in Management. Proficient in QuickBooks and Excel.

PROFESSIONAL EXPERIENCE
1996—present: ACCOUNTING MANAGER, Colwell Corporation, Wellesley, MA
Manager of a staff of six in general ledger and accounts payable
- Designed and refined financial reporting package
- Assisted in month-end closings
- Established guidelines for month-end closing procedures, speeding up closing by five business days
- Implemented team-oriented cross-training program within accounting group resulting in increased productivity of key accounting staff

1994—1996: SENIOR ACCOUNTANT, Franklin and Delany Company, Melrose, MA
- Managed accounts payable, general ledger, transaction processing, and financial reporting
- Supervised staff of two
- Developed management reporting package, including variance reports and cash flow reporting

---

```
1993-1994: STAFF ACCOUNTANT, Franklin and Delany Company,
Melrose, MA
- Managed accounts payable, including vouchering, cash
disbursements, and bank reconciliation
- Wrote and issued policies
- Maintained supporting schedules used during year-end
audits
- Trained new employees

EDUCATION
- MBA in Management, Northeastern University, Boston, MA,
1995
- BS in Accounting, Boston College, Boston, MA, 1993

PROFESSIONAL ASSOCIATIONS
National Association of Accountants
```

Experience and Achievements

Your professional experience should immediately follow the keyword summary, beginning with your most recent position. (If you're a recent college graduate, list your education before your experience.) Be sure your job title, employer, location, and dates of employment are all clearly displayed. Highlight your accomplishments and key responsibilities with dashes (in place of bullets on an electronic resume). Again, try to incorporate as many buzzwords as possible into these phrases.

Education

This section immediately follows the experience section. List your degrees, licenses, permits, certifications, relevant course work, and academic awards or honors. Be sure to clearly display the names of the schools, locations, and years of graduation. List any professional organizations or associations you're a member of; many recruiters will include such organizations when doing a keyword search.

Applicant-Tracking Systems

As the name implies, companies use applicant-tracking systems, or in-house resume databases, to keep track of the hordes of resumes they receive. Many employers, especially large, well-known companies, can receive hundreds of unsolicited resumes per week. Where once these unsolicited resumes may have headed straight for a filing cabinet or even the trash, never to be looked at again, electronic applicant-tracking systems now allow employers to keep resumes in an active file.

Basically, here's how it works: a company receives your resume, either unsolicited, through a career fair, or in response to a classified advertisement. Your resume is scanned into the computer, dated, coded, and placed into the appropriate file (like administrative, financial, or technical). Other systems may simply sort resumes according to date received.

When there's a job opening, the hiring manager submits a search request to the database operator, who is usually someone in human resources or information systems. The database operator performs a keyword search to find resumes that match the criteria.

Advantages

There are numerous advantages of automated applicant-tracking systems. Here are a few that pertain to you, the job seeker:

- A computer is completely impartial.
- You don't have to worry about your resume getting misplaced accidentally.
- Even if you don't get the job, your resume is kept in the database, so you can be considered for later openings.
- You don't need to send in multiple resumes to different department managers at the same company. (If you do send in multiple resumes, the system usually deletes the old one and keeps the most recent one.)

Companies prefer this new technology because it's more efficient, in terms of both time and money. The automated system cuts down on paperwork for many human resources managers and lowers administrative and advertising costs.

Disadvantages

As with anything, there are also some disadvantages or caveats to automated applicant-tracking systems. Those you should be aware of include the following:

- A computer will look for only those resumes that exactly meet the strict criteria of the search. This tends to put recent college graduates, borderline candidates, or those switching careers at a disadvantage, since these job seekers are less likely to have as many keywords included in their resumes.
- No automated system is infallible. If the computer rejects your resume because the scanner is unable to read it or turns it into an unintelligible mess, you're out of luck. Therefore, it's essential to send a clean, computer-friendly resume.

Resume Banks

A resume bank is simply an applicant-tracking system operated by an independent commercial firm. The procedures for submitting resumes to these services vary. Some resume banks charge a fee. What do you get? You get nationwide exposure to hundreds of companies of all sizes, from *Fortune* 500 to smaller, rapidly expanding companies.

In many ways, a resume bank is similar to a traditional employment agency: you send in your resume to a service, and the service begins working to find a job for you. However, with an electronic employment "agency," you are, theoretically, in the running for every job request that comes in. While each resume bank is different, you generally submit your resume to the service either by downloading it or filling out an online form. There are many popular resume banks available on the Internet, including Monster and CareerBuilder, that cater to job seekers in a variety of fields. There are also services that cater to job seekers in specific fields.

How Does It Work?

Resume banks generally give employers online access to their databases, allowing them to search for qualified candidates. Some resume banks may require that client companies call the service with job openings and give the service a list of keywords and desired qualifications. The service then searches the database on the client's behalf, looking for candidates who match the keywords.

How the candidates are presented to the client varies. Some services provide candidate summaries; others provide the actual resume; still others include information from the professional profile. Many resume banks allow you to hide personal information, such as your name and contact information, from employers viewing your resume. Some services contact you before forwarding your resume or any information to the client company.

ALERT!

Before submitting your resume to a resume bank, be sure to read the instructions and usage agreements carefully. You should also be aware of privacy policies. If you want to remain anonymous when looking for work—for example, if you don't want your current employer to know you are doing a job search—make sure the resume bank has that option.

Advantages

Just as with automated applicant-tracking systems, there are numerous advantages to resume banks. Here are a few that pertain to you, the job seeker:

- You benefit because you can make your resume available to hundreds of companies by posting it in one place.
- You are exposed to employers nationwide, not just in your own town or region. If you're willing to relocate, you can find your dream job, even if it's thousands of miles away.

Companies like using resume banks because doing so can potentially save them the cost of advertising and, by prescreening candidates, also save them hours of work. Resume banks also give employers easy access to thousands of candidates.

Disadvantages

Again, there are also a few disadvantages of resume banks to be aware of:

- Since some database searches only turn up a few qualified candidates, many companies may not rely on resume banks.
- Many companies continue to use other methods of recruiting candidates, including in-house applicant-tracking systems, help-wanted ads, and employment agencies, in lieu of resume banks. You should use these databases as a part of your overall job hunt, but should continue to use other methods of job searching as well.

Selecting Resume Banks to Use

Given all the choices available, you may be wondering where to post your resume. Nothing says you can't post to more than one database. Since most online resume databases don't charge job seekers, you could, theoretically, post to every site. You probably don't want to spend the time it would take to do that. You must select resume banks using several criteria.

General Versus Niche Site

A general resume bank has a database that includes resumes of people in a wide variety of fields. A niche site specializes in a particular field. If it is unclear from the description on the site's home page, take a look at the resumes housed on a particular site. For example, if a site has resumes that predominantly showcase technical backgrounds, it's a safe bet that most of the companies that search that database are interested in filling technical positions.

ALERT!

When you post your resume online you make it accessible to virtually anyone with a computer and an Internet connection. That means they can look at your personal information—your name, address, telephone number, and other details. If you don't want that information available, look for services that offer confidentiality, like the option to hide your name and contact information.

If you're thinking of posting your resume to a general job site, like Monster, check out the companies that advertise in the site's job listings section. Often those companies will also utilize the service's resume bank to search for candidates.

Experienced Candidates Versus New Graduates

Some resume banks cater to new or recent graduates with little experience, while others cater to those with a lot of experience. Employers looking for candidates who fit into either of those two categories will visit the appropriate site. Make sure your resume is in the type of database in which it belongs. Also read the information on the Web site. Look for clues about the types of candidates who use their service.

Fees

Most online sites don't charge for posting your resume. Employers and recruiters usually pay to access the resume bank. Some, especially those run by independent recruiters or career placement services, do charge a small fee, which may include resume preparation and advice. These databases are smaller and may not have the wide exposure of some of the larger, free databases, but if you feel you need help composing your resume, the fee might be worth it.

How to Post Your Resume

Most sites have instructions for entering a resume into their database. These instructions should tell you how long resumes remain in the database, how to update and remove your resume, who has access to the database, and the fee (if any). If a database doesn't have instructions, e-mail or call the site administrators for more information.

Before writing a check or giving your credit card number to a company over the Internet, it's a good idea to check its reputation with the Better Business Bureau or a similar agency. While the majority of companies selling services over the Internet are reputable, remember that simply because a company has a presence on the Internet doesn't mean it's legitimate.

Some sites may require you to fill out personal information online, like your name, e-mail address, and resume title, but most allow you to attach your own resume or paste it in a specific area.

Sending Your Resume via E-mail

E-mailing your resume to potential employers is generally done in response to a help-wanted advertisement or simply as a method of direct contact. In fact, many companies now request that resumes be submitted through e-mail, rather than the U.S. mail or by fax. When sending your resume by e-mail, paste it into the body of the message. Do not send an attachment unless instructed to. Many companies won't open an attachment because of the possibility that it may contain a computer virus. You should consider the text of your message preceding your resume a cover letter. Follow the rules for cover letters outlined in Chapter 7.

After e-mailing your resume, wait a few days to be sure the recipient has read it. Call or e-mail the company to confirm that your resume was received intact. As with a paper resume, an e-mailed resume may do you little good unless you follow up to express your genuine interest. If you sent your resume to an individual, ask if he would like you to elaborate on any sections of your resume. If you sent it to a general e-mail address, call the human resources department to check the status of your application.

Dear Mr. Preston:

This e-mail is in response to your advertisement in the Boston Globe for the position of Assistant Controller. My resume follows. I am very interested in the position and believe I have the qualifications you are looking for. Please consider the following:

- I have over twenty years' experience in accounting and systems management, budgeting, forecasting, cost containment, financial reporting, and international accounting.

- I implemented a team-oriented cross-training program within my accounting group, resulting in timely month-end closings and increased productivity of key accounting staff.

- I have an MBA in Management from Northeastern University.

- I am a results-oriented professional and proven team leader.

These are only a few of my credentials that may be of interest to you. I look forward to discussing them with you further in a personal interview.

Thank you for your consideration.

Sincerely,

Madeline Reed

(Your electronic resume will go here)

Advantages

There are some advantages to sending your resume by e-mail. Here are a couple of the most prominent:

- E-mailing your resume is quick and efficient. Instead of spending time printing out a copy of your resume, addressing an envelope, and mailing it, you can send your resume with a few clicks of your mouse. This allows you to respond almost instantly to job listings online as well as to help-wanted ads you see in the newspaper.
- Employers like e-mailed resumes because they cut down on paperwork and lower administrative costs.

Disadvantages

Of course, there are also a few downsides to e-mailing your resume, including the following:

- Some job seekers work very hard at developing a professional-looking hard-copy version of their resumes, printed on high-quality resume paper. An e-mailed resume, while still capable of sounding professional, cannot always offer the same presentation or look as its hard-copy cousin.
- There can be problems with sending or receiving. E-mail may be picked up by a company's spam filter and not reach its recipient. There is also the possibility that e-mail sent to a general e-mail address may not be delivered to the appropriate person.
- Some people just don't check their e-mail all that often. This is a particular problem if you are sending an unsolicited resume. You should follow up your e-mailed resume with a hard copy in the mail. Be sure to indicate that you have done that in the text of the e-mail or snail-mail copy, or both.

Creating Your Own Web Site

Some people choose to create their own Web sites on which to post their resumes. This is particularly useful if you have a portfolio that demonstrates your skills—for example, writing samples or photographs. You can include everything on one site. When creating your own Web page, be sure your employment background is emphasized over all else. It's easy to get carried away with creating a Web page full of elaborate graphics or other links, but your resume should still be the core. Remember also that the home page strategy can backfire. If your design skills are weak and employers aren't impressed, you'll be worse off than before.

Going Live

The first thing you have to do when putting up a Web site is choose a name for it. This is called a domain name (it's the part that goes after the "www" and before the ".com"). You can use your own name or the name of your occupation. Unless your occupation is unusual, it is probably already taken as a domain name. You will have to register your domain name with an Internet registry. When you do that, you will find out if someone else is already using it. InterNIC.com (*http://internic.com*) can direct you to domain registrars.

Next, you must choose a company to host your Web site. There are many companies that do this. Some Internet service providers (ISPs) offer their subscribers free Web space, so that is a good place to start. If not, search for "web hosting" using a search engine. When you find one that you think you want to use, do another search to find reviews of that service.

Building your Web site comes next. Many hosting services provide free tools that can help you get your site up and running pretty quickly. It's as simple as typing your information into a template. You can also use Web editing software like Microsoft FrontPage to help you design your site.

Finally, you must promote your site. If you make sure to include lots of important keywords on your Web site, specifically on your resume, an employer who puts those terms into a search engine will be more likely to have your site come up in his results. Search engines automatically look for sites on the Web to include in their indexes. You can also submit your site to some search engines. You can usually find instructions for this on a search engine's site.

Multimedia and Video Resumes

Multimedia and video resumes are suitable for certain specialized applications. If you're in a creative field where knowledge of cutting-edge technology is valued, a multimedia or video resume may be effective or even essential.

A multimedia resume takes full advantage of the Web's capabilities by incorporating computer technology like graphics, scanned photographs, sound, and links to other sites. The applicant's information is virtually the same as in a regular resume but in an interactive format. For instance, clicking on an icon may present examples of an applicant's work. This type of resume is usually sent directly to an employer on disk or posted on an online resume database. Check out resumes posted online for ideas regarding design and content. (You can do a search on a search engine like Google or Yahoo! for "multimedia resumes.")

Video resumes are generally in the form of dialogues or "question and answer" formats, in which an off-camera participant asks the candidate questions regarding his background. The video itself is short—usually no longer than five minutes, or the equivalent of a three-to-five-page resume.

The simplest advice to give someone considering using a multimedia or video resume is to know your audience. Send it only to companies on the leading edge, where your technological know-how and creativity will be appreciated. Before sending such a resume, call to find out if the company will accept it and if they have the equipment to view it.

Chapter 7

Cover Letters

Do you really need to have a cover letter to accompany your resume? Some people feel that writing one is a waste of time. Employers, they lament, are only interested in your resume and won't even bother to read your cover letter. That may be true of some employers, but not all. A cover letter is your introduction to the employer. Not sending a cover letter is like phoning someone and not bothering to say hello before you begin your conversation.

Always Send a Cover Letter

Whenever you send out your resume, a cover letter should always accompany it. This is true when you are applying for a job in response to a posted job opening or when you are sending an unsolicited resume to a prospective employer. It is true when you are sending your resume to a member of your network or a potential contact. It is also true whether you are sending your resume by snail mail or e-mail. Even when you apply online to a job listing posted on a job-bank site, you will usually have the option of submitting a cover letter along with your resume.

A cover letter lets you introduce yourself to the person to whom you are sending your resume. First, it is your chance to let the recipient know why they are receiving it. That may sound simplistic, but remember that your resume is most likely not the only one landing in the recipient's inbox. An employer may be getting resumes in response to many job openings. You can help him by specifying which job you are applying for.

FACT

Job-search sites like CareerBuilder, Monster, and Yahoo! HotJobs, which will be discussed in detail in Chapter 10, all let users set up cover letters. You must become a member of each site to do this, but don't worry—membership is free. Your cover letter will be stored in a database with your resume and you can access it when applying for jobs listed on each of those Web sites.

Your cover letter gives you the opportunity to highlight your skills and experience that are most relevant to the job opening for which you are applying. Use your cover letter to showcase two or three attributes that the employer will find most desirable. Then don't forget to ask for an interview before closing your letter. If you aren't sending your resume because you are applying for a job, but are instead sending it to a member of your network or a potential contact, then make sure to let the recipient know what you want to happen next. Do you want to set up a meeting with her? If so, specify that. If you plan to follow up with a phone call, say that in your letter as well.

Formatting

You will send your cover letter to an employer in one of three ways. Either you will mail it along with a copy of your resume, send it via e-mail, or submit it along with your resume through an online job-search site in response to a job posting. The content of the body of your cover letter will be the same regardless of how you transmit it. The format of your cover letter will differ depending on whether you send it by mail, e-mail, or electronic submission to a job-search Web site. Generally, if you submit a cover letter through an online job-search site, you will be asked to compose the letter by completing a form. Follow the directions on the site you are using. For a cover letter that you will send by mail or e-mail, use the formatting suggestions in the following sections.

Sending Your Cover Letter by Mail

For many people, writing a business letter—on paper—is an unusual activity. Most of our written correspondence these days is by e-mail. When you compose a business letter you must follow a prescribed format. A business letter is composed of six parts:

1. **Return Address:** This should include your name and address.
2. **Date:** Use the date you are sending the letter. If you plan to write the letter but not send it for a couple of days, don't use today's date, but instead use the date you are going to send it.
3. **Inside Address:** This section includes the recipient's name, title, company name, and address, each on a separate line.
4. **Salutation:** This is where you address the recipient—for example, "Dear Ms. Smith." Avoid addressing your letter to "Dear Sir or Madam," or worse, "To Whom It May Concern." Make every effort to ascertain the name of the recipient.
5. **Body:** Here is the meat of your cover letter. Begin by telling the recipient why you are writing—for example, "I am writing to apply for the administrative assistant job advertised in the *Delaware Sun*." Go on to tell the recipient why you are qualified for the job, and close by asking for an interview. Look for more on the body of your cover letter below.

6. **Closing:** Close your letter by saying either, "Thank you," "Yours truly," or "Sincerely." Then leave room for your signature beneath that, and follow that, on the next line, by typing your name.

There are two styles to choose from when writing a business letter. You can use indented paragraphs or block paragraphs. If you use indented paragraphs, you should place your return address and date at the top right side of your paper and the inside (recipient) address on the left, followed by the salutation and the body. You will begin all paragraphs by indenting five spaces.

If you use block paragraphs, all content is flush left. Rather than indenting each paragraph, you will separate paragraphs with a blank line. Block paragraphs are more commonly used than indented paragraphs, and that style will be the one used in sample letters in the following two chapters. Some people, however, still prefer to indent paragraphs. Here are samples of each style.

Strong writing skills are a requirement for many different types of jobs. Think of your cover letter as the first chance you have to demonstrate your writing skills to a potential employer. You want the body of your cover letter to clearly convey your intent. To achieve this goal, your writing must be concise. Use simple language. You want your words to stand out in the reader's mind, so avoid using clichés.

ALERT!

The spell checker that came with your word processing software is a wonderful tool. Don't rely on it solely, though. If there are multiple spellings for a word, each with a different meaning, the spell checker won't tell you if you use the wrong one. For example, the sentence, "I went too the park two play bawl" could be entirely missed by a spell checker. Try it and you'll see!

Always make sure you use correct spelling and proper grammar. After you write your letter, put it aside for a little while before you proofread it. You may not catch your mistakes immediately after writing it. If possible, have someone else proofread it as well. It is difficult for most people to find

INDENTED PARAGRAPH STYLE

Robert K. Lynn
114 Remsen Avenue
Brooklyn, NY 11236

March 17, 2007

Samantha Rich
Vice President
Fillmore Savings Bank
456 Seventh Avenue
New York, NY 12234

Dear Ms. Rich,

I saw your advertisement for a customer service representative that appeared in Sunday's *New York Star*. I would like to apply for this position. I am enclosing my resume.

I recently completed my studies at Brooklyn College, earning a Bachelor's degree in Business. As you can see from my resume, I worked in the banking industry part-time during my four years in college. I began as a teller in 2002 and in 2004 I was promoted to assistant customer service representative. My two years of experience and success in this job qualifies me to take the next step to customer service representative.

I would like to set up an appointment for a job interview at your convenience. I can be reached at (718) 555-8288. I will call you at the beginning of next week after you have had a chance to look over my resume, unless I hear from you before then.

Yours truly,

(Signature)

Robert K. Lynn

BLOCK PARAGRAPH STYLE

Robert K. Lynn
114 Remsen Avenue
Brooklyn, NY 11236
March 17, 2007

Samantha Rich
Vice President
Fillmore Savings Bank
456 Seventh Avenue
New York, NY 12234

Dear Ms. Rich,

I saw your advertisement for a customer service representative that appeared in Sunday's *New York Star*. I would like to apply for this position. I am enclosing my resume.

I recently completed my studies at Brooklyn College, earning a Bachelor's degree in Business. As you can see from my resume, I worked in the banking industry part-time during my four years in college. I began as a teller in 2002 and in 2004 I was promoted to assistant customer service representative. My two years of experience and success in this job qualifies me to take the next step to customer service representative.

I would like to set up an appointment for a job interview at your convenience. I can be reached at (718) 555-8288. I will call you at the beginning of next week after you have had a chance to look over my resume, unless I hear from you before that.

Yours truly,

(Signature)

Robert K. Lynn

their own errors because often they see what they expect to see rather than what is actually there on the paper.

Sending Your Cover Letter by E-mail

When you send your cover letter by e-mail, the format you should use is much different than the one you would use for a printed letter as described in the preceding section. You shouldn't use a return address at the top, although you should include contact information in your signature. You don't need to use an inside address, either. The date is automatically inserted into the header of your e-mail so you don't need to type one in.

Be certain to always put something in the subject line. This should be the title of the position for which you are applying. Your salutation should be similar to the one you would use if you were sending the letter by snail mail. Never address the recipient by her first name.

You can set up an automatic e-mail signature in most e-mail software programs like Eudora and Outlook, as well as in Web-based e-mail like Gmail or Yahoo! Mail. Doing this will save you time since you won't have to type the information into each message you send. Your signature should include your full name and your contact information, including your mailing address, your telephone number, and your e-mail address.

When composing the body of your e-mail cover letter, follow the same rules as you would when writing a letter to be printed: State the reason for your message, explain why you are worthy of consideration, ask for an interview, and tell the recipient how you are going to follow up. Be concise and make sure you proofread your message.

Don't trick yourself into believing that an e-mail cover letter is any less formal than one you send by snail mail. Remember that you aren't writing a message to a friend. Don't use slang, e-mail shorthand, or emoticons (those little smiley faces many people use to express emotions). Avoid any fancy fonts, special formatting, or colored text.

Unless you are asked to do so, don't attach any files to your e-mail message. With viruses running rampant on the Internet, most people are reluctant to open unexpected attachments. Instead, put everything you are sending, including your resume, in the body of your message. See Chapter 6 for instructions on formatting a resume for e-mail.

Avoiding Common Mistakes

One of the most common mistakes job seekers make is sending a form letter rather than a letter individually written to each employer. Even if you use a basic template for all your cover letters, make sure you customize each one you send out.

Address your letter to a person, not "To Whom It May Concern" or "Dear Sir or Madam." If a person's name is not indicated in the job listing, call the company if a phone number is given. If you have tried and you still can't obtain the actual name of the intended recipient, then address your cover letter to the job title of the recipient, e.g., "Dear Hiring Manager."

Many job seekers forget to say what job they are applying for. State the job in your letter. As mentioned earlier, human resources departments receive hundreds of letters for many different positions. You want to be clear about which one you want.

Look through your resume and pick out attributes—skills and experience—that are most pertinent to each position you apply for. Highlight those attributes in the appropriate cover letters. If you send the same letter for every job opening, merely highlighting a few of your (possibly unrelated) qualifications, you won't come across as a strong candidate for the job at hand.

Remember to ask for an interview. Include a way for the employer to contact you, such as a phone number and e-mail address. State when and how you will follow up with the employer. For example, you can say, "I will call you in one week to schedule an interview unless I hear from you before that." Of course, you can only say you will call the employer if the job announcement provides the company's name. Not all include that information. If you say you're going to follow up, make sure you do!

Identified Employers Versus Unidentified Employers

Most help-wanted ads and job announcements include the name of the employer. Some do not. When an employer is identified, it will be much easier to customize your cover letter. For example, when possible, you should write your letter to a specific person. Often that information is included when an employer is identified. Sometimes, although an employer is identified in a help-wanted ad, the person to whom you will send your resume and cover letter is not. If you have the name of the company, you should call their offices to find out to whom you should address your letter.

When you see a job listing without a company name, remember that a staffing firm or a recruiter may have posted it. There may or may not even be a specific job available, since these firms sometimes place these ads in order to build up a list of viable candidates for future job openings.

In your cover letter you always want to highlight those attributes, including your skills and experience, most relevant to the position for which you are applying. If you know the name of the company, you can do a little research to find out more about it. Find out what products and services they sell by visiting the company's Web site. If you have experience with those products and services, you can showcase that information in your cover letter.

It is more difficult to write a cover letter when the employer is unidentified. You most likely won't be able to address your letter to a specific person, although sometimes that information is given even when the company name is not. Because it will be more difficult to decide which of your skills and experience to highlight if you don't know anything about the employer, choose those attributes that you know to be most valued in your field. Ask your network contacts for their opinions if you have trouble figuring this out.

Cold Contact Letters

When you are engaged in a job search, you aren't limited to sending your resume only to employers who have advertised job openings. You can send your resume to companies that interest you as well, even if there is no indication that they have any opening right now. This is referred to as making a "cold contact" and the cover letter you send to accompany your unsolicited resume is called a "cold contact letter."

When you send a cold contact letter it is important that you always specify the position for which you are applying. It doesn't matter that they aren't currently seeking someone to fill that position. If you don't specify a position, you will come across as seeming unfocused about your goals.

Many companies maintain files of resumes they receive that aren't in response to an announced opening. Some put these unsolicited resumes in a database that the employer will eventually search to find matches for open positions.

Just as you would do when sending a cover letter in response to an advertised job opening, highlight your attributes. You want to tell the employer why you are the best person to fill the position in which you're interested. Use keywords associated with the skills required for that position. Should your resume end up in a database, the employer will easily find it when searching for those words.

Before you close your letter, indicate the action you want the recipient to take. Do you want him to call you when an opening comes up or do you want to arrange for a meeting so you can discuss possible future openings? Also tell him what you plan to do next—for example, call in a week to follow up.

Following Up on Your Cover Letters

Sometimes when you send a cover letter to an employer, whether it is a cold contact or one made when there is an advertised job opening, it feels like you are sending it into an abyss. You wonder, "Will I ever hear anything about this?" Sometimes the answer is no. Some employers only call back candidates in whom they are interested, leaving others to assume that if they haven't heard anything, they aren't going to be called in for a job interview.

QUESTION?

How long after I send them should I wait before I follow up on my resume and cover letter?

Follow up about one week after you submit your cover letter and resume. This will give the employer a chance to review it. If you send them by e-mail, you can call even sooner than that, though some job postings will specifically ask for no calls.

Don't send your resume into an abyss. First of all, as mentioned throughout this chapter, indicate on your cover letter that you will follow up if you don't hear from the employer. Then do it! When you call the employer, ask her if she has received your resume and when you can set up an appointment to discuss it. Even if she isn't ready to do that yet, your name will stand out in her mind. But be careful—you don't want your name to stand out for the wrong reasons. Don't call repeatedly. If she isn't ready to set up an interview when you make your follow-up call, ask her when you can call back. If she says she'll call you, wait a couple of weeks before you call again, but do call again. You don't want to sound too desperate but you do want to be assertive.

Chapter 8
Cover Letter Samples

Chapter 7 dealt with the how-tos of writing cover letters, including formatting them for snail mail and e-mail. You found out what to do when you have an unidentified employer versus an identified one. Now here are sample cover letters you can use to guide your own cover-letter writing. Included are cover letters that address special circumstances you may be facing.

Last-Minute Cover Letter Tips

Do you remember all you've learned about writing a cover letter? You may feel like this is a difficult task, but it does get easier with practice. And just as with putting together your resume, common sense is always the most helpful tool at your disposal. You want to present yourself clearly and professionally, and you want to keep your letter concise. Nothing will turn off a prospective employer more quickly than a multiple-page rambling cover letter. The following are some other helpful tips to keep in mind when writing a cover letter:

- State the job you are applying for in the first paragraph of your cover letter.
- Address your letter to a specific person if at all possible.
- Do not send the same letter to every employer.
- Showcase your relevant attributes.
- Ask for what you want—an interview, for example.
- Tell the recipient when and how you will follow up.
- Proofread your cover letter to make sure there are no spelling or grammatical errors or typos.

If nothing else, your cover letter should clearly state your intent and the reason for your interest in the job. If the person reading your letter does not get a sense of why you want the job you're applying for, or why she should hire you to do that job, that letter—and your chances—will probably end up in the trash.

SAMPLE LETTER TO IDENTIFIED EMPLOYER James Luther is applying for an advertised position where the employer was identified. The contact person's name was not given in the ad. Since James knew the name of the company, he was able to call them to find out to whom he should send his resume.

James Luther
24 Shell Street
Miami, FL 33132

September 21, 2007

Julie J. Brynn
Executive Producer
Beta-Up Production Company
2 Pete's Circle
Hialeah, FL 33012

Dear Ms. Brynn:

I am writing to express my interest in the production assistant position at Beta-Up Production Company that was advertised in the *Miami Herald*. My resume is enclosed.

I possess extensive experience in all aspects of video production, including positions as writer, researcher, director, and editor. For the past three years, I have been a freelance production assistant working on several commercial and documentary pieces. As chief assistant on *Milk Carton Kids: An American Crisis*, I assisted in preliminary research and writing, scheduled location shooting, and screened potential interview candidates. I also helped complete two public service announcements for Miami Child Services, where my duties included camera operation and heavy editing work.

I have admired Beta-Up Production Company's work for some time and attended your screening of *Silent Victims* at the Miami Crime Awareness Convention last month. I would like the opportunity to contribute to such remarkable work.

Please contact me at (305) 555-5555 during the day or (305) 555-4444 in the evenings if you need any additional information or to arrange a meeting. I will be in touch in a week to confirm that you have received my resume.

I look forward to hearing from you.

Sincerely,
(Signature)

James Luther

SAMPLE LETTER TO UNIDENTIFIED EMPLOYER   David Goff is applying for a job he saw advertised in a local newspaper. Neither the name of the employer nor the name of a contact person was given.

David Goff
473 Blueberry Lane
Bangor, ME 04402

February 6, 2007

P.O. Box 7777
Bangor, ME 04401

Dear Hiring Manager:

I saw your advertisement for a financial analyst in the *Bangor Daily News*. I am interested in applying for this position. I am enclosing my resume.

I am a 2004 graduate of the University of Maine's Graduate School of Business with over six years of business and financial analysis experience, including two years of domestic and international travel as an internal auditor for Botanee Bay Foods, Inc., two years of credit analysis at Millbury, and a treasury internship at Envirlab.

I have been recognized for my creative spirit and ability to identify and implement solutions to current business problems. The following list highlights some of my achievements:

- Participated in the due diligence and/or post-acquisition reviews of five acquisitions
- Planned, coordinated, and/or participated in the compliance and productivity audits of forty-one independent business units
- Participated in the fraud review of a major business unit
- Researched, developed, and planned a cash collection reorganization that, when implemented, will save $120,000 per year

Based on my job experience and educational qualifications, I am confident I can make an immediate contribution to your firm. I would appreciate the opportunity to further discuss my credentials with you. You can reach me at (207) 555-5555.

Sincerely,

(Signature)

David Goff

SAMPLE COLD COVER LETTER Cecil Ives is sending an unsolicited resume to an employer with the following cover letter. In his letter, Cecil explains why he is interested in working for this employer.

Cecil Ives
49 Wilson Street
Miami, FL 33054

November 11, 2007

Jenny Ryan
Personnel Manager
Frohman Corporation
6 Jefferson Road
Chicago, IL 60605

Dear Ms. Ryan:

I am writing to you to inquire about positions in new business development at Frohman Corporation. I am enclosing my resume for your perusal.

I have worked for five years as a district sales manager. During the last two years I have expanded my territory to include 25 new corporate clients. I am confident I can use my skills to contribute to Frohman Corporation's growth. I also have experience in the women's apparel industry. I see from my research that many of your clients are in that industry.

Please contact me at (305) 555-5555 or CecilIves@mail.net. I will call you in about a week to confirm that you have received this letter and to discuss career opportunities with Frohman Corporation. Thank you for your consideration.

Sincerely,

(Signature)

Cecil Ives

SAMPLE LETTER FROM A STUDENT/NEW JOB SEEKER Diane Fenton, a recent college graduate, is applying for a job as a marketing assistant. She is not applying for an announced job opening, but is instead sending an unsolicited resume.

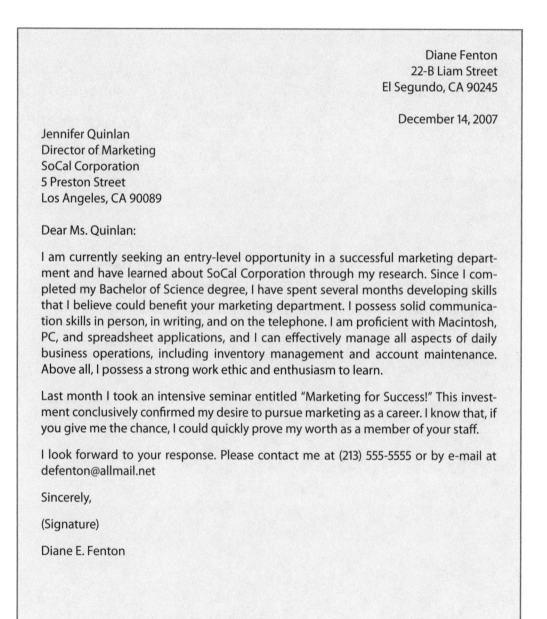

Diane Fenton
22-B Liam Street
El Segundo, CA 90245

December 14, 2007

Jennifer Quinlan
Director of Marketing
SoCal Corporation
5 Preston Street
Los Angeles, CA 90089

Dear Ms. Quinlan:

I am currently seeking an entry-level opportunity in a successful marketing department and have learned about SoCal Corporation through my research. Since I completed my Bachelor of Science degree, I have spent several months developing skills that I believe could benefit your marketing department. I possess solid communication skills in person, in writing, and on the telephone. I am proficient with Macintosh, PC, and spreadsheet applications, and I can effectively manage all aspects of daily business operations, including inventory management and account maintenance. Above all, I possess a strong work ethic and enthusiasm to learn.

Last month I took an intensive seminar entitled "Marketing for Success!" This investment conclusively confirmed my desire to pursue marketing as a career. I know that, if you give me the chance, I could quickly prove my worth as a member of your staff.

I look forward to your response. Please contact me at (213) 555-5555 or by e-mail at defenton@allmail.net

Sincerely,

(Signature)

Diane E. Fenton

SAMPLE LETTER FROM A RETURNEE TO WORK George Klass is applying for a job as an account manager. He has a lot of experience, but none of it is recent. While discussing his qualifications, he doesn't mention that he is returning to the job market after an absence, nor does he need to do that.

George Klass
1547 South Street
Cheeseville, CA 96037

July 21, 2007

Samuel Brooks
Hiring Manager
Davis Accounting Associates
17 Alice Circle
Davis, CA 95616

Dear Mr. Brooks:

I am very interested in a staff accountant position at Davis Accounting Services. I saw the job announcement you posted on jobjobsjobs.com and I am sending my resume for your consideration.

I would bring the following to this job:

- A Bachelor of Science degree, with a major in accounting
- Four years of collections experience
- Successful collection of 90 percent of company's overdue accounts
- Experience in accounts payable and accounts receivable
- Knowledge of Microsoft Excel, Microsoft Word, and accounting software

I will be in touch with you in one week to confirm that you have received my application. If you want to reach me before then, I can be contacted at (530) 555-5555. Thank you for your consideration. I look forward to speaking with you.

Sincerely,

(Signature)

George Klass

SAMPLE LETTER TO AN EMPLOYMENT AGENCY   Dina Linsky is relocating. She is contacting an employment agency she hopes will be able to help her find a job.

Dina Linsky
362 North Main Street
Reston, VA 22091

December 19, 2007

Natalie Goldword
Staffing Manager
Elbonia Employment Agency
7 Bones Street
Taos, NM 87571

Dear Ms. Goldword:

I am searching for a managerial position in the fast-food industry in which work experience and a commitment to excellence will have valuable application.

Currently, I am the manager of a large restaurant in Reston, Virginia. I am responsible for staffing, inventory, cash receipts, and conflict resolution. I work well in both fast-paced, high-pressure environments or in relaxed environments.

I will be relocating to Taos next month and I would like to continue my career in food services. I understand your agency specializes in this industry. I would appreciate your assistance in obtaining employment. I can be reached at (215) 555-5555 until January 1st. After that date, I can be reached at (703) 555-5555. If I don't hear from you before then, I will contact you as soon as I arrive in the area. Thank you for your time.

Sincerely,

(Signature)

Dina Linsky

SAMPLE LETTER FROM SOMEONE SEEKING PART-TIME WORK   Tim Concorde is applying for a job as a part-time art instructor. The employer was identified in the job listing Tim saw, so he can address the letter to a specific person. In his cover letter, he discusses why a part-time schedule is a good fit for him.

Tim Concorde
178 Armour Street
Kingsdale, PA 17340

January 28, 2007

Kay Nichols
Principal
Knightsville Elementary School
11 Cleese Lane
Knightsville, PA 17052

Dear Ms. Nichols:

I would like to apply for the part-time art instructor position advertised in the *Philadelphia Daily News*. I am enclosing my resume for your consideration.

I am a trained elementary art instructor with expertise in arts and crafts instruction as well as program conception and coordination. For four years, I taught art classes on a part-time basis for the Camelot School in Kingsdale. Also, I hold a State of Pennsylvania Elementary Education Certificate in Art and a Bachelor of Fine Arts in Art Education.

For the past year, I have been spending weekends as arts and crafts program director for the Knightsville Parks and Recreational Association. I create and facilitate programs for children, control a budget, select and purchase supplies, and supervise aides in various duties. Since this work is restricted to weekends, my weeks would be open to fulfill my responsibilities as your art instructor. I am confident I could create and maintain an exciting program at Knightsville Elementary School.

I would like to discuss my relevant experience further in a personal interview as well as share my portfolio with you. You can reach me by telephone at (215) 555-5555 or by e-mail at tconcorde@email.com. I will call you in one week to find out the status of my application.

Sincerely,

(Signature)

Tim Concorde

Chapter 9
Other Letters

Your written correspondence during a job search doesn't end with composing cover letters. Sending a thank-you letter is a must after a job interview and when someone provides a reference for you or helps you get an interview. A successful job search means writing a letter to your future boss accepting a job offer and a letter of resignation to your current boss. You may have to write a letter to follow up after submitting your resume to an employer.

Thank-You Letters

Always, always, always send a thank-you letter immediately after a job interview. The reason for sending a thank-you letter following a job interview is threefold. First of all, it's the polite thing to do. The interviewer has taken time out of his busy day to meet with you. Secondly (and most important) is that a thank-you letter gives you the chance to reiterate why they should hire you. You can also use the opportunity to call something to the interviewer's attention that you didn't discuss on the interview. Finally, sending a thank-you letter will make you stand out in the employer's mind. When he is deciding between hiring you and hiring another candidate with similar qualifications, your thank-you letter will give you the edge.

You should send your thank-you letter by e-mail, but if you can't, send a typed letter using the format described in Chapter 7. Remain formal—don't address the interviewer by his first name. Even though you have already met him, you shouldn't be on a first-name basis at this point.

If more than one person interviewed you, you should send a thank-you letter to each one. Jot down their names before you leave the office if possible. Check with the receptionist to get the proper spelling. Each letter should be personalized. That means, don't say exactly the same thing in each one. Talk about something that is relevant to a question the recipient asked, or something that would be important to her.

When someone helps you in your quest for a new job, you should also send a thank-you letter, whether or not that person's help leads to your getting hired. Send a thank-you note to a network contact who helps you get a job interview immediately after the interview. That will give you the opportunity to let her know how the interview went. It may also spur her to contact the employer to put in a good word for you. Send thank-you notes to anyone who provides a reference to a potential employer on your behalf.

SAMPLE LETTER AFTER A JOB INTERVIEW   The following is an example of a thank-you letter to send to your interviewer after a job interview. (If you are sending your letter by e-mail, you can omit the return and inside addresses.)

James Luther
24 Shell Street
Miami, FL 33132

October 12, 2007

Julie J. Brynn
Executive Producer
Beta-Up Production Company
2 Pete's Circle
Hialeah, FL 33012

Dear Ms. Brynn,

Thank you for meeting with me yesterday to discuss the production assistant position at Beta-Up Production Company. I am very enthusiastic about many of the projects we discussed during our interview.

Your upcoming documentary on violence in suburban schools is of particular interest to me. I have worked on several projects that dealt with issues related to this epidemic. Because of my background in this area, I feel I can make significant contributions to this documentary's success.

Again, thank you for speaking with me. If you need any additional information to help you make your hiring decision, please let me know. You can reach me at (305) 555-5555 during the day or at (305) 555-4444 in the evenings. I look forward to hearing from you soon.

Yours truly,

(Signature)

James Luther

SAMPLE LETTER TO A REFERENCE

David Goff
473 Blueberry Lane
Bangor, ME 04402

February 20, 2007

Paul John
Envirlab
Bangor, ME 04402

Dear Paul,

Thank you for writing a letter of reference to Peter Paulson at Interfinance Corp. I spoke with Mr. Paulson yesterday and he says I am a strong candidate for the financial analyst position! That certainly is good news. I'll let you know how it turns out.

Once again, thank you for providing a good reference for me. If there's anything you need, please let me know.

Sincerely,

(Signature)

David

SAMPLE LETTER TO SOMEONE WHO HELPED YOU GET AN INTERVIEW

Penny Coppersmith
40 Alton Lane
Cranbury, NJ 08512

April 14, 2007

Victoria Beckett
57 Spruce Street
Cherry Hill, NJ 08002

Dear Vicki,

Thank you for arranging for the opportunity for me to be interviewed by Mrs. Parker at Johnson Elementary School. I just got back about an hour ago. I think it went very well. The reading program sounds wonderful. I can see why you thought it would be a good fit for me—this job would utilize all my skills and training.

Mrs. Parker says she will get back to me by the end of next week. I'll let you know what happens!

Best,

(Signature)

Penny

THE EVERYTHING GET-A-JOB BOOK

LETTER ACCEPTING A JOB OFFER   Congratulations! You've been offered a job. Don't just stand there smiling—do something. First, of course, you have to decide whether to accept it. Jump ahead a bit and take a look at Chapter 17 to get help making your decision. Once you've decided this job is right for you, inform your future employer of your decision in writing. Thank her for the offer and tell her that you can't wait to get started. Then confirm the terms of the offer. This will help you avoid future misunderstandings.

Diane Fenton
22-B Liam Street
El Segundo, CA 90245

January 15, 2007

Jennifer Quinlan
Director of Marketing
SoCal Corporation
5 Preston Street
Los Angeles, CA 90089

Dear Ms. Quinlan,

Thank you for offering me a job as a marketing assistant at SoCal Corporation. I am accepting your offer and look forward to working with you.

As we discussed last week, my start date will be February 1st. The terms of the offer are as follows:

Salary: $30,000

Schedule: Monday through Friday, 8:30 A.M. to 5:30 P.M., with additional hours possible at least two days each week

Vacation/Personal Days: Two weeks' vacation and three personal days per year

Please let me know if that information is correct. I am enclosing the completed forms you sent to me.

Yours truly,

(Signature)

Diane Fenton

LETTER REJECTING A JOB OFFER If you decide to reject an employment offer, inform the employer through a formal letter. Even if you rejected the offer over the phone, confirm your decision in writing. Begin by thanking the interviewer for both the offer and the time he or she spent with you. Stating a reason for rejection is optional. Above all, keep your letter upbeat—you never know if you'll reapply to the company in the future.

Steven Jeffries
178 Green Street
Menomonee Falls, WI 53051

January 30, 2001

Donnie Sloan
Vice-President, Sales
Onyx Corporation
1140 Main Street
Milwaukee, WI 53202

Dear Mr. Sloan:

I enjoyed our meeting Friday to discuss the possibility of my joining Onyx Corporation in a sales position. Your staff seems enthusiastic, and your semiannual sales record is very impressive. That is quite an achievement.

Although I greatly appreciate your confidence in my abilities, I am afraid I must decline your employment offer. I understand that this position requires a great deal of travel. At this point, I would be unable to do that. If a position comes up in the future that doesn't require as much travel, please keep me in mind.

Once again, thank you for your consideration.

Sincerely,

(Signature)

Steven Jeffries

RESIGNATION LETTER   No matter how much you hate the job you are leaving, don't slam any doors behind you. Respect the old adage "Don't burn any bridges." You really don't know what the future holds for you and who you will meet when you get there. None of us does. You may end up working with your former boss again at some point (okay, stop cringing). A well-written resignation letter to your employer stating when you are leaving is imperative. In this letter you may or may not want to explain why you are leaving. Only do so if you can be polite and not lay blame on anyone.

Christine Wilson
2656 Hartman Road
Lancaster, PA 17573

August 25, 2007

Bob Randolf
President
Randolf Advertising, Inc.
92 Fifth Street
Lancaster, PA 17699

Dear Bob,

I will be resigning from my position as accounts supervisor effective September 15th. I am leaving to join a large agency that will afford me the opportunity to further advance my career in advertising.

It has been a pleasure working for you. Thank you for your continued confidence in me over the last three years. I will be happy to train the person who will be replacing me if you hire someone while I am still here. If not, I can answer any questions he or she has by e-mail or telephone.

Sincerely,

(Signature)

Christine Wilson

FOLLOW-UP LETTER AFTER SENDING A RESUME   When you reply to an ad and the employer is unknown, generally you will be asked to send your resume and cover letter to a post office box. You won't have a phone number and therefore will not be able to call the company to follow up on your resume and cover letter. You must do so in writing. Send a follow-up letter about a week after you mail your resume. Reiterate your interest in the job and your qualifications for it. Always enclose another copy of your resume and don't forget to ask for an interview.

David Goff
473 Blueberry Lane
Bangor, ME 04402

P.O. Box 7777   February 15, 2007
Bangor, ME 04401

Dear Hiring Manager:

On February 6th I replied to your advertisement for a financial analyst that appeared in the *Bangor Daily News*. I want to confirm that you have received my letter and resume. I am enclosing another copy of my resume.

To reiterate what I said in my prior letter, I am a 2004 graduate of the University of Maine's Graduate School of Business and have more than six years of business and financial analysis experience. This includes two years of domestic and international travel as an internal auditor for Botanee Bay Foods, Inc., two years of credit analysis at Millbury, and a treasury internship at Envirlab.

I think I would be a perfect fit for the financial analyst position at your company. Here, again, are highlights of some of my achievements:

- Participated in the due diligence and/or post-acquisition reviews of five acquisitions
- Planned, coordinated, and/or participated in the compliance and productivity audits of forty-one independent business units
- Participated in the fraud review of a major business unit

Please call me at (207) 555-5555 to set up an appointment for an interview. I look forward to discussing my qualifications in further detail.

Yours truly,

(Signature)

David Goff

Sending Letters via E-mail

When you e-mail a letter, it arrives at its destination almost instantly. This is quite a contrast to snail mail, which is nicknamed that for a reason. This makes e-mail a very good medium for sending something you want the recipient to have quickly.

If you want to send a letter accepting a job offer by e-mail, make sure to follow that up with one sent by snail mail. Since that letter includes the details of your job offer, you want a hard copy of it. Both letters can say exactly the same thing. You should indicate in the e-mail version that you are going to send a copy through the regular mail. You can reject a job offer by e-mail alone, though. You should not send a resignation letter to your boss by e-mail. You should send it through regular mail, interoffice mail, or preferably by delivering it to him in person.

Send thank-you letters by e-mail if you can. It will wind up in the recipient's inbox immediately, as opposed to sending it by regular mail when it might arrive after he has decided who to hire. While time is not as much of the essence when it comes to thanking someone for a job reference or for setting up an interview, you can also send those by e-mail.

Before you hit send when e-mailing a letter, make sure it conforms to professional standards. Address the recipient by title (Ms., Mrs., Mr., etc.) and last name if it is someone you don't know well. Though it is tempting to be less formal in an e-mail than you would be in a printed letter, remember that this is still business correspondence. Avoid using e-mail shorthand, although you may do that when you are sending messages to friends. Although you've now established a relationship with the recipient, you should still remain on professional terms. Don't use emoticons, fancy typefaces, or colored text.

Chapter 10

Looking for a Job Online

According to the business membership research organization The Conference Board in their Help-Wanted Online Data Series™ reports, there were over two million jobs posted on Internet job boards as of April 2006. Given this staggering statistic, the Web should be part of everyone's job search. From major job-search sites to smaller niche sites, you can do almost all your job hunting online. You can even find tools to aid you in your job search, like fax services and free e-mail accounts.

10

Major Job-Search Sites

It doesn't matter what type of work you do; if you are looking for a job, there's a good chance you will find one that interests you on one of the major job-search sites. These sites are also called job banks. Employers in all industries post jobs on these Web sites. Those looking for work can search for jobs by keyword, location, or job category. Job seekers can often apply for jobs online or get further information on where to send their resumes.

Why You Should Visit the Major Job Banks First

If you were looking for a pair of shoes, would you first go to a tiny shoe store with a limited selection or would you turn to a big store with a large selection from which to choose? Most people would turn to the big store with the idea that they would be more likely to find something they wanted when there was more to choose from. Looking for a job on a major job bank is similar to shopping in that big store. You will find more jobs listed on those sites and therefore you will be more likely to find one for which you qualify.

You can often find job listings on corporate Web sites. Look for links to "Careers" or "Jobs." If you can't find a link on the front page, look for a link to "About the Company." Once you get to that page, you may see a link to job openings.

Which Job-Search Sites Should I Use?

There are several big job-search sites, but the biggest four are Monster (*www.monster.com*), CareerBuilder (*www.careerbuilder.com*), Yahoo! Hot-Jobs (*http://hotjobs.yahoo.com*), and America's Job Bank (*www.americas jobbank.com*). You don't have to choose just one, since you can use all of them for free. It's only a matter of finding the time to sit down and look at the jobs listed on each one.

Monster

You can search for a job on Monster without registering. However, if you want to take advantage of some special features, you should register. For example, to apply for a job through Monster, you must register. Registered members may also build a resume online that is searchable by employers. If you are a member you can also set up a job search agent by indicating the type of job you want along with its desired location. You will receive search agent results when there is an appropriate match. You can also save a search as an RSS feed, or news feed. Using a news-feed reader, you can receive updates on jobs that match your specifications. For more on how to set up RSS feeds, see the section titled "Step Five: Get the Latest News" in Chapter 12.

FACT

Monster is the number one job-search site, according to TopJobSites. com (*www.topjobsites.com*), a company that ranks the top job-search sites on the Web in terms of page views and popularity. Also according to TopJobSites.com, Monster lists over 800,000 jobs and 130,000 employers.

CareerBuilder

CareerBuilder is another very large and very popular job-search site. Through its partnership with several large newspaper publishers, Career-Builder provides job listings from many local markets. Employers may also post listings to this site.

Anyone can search for jobs on CareerBuilder, but if you want to apply to any of them online, you must sign up to be a member. Membership also allows you to upload a resume or build one online. Your resume, if you wish, will become part of a resume database that employers can search. You can use your resume when you apply for jobs online. Members can set up job alerts by specifying certain criteria. CareerBuilder will send you these job alerts by e-mail.

Yahoo! HotJobs

Search-engine powerhouse Yahoo! is the parent company of HotJobs. When you search for a job on Yahoo! HotJobs, your results will include jobs employers have posted on this site, as well as jobs listed on other sites across the Web. In this sense, HotJobs is a hybrid of a job-search site and a job search engine. Job search engines will be discussed later.

Taking full advantage of Yahoo!'s search engine experience, HotJobs has some unique search capabilities. For example, once you begin your search, you can refine it by using the HotJobs Guided Search tool. You can limit your search to jobs that have been posted today or over the past two days, seven days, or 30 days. You can also narrow your search by company, experience required, or location. In addition to these criteria, you can have your results show only those jobs that have been posted by employers as opposed to staffing firms.

ALERT!

You want to apply for newer job listings before you apply for older ones. Jobs that have been listed for a while may already have a glut of candidates applying for them, or those jobs may have been passed over because they are in some way undesirable.

If you want to apply for a job online, you will need to become a registered member of Yahoo! If you have ever signed up for any other Yahoo! service you are already a member (you just need to remember your username and password). You can upload or create a resume that you can choose to make searchable by employers. You can also block specific companies from viewing your resume. HotJobs will send you alerts when jobs that fit your criteria are posted.

America's Job Bank

One of the largest job-search sites is America's Job Bank. This site is administered by the U.S. Department of Labor. It comprises job postings submitted by employers as well as by state labor departments. Job seekers can search America's Job Bank by job category or keyword, and location.

ESSENTIAL

Use the CareerOneStop Online Coach feature on America's Job Bank to help you with your job search. This service will help you search for jobs, find unemployment information, identify and upgrade your skills, and locate career advancement tools.

If you sign up for an account with America's Job Bank, you can create and post your resume online. It will be put into a database that employers can search. You can also set up job scouts that will alert you, by e-mail, of job openings that meet your specifications.

Job Search Engines

When you use a general search engine like Yahoo!, Google, or Ask.com to do a search about something, it looks for information on the Web. It combs through thousands of Web sites to find what you are looking for. Job search engines work in much the same way general search engines do. You put in your search terms, usually the type of job you want and the location, and the job search engine will look through job listings on a variety of Web sites. Three popular job search engines are Indeed (*www.indeed.com*), SimplyHired (*www.simplyhired.com*), and Jobster (*www.jobster.com*).

Indeed

According to information on the Web site, Indeed includes all the job listings from major job boards, newspapers, associations, and company career pages. After you search using your initial terms, you can then refine your search further by selecting key phrases, company names, location, and job type—for example, part-time, full-time, or temporary.

Anyone can search Indeed, but if you become a member you can set up job alerts that will be sent to you by e-mail when jobs that match your criteria are posted. You can also save your searches in order to run them again without having to type in all the terms. Membership also lets you save individual job listings. You can then add notes, visible only to you, to each listing. This can help you stay organized.

SimplyHired

SimplyHired claims to list "thousands of jobs from job boards, classifieds, and company sites." This site allows you to narrow down your search by setting up filters. You can refine your search by job type, company, required education, or the date the job was posted. You can also ask this search engine to only display jobs with employers that appear on a ranked list, such as the *Fortune* 500.

Signing up for a SimplyHired account gives you access to services similar to those offered by Indeed. For example, you can save your searches and set up e-mail alerts. You can also save individual jobs, rate them, and type in notes about them.

Next to each job listing on Indeed, you will see a link that says "more actions." Clicking on that link will reveal a set of links to useful tools including a Google search on the company, a map, and general salary information for that job title.

Jobster

Jobster works like the other job search engines listed here as far as its search function is concerned. The similarities end there. The first noticeable difference is that when you do a search the results page tells you how long ago the job arrived on Jobster, and what job bank it came from. When you return to the Web site, Jobster remembers your previous searches—updated results appear on the front page. You must have cookies enabled in your Web browser for this to occur (use the Help feature of your browser to learn more about cookies).

Signing up for MyJobster lets you create a profile that highlights your skills and qualifications. You can choose whether or not to make your profile public. You can also set up job alerts to notify you, by e-mail, about new job openings that match your criteria.

The biggest difference between Jobster and its competitors is the networking opportunities it can help facilitate. Jobster operates on the premise that employers are more likely to hire candidates whom their employees recommend. In addition to listing job openings from job banks and company Web sites, Jobster has client companies for which it also lists job openings. If you know someone who works at one of these companies (or if you know someone who knows someone), you can ask that person for a referral. Once Jobster has that referral, it is passed along to the hiring team at the company. You can also receive "Insider Alerts" about other job openings with that employer.

Niche Job-Search Sites

Niche job-search sites are those that focus on a particular industry or field. While the large job-search sites and the job search engines provide a broad base of job openings, these more specialized sites allow you to focus on your particular field of interest. The job search engines may turn up some of the jobs posted on these job lists, but they are still worth looking at.

Professional journals often list job openings. You should be reading the ones for your field anyway. If the journal has a Web site, visit it to see if they have job listings. You may have to subscribe to the journal in order to access them.

TopJobSites.com (*www.topjobsites.com*) lists the most popular niche job sites. The fields covered by those sites include law, finance, engineering, human resources, and communications. What should you do, though, if your field isn't covered by one of these sites? The About.com Job Searching page has a huge list of job banks arranged by career field: *http://jobsearch. about.com/od/jobsbycareerfieldaz/a/topsbytype.htm*. You can also visit the Web site of the trade or professional associations for your field.

Using Resume Banks

You already learned quite a bit about resume banks in Chapter 6, but the option is worth reiterating in the discussion of looking for a job online. Many of the job-search Web sites mentioned in the last section let you upload your resume or create one online. Your resume then gets put into a database that employers may search when looking for job candidates. Some of these services allow you to keep your resume private, or at least invisible to employers you specify. Why would you choose to do this? Let's take this likely scenario: you are looking for a new job without your current employer's knowledge. You upload your resume to one of these services. Your boss has to fill a job opening and decides to look for candidates on the same site to which you just uploaded your resume. Now, wouldn't that make for an awkward situation?

ALERT!

If you do decide to make your resume public, make sure you can keep your personal information—address and phone number—private. That is information you don't want to make available to the world at large.

All of that said, posting your resume to a resume bank or other job-search site can be a big help to you as a job seeker. Someone may contact you from out of the blue to see if you are interested in a particular opportunity. These opportunities may not always be exactly what you're looking for, but this is still a good way to become more educated about your options and to reach a broader "audience." You never know; an option you might never even have considered may turn out to be the perfect choice for you.

Government Jobs

Government jobs have a reputation for being stable and for having excellent benefits. That is why many people turn to this venue, also called civil service, when looking for work. Whether you are looking for federal jobs or for jobs in local governments, you can easily access job openings on the Web.

Federal Job Listings

USAJOBS (*www.usajobs.opm.gov*) is the official job search Web site of the United States government. All vacancies in every federal government agency are listed here. You can do a basic search by keyword, job category, and location. You can also search for jobs within specific agencies or by Occupational Series (all federal jobs are assigned a series number). Additionally, you can specify a salary range when you search for a job. To create an online resume you must become a My USAJOBS member. Membership also allows you to apply for jobs online. As you can with the other job-search sites, you can create automated job alerts.

QUESTION?

Should I ever pay a fee for government job listings?
No. Beware of Web sites and other companies that charge a fee for government job listings. Access to this information is available to anyone who wants it, free of charge. The only fees you may encounter are application and exam fees charged by the government entity with which you are applying for a job.

U.S. Postal Service

You can find some jobs with the U.S. Postal Service listed on USAJOBS. However, Postal Service employees are not considered federal workers. For a more extensive list of Postal Service jobs, you should visit the U.S. Postal Service Web site: *www.usps.gov.* You can look for mail processing jobs and corporate jobs. You can also apply for exams, a necessary evil if you want all but a corporate job with the U.S. Postal Service.

Local Government Jobs

Many local governments, including states, counties, and cities, have their own Web sites on which they list, among other information, job openings. There are also several Web sites dedicated to local government employment. One of these sites is govtjobs.com (*www.govtjobs.com*). You can search through job categories for a position or you can use the search box to specify a job title. Another Web site on which to search for local government jobs is Careers In Government (*www.careersingovernment.com*). Search for jobs by selecting a job category, organization type, location, and salary.

Online Tools to Assist You in Your Job Search

Conducting a job search is almost like running a small business. You have a product to sell (yourself). You have an advertising campaign, which consists of your resume and other job-search tools that will get your name out there. Just as you would if you were running a small business, you are going to need some tools to help you with the demands of your job search.

You will need a personal e-mail account, since you never want to use your work account for your job search. Many employers will ask you to send your resume by fax. If you don't have a fax machine, you will run up quite a bill faxing resumes from your corner drugstore or print shop. What about receiving phone messages from employers when you aren't available to take calls? Do you want to change your home voicemail message to make it sound more formal, or would you prefer to have a voicemail service dedicated to your job-search campaign? Fortunately, there are Web-based resources that provide many of these services.

Free E-mail

Is your only e-mail address your work account? Or does the personal e-mail address that you use to communicate with your friends not sound very professional (for example, honeybabe@email.com)? You should never use your work e-mail account for your job search, nor should you use an address that sounds less than professional. You can set up a free e-mail account dedicated specifically to your job-search campaign. You will put this address on your resume, cover letters, and anywhere else you are asked to put contact information.

Google offers free e-mail accounts through their Gmail service. You can store an almost unlimited number of e-mail messages on their server. You can also get a free Yahoo! e-mail account. Other free e-mail services are AIM (*www.aim.com*) from AOL (you don't need to subscribe to AOL), MSN Hotmail (*www.hotmail.com*), and Inbox.com (*www.inbox.com*).

Fax Services and Voicemail

Web-based fax services let you send and receive faxes online. You send a file to the fax service as an e-mail attachment. They then convert it into a document that is sent to the recipient's fax machine. You can even send a scanned document by saving it as a file and attaching it to an e-mail message. When you use one of these services, you also receive faxes as e-mail attachments. These services give you a local or toll-free telephone number.

MaxEmail (*www.maxemail.com*), eFax (*www.efax.com*), and jConnect (*www.j2.com*) are Web-based fax services. They all charge a monthly fee and a small fee per fax. If you only need to send and receive faxes during your job search, it may not be worth buying and setting up a fax machine. This type of service will fit your needs.

MaxEmail, eFax, and jConnect also offer voicemail services for an additional fee. Messages are sent to you as e-mail attachments. MaxEmail and jConnect also let you listen to your messages over the phone, which is great if you are away from a computer.

Chapter 11

Employment Services

Many people turn to temporary agencies, permanent employment agencies, or executive recruiters to assist them in their respective job searches. At their best, these resources can be very valuable—it's comforting to know that someone is putting his wealth of experience and contacts to work for you. At their worst, they're more of a friend to the employer or to more experienced recruits than to you personally. For this reason, it's best not to rely on them exclusively. Employment services fall into several categories, each of which is described here.

Types of Employment Services

There are several types of employment services you may encounter in your job search. There are temporary employment agencies, contract services firms, and permanent employment agencies. Each one serves a different purpose, but all have the primary goal of finding qualified candidates to fill job openings. Most employment services work on behalf of the employer. Generally, it is the employer who will pay them, so beware of agencies that ask for a fee before they will place you.

Temporary Employment Agencies

Temporary, or "temp," agencies can be a viable option. Often they specialize in clerical and support work, but it's becoming increasingly common to find temporary assignments in other areas, like accounting or computer programming. Working on temporary assignments will provide you with additional income during your job search and will add experience to your resume. It may also provide valuable business contacts or lead to permanent job opportunities.

Temporary work appeals to people for a variety of reasons. It can be a wonderful way for a recent college graduate to gain much needed experience. Those who like variety might find that temping is just what they need. Parents who want flexibility in work hours might also benefit from temporary jobs.

Temporary agencies often advertise in the help-wanted sections of newspapers. You can also find them listed in local telephone directories.

Contract Services Firms

Firms that place individuals on a contract basis commonly receive job orders from client companies for positions that can last anywhere from a month to over a year. Most often, contract services firms specialize in placing technical professionals, though some do specialize in other fields, including clerical and office support. Most contract services firms don't charge a fee to the candidate. For more information on contract services, visit Contract Employment Weekly at *www.ceweekly.com*.

Permanent Employment Agencies

Permanent employment agencies are commissioned by employers to find qualified candidates for job openings. The catch is that their main responsibility is to meet the employer's needs—not necessarily to find a suitable job for the candidate. This is not to say that permanent employment agencies should be ruled out altogether. Permanent employment agencies specializing in specific industries can be useful for experienced professionals. However, they're not always a good choice for entry-level job seekers. Some will try to steer inexperienced candidates in an unwanted direction or offer little more than clerical placement to experienced applicants. Others charge a fee for their services—a condition that job seekers should always ask about up front.

ALERT!

Some employment agencies are looking to simply fill positions as quickly as possible. These agencies are interested only in what work you can do, not what work you want to do. To them a job seeker is simply a commodity from which they hope to earn money, in the form of a commission or fee from an employer. As long as you stay at a job for a specified length of time, they will earn their money. If you are not interested in a particular job, speak up.

Some permanent employment agencies dispute the criticisms mentioned above. As one recruiter puts it, "Our responsibilities are to the applicant and the employer equally, because without one, we'll lose the other." She also maintains that entry-level people are desirable, saying that "as they grow, we grow, too, so we aim to move them up the ranks."

Finding an Agency

If you decide to register with an employment agency, your best bet is to find one recommended by a friend or associate. As mentioned previously, you can find local employment agencies advertised in the help-wanted sections of local newspapers. You can also find them listed in local telephone directories. Of course, you can always search for employment agencies on the Web. One Web site that lists agencies is the American Staffing Association. Go to *www.americanstaffing.net* where you can search by type of agency, location, and occupational category.

Once you gather names and phone numbers of several employment agencies, it's time to make contact with them. Call the firm to find out if it specializes in your area of expertise and how it will go about marketing your qualifications. After selecting a few agencies, send each one a resume with a cover letter. They will probably ask you to send it via e-mail, so be sure to read Chapter 6, which will help you design an electronic resume.

Making contact with an agency is no different than making contact with an employer. You should always be professional whether you are contacting an agency on the telephone, in person, by mail, or by e-mail. Treat them as you would a potential employer. If you are visiting an agency, even just to drop off a copy of your resume, dress professionally.

Make a follow-up call a week or two later and try to schedule an interview.

Above all, don't expect too much. Only a small number of all professional, managerial, and executive jobs are listed with these agencies. Use them as an addition to your job-search campaign, not as a centerpiece.

Executive Search Firms

Also known as "headhunters," executive search firms seek out and carefully screen (and weed out) candidates, typically for high-salaried technical, executive, and managerial positions (although lower-salaried positions are handled by many such firms as well). Executive recruiters are paid by the employer; the candidate is generally not charged a fee. Unlike permanent employment agencies, they often approach candidates directly, rather than waiting for candidates to approach them. Some prefer to deal with employed candidates.

QUESTION?

What should I do if a recruiter calls me at work?
Since executive recruiters often prefer to work with those who are currently employed, they usually contact people at work. That can make for an uncomfortable situation if your boss, or anyone else, is hovering nearby. If you are interested in working with the recruiter, ask him if you can return the phone call at a later time. Then do so on a break or lunch hour using your cell phone and not an office phone.

Whether you're employed or not, don't contact an executive search firm if you aren't ready to look for a job. If a recruiter tries to place you right away and finds you aren't really looking yet, it's unlikely he will spend much time with you in the future.

Types of Executive Search Firms

There are two basic types of executive search firms—retainer-based and contingency-based. Essentially, retainer firms are hired by a client company for a search and paid a fee by the client company, regardless of whether a placement is made. Contingency firms receive payment from the client company only when their candidate is hired. Some firms conduct searches of both types. The fee is typically 20 to 35 percent of the first year's salary, with retainer firm fees at the higher end of that scale, according to Ivan

Samuels, president of Abbott's of Boston, an executive search firm that conducts both types of searches.

Retainer Firms

Generally, companies use retainer firms to fill senior-level positions, with salaries over $60,000. In most cases, a company will hire only one retainer firm to fill a given position, and part of the process is a thorough, on-site visit by the search firm to the client company, so the recruiter can check out the operation. These search firms are recommended for a highly experienced professional seeking a job in her current field.

Confidentiality is more secure with these firms, since a recruiter may use your file only in consideration for one job at a time, and most retainer firms will not freely circulate your resume without permission. This is particularly important to a job seeker who is currently employed and insists on absolute discretion. If that's the case, make sure you don't contact a retainer firm used by your current employer.

Contingency Firms

Contingency firms make placements that cover a broader salary range, so these firms are preferable for someone seeking a junior or midlevel position. Unlike retainer firms, contingency firms may be competing with other firms to fill a particular opening. As a result, they can be quicker and more responsive to your job search. In addition, a contingency firm will distribute your resume more widely. Some require your permission before sending your resume to a company; others ask that you trust their discretion. Inquire about this with your recruiter at the outset, and choose according to your needs.

Finding an Executive Recruiter

Look for executive recruitment firms that specialize in your field of interest or expertise as well as generalist firms that place people in a variety of fields. You don't need to limit yourself to firms in your geographic area, as many firms operate nationally or internationally. Once you've chosen the specific recruiter or recruiters to contact, keep in mind that they are working for the companies that hire them, not for you. Attempting to fill a position—especially among fierce competition with other firms — means your best interests may not be the recruiter's only priority. For this reason, contact as many search firms as possible to increase your chances of finding your ideal position.

Making Contact with an Executive Recruiter

A phone call is your first step, during which you should speak with a recruiter and exchange all relevant information. Find out whether they operate on a retainer or contingency basis (or both), and ask some brief questions, if you have any, regarding the firm's procedures. Offer the recruiter information about your employment history and the type of work you are seeking. Make sure you sound enthusiastic and assertive, but not pushy. The recruiter will ask you to send a resume and cover letter, probably by e-mail.

Occasionally the recruiter will arrange to meet with you, but most often this won't occur until she has received your resume and found a potential match. James E. Slate, president of F-O-R-T-U-N-E Personnel Consultants, advises that you generally should not expect an abundance of personal attention at the beginning of the relationship with your recruiter, particularly with a large firm that works nationally and does most of its work over the phone. You should, however, use your recruiter's inside knowledge to your best advantage. Some recruiters will coach you before an interview, and many are open to giving you all the facts they know about a client company.

FACT

It's common for recruiters to try to match job seekers with jobs in other states. For example, recruiters in Boston sometimes look for candidates to fill positions in New York City, and the reverse is true as well. If you are not interested in relocating, be up front with the recruiter from the start so she can look for local jobs only.

Names of executive recruiting firms nationwide can be found in *The Directory of Executive Recruiters* published by Kennedy Information. This directory is also available online (*www.kennedyinfo.com*) for a fee.

Contacting an Executive Search Firm

Although executive search firms actively recruit candidates for client companies, don't let this discourage you from contacting them. A well-crafted cover letter can alert an otherwise unknowing recruiter to your availability. Remember, this is your chance to shine. Highlight your most impressive accomplishments and attributes and briefly summarize all relevant experience. If you have certain preferences, like geographic location, travel and salary, mention them in your cover letter. Generally, if executive search firms are interested, they'll call you, so keep your closing succinct.

Here's a sample of a "cold" cover letter to an executive search firm:

1441 Pistash Park
Flandreau, SD 57028
March 4, 2007

Heidi Button
Director
First Search Corporation
1140 Main Street
Chicago, IL 60605

Dear Ms. Button:

During the past ten years I have worked in the liability insurance field, in positions ranging from transcriber to senior field claims representative. Currently, I am seeking a new position with an underwriter or a corporate liability insurance department with a need for expertise in claims settlement, from fact-finding analysis to negotiation.

I am hoping that among your clients, one or two may be looking for someone knowledgeable in the area of corporate liability insurance. If so, I would like to explore the opportunity. I can be reached at (605) 555-5555.

I look forward to hearing from you.

Sincerely,

Jennifer-Anne Kelly

Outplacement Services

Outplacement services, also called outplacement counseling services or employment marketing services, charge a broad range of fees depending on the services they provide. These include career counseling, outplacement, resume development and writing, interview preparation, assessment testing, and various workshops.

If you decide to work with an outplacement firm, choose one wisely. Fees can range from hundreds to thousands of dollars! Get recommendations from trusted friends and acquaintances. Ask the firm for references. Don't be afraid to ask to interview the person with whom you would be working, before you hire the outplacement firm. As results are not guaranteed, you may also want to check on a firm's reputation through the local Better Business Bureau.

While employers pay employment agencies and executive recruiters, job seekers pay an outplacement service (often thousands of dollars) to help them find a job. These companies will send out letters, make phone calls for you, and basically do the things you should be doing in your job search. If you go out and do it yourself, not only will you save a great deal of money, you'll gain important experience and probably make invaluable contacts.

Community Agencies

There are many nonprofit organizations that offer free or inexpensive job counseling services. Many nonprofit organizations—colleges, universities, public libraries, and private associations—offer free or inexpensive counseling, career development, and job placement services. Often these services are targeted to a particular group—for example, women, minorities, the blind, and the disabled—although there are also agencies that are available to the general public. Many cities and towns have commissions that provide services for these special groups.

The United States Department of Labor also offers job placement services through One-Stop Career Centers located throughout the country. You can search for a local center by visiting America's Service Locator on the Web at *www.servicelocator.org* or by calling 1-877-US-2JOBS.

Employment Services for Students and Recent Graduates

If you're just starting out fresh from academia, don't expect headhunters to help you out. Executive search firms are paid by employers, and your lack of professional experience puts you straight into the unprofitable bin. Consider this resource later on down the line, once you've added some kick to your resume.

Permanent employment agencies are probably more your speed at this career juncture. The reputable agencies are usually compensated by employers, so if you're asked to pay up front, run for the door.

Temporary agencies are a great way to get in on the corporate ground floor; just make sure you request placement with a company specializing in your area of interest. Once so installed, you can make all the right contacts while watching for a more upscale position to become available.

ESSENTIAL

Treat a temporary assignment just as you would a permanent one. That means be on time, dress professionally, and take your work seriously. Even though you may not end up with a permanent position at this company at this point, you don't know what will happen in the future.

Outplacement services, which were discussed earlier, can be costly and may be unnecessary. A lot of the work they do, you can do yourself. You need only be diligent, ambitious, and organized. Turn to your college placement office first. The services are probably free to you, and the people who staff those centers are experts at working with recent graduates. Nonprofit agencies, also discussed earlier, can be a wonderful resource for you.

Chapter 12

Researching Companies

Finding information about a prospective employer should be on your "must do" list before you set off on any job interview. Learning about the industry the company is part of is also imperative. Taking the time to do this research will benefit your job search in several ways and it could help you get the job you desire. Follow the steps laid out here as you go about the task of gathering company and industry information.

Why You Need to Do Company Research

In the business world, corporations spend significant amounts of money on competitive intelligence. Competitive intelligence involves gathering information about the company's clients, competitors, and the industry in general. Large companies often maintain research departments, or libraries, where professional librarians do this work. Before a company goes out and tries to woo a new client, the research department will learn as much as it can about that client and the industry of which it is a part. This will help the company compete more effectively with the other companies that are pursuing the client. Take your cue from those companies. While you won't, of course, be able to hire a staff of researchers, you should spend some time and energy researching prospective employers.

There are several reasons you need to do company research as you prepare for a job interview. You want to be able to intelligently discuss the company and the industry on a job interview. Because you did the research, you will know what you are talking about. You will also be able to ask the interviewer meaningful questions about the company. For example, if your research tells you that the company is about to introduce a new product, you might ask if you will be involved in that product introduction (yes, ask the question as though you know they will hire you!).

ESSENTIAL

One reason for doing company research is simply to demonstrate to the employer that you have taken the job interview seriously, just as you will take seriously any project you are assigned. Don't be afraid to show off what you learned through your research.

If you get a job offer, the information you gathered about the company while doing your research will help you decide whether you should accept it. Your research will help you learn about a company's financial health. You will feel comfortable accepting an offer from a company that is financially sound versus a company that is teetering on the edge of bankruptcy.

What Information Do You Need?

Before you begin your research, you need to establish goals. Begin by listing the questions you want to answer. Here is a list of some important questions you should be able to answer by the time you finish your research.

- What does the company do—what products or services do they sell?
- What industry is the company part of?
- Who are the company's customers or clients? Are they big companies, small companies, or individuals?
- Does the company have any subsidiaries?
- Does the company have a parent company?
- Who are the company's leaders?
- Where is the company's corporate headquarters?
- Does the company have regional locations? Where are they?
- Is the company publicly or privately held?
- Who are the company's competitors?
- How does the company rank in its industry? Is it considered a big player, a small player, or somewhere in the middle?
- What are the company's sales and profits trends?
- What are the company's plans for the future?
- Has the company been in the news lately? If so, why?
- What other companies are in the industry?

You should be able to answer all of these questions for many companies. However, information about some companies will be more readily available than for others. Publicly held companies, those that have shareholders (also called stockholders), are required to release a great deal of information to the government. Finding information on them is as simple as locating a copy of their annual report, which will be discussed later in this chapter. Privately held companies, by contrast, aren't required to release much information to the public. It could take much more digging to find what you are looking for.

Step One: Getting Started

Once you have determined what questions you want to answer, you can begin your research. This guide will help you stay organized as you proceed through the task of finding information about your prospective employer.

Keep a separate folder for each company on your list. This can be either a paper folder or an electronic one that you store on your computer. The first page in your folder should include basic information about the company: the location of the company's headquarters and regional offices, its parent company, the names of its subsidiaries. Subsequently you will gather information about the company's products and services and its leadership team. You will obtain financial reports as well. Finally, you will look for current news about the company.

FACT

Most industry trade groups and professional associations have Web sites. You can learn a lot about an industry by looking at these sites. If you don't know the name of the association for the industry in which you want to work, look in *Gale's Encyclopedia of Associations*. This annually updated publication is available in many public libraries. There is also an online version, Associations Unlimited. If your library subscribes to it, you may be able to access it from home. Keep reading to learn more about library resources.

You will need access to the Internet to do most of your research. If you don't have a computer or Internet service at home, find out if your local library has computers for public use. If they don't, find a friend who is willing to let you use his computer.

Step Two: Find the Company's Web Site

Most companies have Web sites. That is the first place you should look for information about your prospective employer. You will usually find a wealth of information there. It is almost like walking into the company's offices and saying "Tell me about yourself." A corporate Web site is also the "face of the company"—it conveys its personality, or at least the personality it wants to share with the public.

Use a search engine, such as Google or Ask.com, to find a company's Web site. Type the company's full name (with quotation marks around it) into the search box. Use lowercase letters. For example, search for "xyz group incorporated." If you can't find it under its full name, try searching for a name by which the company is commonly known. The company's name will usually appear in the URL (Uniform Resource Locator), which you may know as the Web address. If the company is a subsidiary of a larger company and you can't find its Web site, try searching for the parent company's site.

Once you are on the company's Web site, begin clicking around. You will usually find a link that directs you to information about the company. Hint: Look for links that say "About XYZ Company" or "About Us." Try to find a link to company news (these links may be called "News", "Press Releases", "Media Relations" or "Press Room"). You will even find a link to jobs or careers. This can be very helpful if you need a detailed job description. Larger companies may have links to their subsidiaries on their Web sites. You can often find a company's annual report on its Web site.

QUESTION?

What is an annual report?

An annual report is a document that most publicly held companies must make available to their shareholders. It contains financial information about the company as well as information about key personnel and newsworthy items, such as new product introductions.

If you had no luck hunting down a company's Web site, there are still other resources to try. Let's move on to the next one—company directories.

Step Three: Look in Company Directories

You will probably learn more about a company from its Web site than from a company directory, which is just a compilation of basic facts about many different companies. A company directory, in book form, is generally arranged alphabetically, much like an encyclopedia or dictionary. Many of these directories are available online and can be searched using the internal search engine on that site. By using these directories you will be able to learn what industry a company is in, what products and services they sell, where their regional offices are located, and who their parent company is.

FACT

There are some free directories available on the Web. One example is Hoover's (*www.hoovers.com*). You can use Hoover's to find basic information about public and private companies. There is a fee if you want to see more information than that. For example, the free service will give you an overview of a company, a few names from its leadership team, and some key dollar figures. If you want anything additional, you will need to pay a fee. The good news is that, at the time of this writing, Hoover's offers a "Hoover's Lite" subscription to students and job seekers.

Many online company directories charge a fee before they will grant a researcher access to their information. These are called proprietary databases, but you might also see them referred to as electronic databases or directories. You may be able to access these databases through your public library or through your college library at no charge if that institution has a subscription. Many libraries even allow their patrons remote access to the proprietary databases to which they subscribe. That means you can enter the directory through your library's Web site with your library card number and a username and password. Call the reference desk of your library to find out what resources they subscribe to and how to access them.

Step Four: Obtain Annual Reports

As mentioned earlier in this chapter, another good resource for company information is an annual report, which many companies publish on their Web sites. Unfortunately, only publicly held companies are required to publish annual reports. The U.S. Securities and Exchange Commission (SEC) requires most companies that have stockholders to send those stockholders annual reports. If you can't find an annual report on a prospective employer's Web site, you can call the company's investor relations department to ask them to send you a copy of the latest one. You don't even have to identify yourself as a job candidate—corporations send these reports to anyone who requests them.

ALERT!

You always want a company's most recent annual report. A company has a few months to file its annual reports following the end of its fiscal year (which isn't necessarily the same as the calendar year), so there may be a time lag between the date of the financial data contained in an annual report and the date the report is published.

In addition to sending shareholders annual reports, companies also file a more detailed version of this report with the SEC. It is called a Form 10-K. They also file quarterly reports, called Form 10-Qs, with the SEC. You can search for company filings on the SEC Web site, *www.sec.gov*. Bear in mind, though, that these reports can be difficult to understand for those not well versed in reading financial statements.

Step Five: Get the Latest News

Once you've gathered all the basic information you can about the company, you'll want to find out what's happening with the company now and what has happened in the recent past. You'll want to look for newsworthy information about the company. This could include new or anticipated product introductions or changes in key personnel. It may even include some negative news, such as lawsuits filed against the company or financial problems that company may be experiencing.

You should look for news about the company that occurred during the past year, with a focus on the most recent news. These newsworthy items may have shown up in newspapers, magazines, and business journals.

It would be an enormous (and probably an impossible) task to search through these publications individually to find the information you need, even though many have Web sites on which they archive past issues. Fortunately there are several tools that will help expedite this process.

Searching for News on the Web

Google, Yahoo!, and Ask.com all have news sections that you can use to find current headlines about a company (or any topic). Click on the "News" link located on the front page of any of these search engines. Once you get to the news search page, you simply type in your search term (the company name, for example), just as you would if you were doing a regular search. The only difference is that the search engine looks through news sources rather than regular Web sites. Topix.net is a search engine devoted exclusively to news.

Since news occurs continuously, there is a chance that something can happen after you've done your search. All the search engines mentioned above are updated throughout the day and the news headlines you find on them could be only minutes old.

If you want to keep track of breaking news for your company—and you should—you can subscribe to a news alert, which you may also see referred to as a news feed. A news alert will let you know, by e-mail, when there is breaking news on the topic you specify. A news feed sends current headlines to a news-feed reader or news aggregator. (This will be covered in more detail later.) Google and Yahoo! offer alerts through both e-mail and news feeds, while Topix.net only offers a news feed. In any of these search engines, you simply do a search for your topic and then look for a link to "news alerts." Provide your e-mail address and specify how often you want to receive alerts, and you're set.

Bloglines.com is a free Web-based news-feed reader. You can subscribe to feeds from news sites and blogs and use them to create a personal page on Bloglines. You can choose to share your page with others or you can keep it private.

Subscribing to a news feed is a bit more involved, but it isn't difficult to do. First you must sign up for a news-feed reader or an aggregator. You may also see this referred to as an RSS (Really Simple Syndication) reader. This is a type of software that collects news feeds to which you subscribe. A few of these are Web based—you access them through a Web site using a personal username and password. There are other types of news-feed readers available, but we will focus only on the Web-based ones here. Once you've signed up for a news-feed reader, you can subscribe to a Web feed on one of the news search engines described previously. After doing your search, click on the orange button that says either XML or RSS. For a good primer on RSS and news feeds, read the article "What Is RSS?" (*www.whatisrss.com*).

Business Databases and Newspaper Indexes

There is one major drawback to news search engines. All of them only post news from the last thirty days. Since, ideally, you should get news that occurred during the entire year, you must look to other sources. One source is a business database. Business databases are usually available by subscription only. Fortunately, most public libraries subscribe to them and allow their patrons access. Check with the reference librarian at your library to find out which databases they have available. Then find out if you can use them at home, through the library Web site, or if you must use them at the library.

Your library may subscribe to one or more of the following databases: General BusinessFile ASAP from Gale, Predicasts PROMT, Mergent Online, and Business Source Premier from EBSCO. You should also look in a national newspaper index, particularly one that lists articles from the *New York Times* and the *Wall Street Journal*. A good one is EBSCO's Newspaper Source.

Press Releases

Press releases are another good source of company information. When a company has news it wants to share with the public, very often it issues a press release. It will send the press release to various news organizations that may or may not choose to publish the information. PR Newswire distributes press releases on behalf of public relations professionals. You can search for press releases, by company on PR Newswire's Web site:

www.prnewswire.com. You can also search for press releases about various industries on this Web site.

Blogs

Blogs, shorthand for weblogs or Web logs, are online journals or diaries. Although in the past they have been frequently associated with teens writing about the details of their daily lives, they have come into their own as a place to post continuously updated information on a variety of topics. There are blogs that focus on every topic you can think of.

Companies use blogs to help make the public aware of the latest news about their products and services. Employees maintain these corporate blogs, often writing about their areas of expertise.

FACT

The *Fortune* 500 Business Blogging Wiki, which can be found at *www .socialtext.net/bizblogs/index.cgi*, lists blogs maintained by employees of *Fortune* 500 companies. All blogs listed on this site are open to the public. There is also a link to the Global 1000 Business Blogging page, which lists blogs from large companies that aren't in the *Fortune* 500.

While some companies encourage their employees to post information to official company blogs, there are many unofficial blogs floating around the Web. Those blogs are where you might find information employers might not want the public to see. For example, ex-employees might post unfavorable comments about the companies for whom they worked. You may learn something by looking at these blogs, but remember not to believe everything you read.

In addition to learning about prospective employers by reading blogs, you can also learn a lot about various industries. Many trade and professional associations publish blogs. One way to find out if your trade or professional association publishes a blog is by going to their Web site. If they do have a blog, you might see it right on their front page, or you might see a link to it on the menu. You can also find blogs published by people who work in different industries. Those who write those blogs often are the movers and shakers in their fields. If you want to know what's going on in an industry, reading a blog is often the best way to do it.

It seems that a lot of people have a lot to say! There are many blogs out there but your time is limited. So, how do you figure out which industry blogs you should be reading? Ask people who work in the industry in which you are looking for a job. They should know which blogs are "must-reads" and which you can skip.

You can search for blogs in several ways. Technorati.com (*www.tech-norati.com*) is a blog search engine. Use the "Blog Finder" tool to search in Technorati's directory of blogs. Many of the standard search engines have blog-search tools. Try Google's Blog Search (*http://blogsearch.google.com*) or Ask.com's Blogs and Feeds (*www.ask.com/#subject:bls|pg:1*) to find blogs about the industries or companies for which you need to find information.

To keep up with the latest postings on a blog, you can subscribe to its RSS news feed. You would use a news-feed reader or aggregator, as described earlier. You can use the same one you use to read feeds from news sites. Click on a link that says "subscribe" or on an RSS or XML button on each blog you want to subscribe to.

Chapter 13

Interviewing

At last, you've reached your long-sought goal. All your efforts spent writing an excellent resume and cover letter, finding and responding to job openings, and networking have paid off—you've been invited to come in for a job interview. Congratulations! You have made significant progress so far and it wouldn't have happened had you not worked so hard. Keep going and you will succeed in the interviewing phase of the job search as well.

Preparing for the Job Interview

While you may be tempted to just take a little break now until the day of your interview rolls around, this isn't the time for it. There's much work to be done as you prepare for the big day. Now is the time to learn as much as you can about the company. It is also the time to get to know yourself better as you get ready to answer the interviewer's questions.

Learning about the Company

You may have taken the time to gather some information about prospective employers as you prepared to send your resume to them. Now you need to get serious about gathering information. As each interview is arranged, begin your in-depth research. You should arrive at an interview knowing the company upside down and inside out. You need to know the company's products, types of customers, subsidiaries, parent company, principal locations, rank in the industry, sales and profit trends, type of ownership, size, current plans, and much more. You should be familiar with common industry terms, the trends in the firm's industry, the firm's principal competitors and their relative performance, and the direction in which the industry leaders are headed.

ESSENTIAL

Librarians are a tremendous source of help when it comes to doing research. Visit your public library and tell the librarian exactly what you are doing. He will be able to point out the most useful resources to help you in your research. The bigger the library, the more likely you will be to find what you need.

Dig into every resource you can! Surf the Web. Read the company literature, the trade press, and the business press. If possible, speak to someone at the firm before the interview, or if not, speak to someone at a competing firm. The more time you can spend on this, the better. Even if you feel extremely pressed for time, set aside several hours for pre-interview research.

Developing Your Personal Themes

Too many job seekers jump into a full-scale search without much preparation other than putting together a resume. Be aware that this is a serious mistake! Although your resume may get you interviews, in order to win offers, you must prepare yourself a little further. It's vital to distinguish yourself in some positive way from other candidates. One way is to develop themes to which you refer throughout the interview. This enables you to emphasize your strongest points and ensures that you'll leave a positive impression.

Interviewers seek certain types of information about candidates. Knowing this and considering your responses in advance will make you feel more confident and in control. Think of your themes as sales messages. Each is designed to showcase your best skills and qualifications. Together, they make up a strategy that will enable you to sell your qualifications in virtually any interview. The topics about which you will need to establish themes include your personality, skills and abilities, professionalism and leadership, and interest in the field and in the company. The four items are among those that will be covered in depth in Chapter 14 where you will be presented with practice interview questions.

Mapping Out Your Route

One of the worst things you can do is get to your interview late. Even if the interviewer is forgiving and understands your reasons for arriving late, you will be so flustered you may not be able to present yourself as you would have otherwise.

One way to avoid arriving late for an interview is to not get lost. Plan your route in advance. You can use an online mapping service to get directions, or even just a good old-fashioned road map.

Plan some alternate routes as well, just in case of a traffic tie-up or road closure. If you are taking public transportation, get the schedules in advance and know which buses or trains you need to take. Again, plan alternate routes if possible.

By the way, if something unavoidable happens, call the interviewer to let him know you will be delayed (and apologize).

The Night Before the Interview

Prepare everything you will need on the day of the interview before you go to bed the night before. Make sure your clothes are pressed and your shoes are polished. Print out a clean copy of your resume so you can take it with you.

Get a good night's sleep the night before the interview. Don't go to bed hours before you normally would. You may not be able to get to sleep that early and that may make you more anxious. To help insure that you are able to sleep soundly, avoid caffeine for several hours before bedtime. Even those who claim not to be affected by caffeine do not sleep soundly after consuming it. Caffeine can have a heightened effect when your body is already in stress mode, so even if you don't normally have a reaction, you might have one if you are dealing with something else that is making you anxious—like a job interview, for instance.

The Day of the Interview

Give yourself enough time to get ready the day of the interview, but not so much time that you're hanging around waiting to leave your house. If your interview is in the morning, wake up early enough so that you don't have to rush around the house. If your interview is later in the day, find something to do until you have to be there. Perhaps you can meet a friend for lunch.

Looks Matter

If you think that your skills and abilities will speak for themselves when it comes to getting hired, you are wrong. First impressions are extremely important, and the first thing an interviewer will notice about you is how you look. Although it may sound superficial, your prospective employer gathers information about you based on how you look. If your appearance is neat and clean, you will give the impression of being someone who is organized and pays attention to detail. You must also look the part of the person who will fill the position for which you are interviewing.

Attire

How important is proper attire for a job interview? Buying a complete wardrobe, donning new shoes, and having your hair styled every morning aren't enough to guarantee you a career position as an investment banker. On the other hand, if you can't find a clean, conservative suit or won't take the time to wash your hair, you're wasting your time by interviewing at all.

Men applying for any professional position should wear a suit, preferably in a conservative color like navy or charcoal gray. It's easy to get away with wearing the same dark suit to consecutive interviews at the same company; just wear a different shirt and tie for each interview.

Women should also wear a business suit—a skirt or pants are appropriate. The suit should be in a dark color like black, charcoal gray, or navy. Wear a conservative shirt under the suit and a simple necklace or scarf.

ESSENTIAL

When choosing your clothes for a job interview, the way employees dress at that company should guide you. Plant yourself in the company parking lot one day, or hang out near the building, to see what employees are wearing when they arrive for work. Avoid Fridays, which are "dress-down days" in many offices. Always dress a little more formally than the employees you see—after all, an interview is a special occasion.

The final selection of candidates for a job opening won't be determined by dress, but inappropriate dress can quickly eliminate a first-round candidate. So while you shouldn't spend a fortune on a new wardrobe, be sure your clothes are adequate. The key is to dress at least as formally and conservatively as the position requires, or slightly more so.

Women should avoid wearing skirts that are too short or blouses with plunging necklines. If you are a student or recent graduate, you may be accustomed to wearing low-cut pants and short tops that reveal your bellybutton. This is inappropriate for a job interview—and for work, for that matter.

Both men and women should make sure their clothing fits well. You certainly don't want to feel like your pants are falling down or are too tight. Your shoes should be comfortable, too. You want your mind to be on the interview and not on your aching feet.

Personal Grooming

Personal grooming is as important as finding appropriate clothes for a job interview. Careful grooming indicates both a sense of thoroughness and self-confidence. Women should not wear excessive makeup. Both men and women should refrain from wearing perfume or cologne—it only takes a small spritz to leave an allergic interviewer with a fit of sneezing and a bad impression of your meeting. Men should be freshly shaven, even if the interview is late in the day.

Your hair should be clean and neat. Your nails should be nicely manicured. Ladies—excessively long nails are not a good idea. Keep jewelry to a minimum. Don't wear large earrings, bulky bracelets, or big rings.

What to Bring

You now know how to prepare for the interview and what to wear, but there is still the question of what to bring with you. While you don't want to show up with a briefcase that's bursting at the seams, you don't want to show up empty-handed either. At the bare minimum you should bring a pen and a notepad to an interview. This will show that you're interested in making notes about what you learn, and it will allow you to jot down any items of importance, such as your interviewer's phone number. A slim briefcase or a leather-bound folder (containing extra, unfolded copies of your resume) will help complete the look of professionalism.

Sometimes the interviewer will be running behind schedule. Don't be upset—be sympathetic. Recruiters are often under pressure to interview a lot of candidates to quickly fill a demanding position. Come to your interview with some reading material to keep yourself occupied and relaxed while you wait. A good choice would be a trade journal or a book about your field; this will show your interest in the job and keep your brain on topic.

The Crucial First Moments

The beginning of the interview is the most important, because it determines the tone. Do you smile when you meet? Do you establish enough eye contact, but not too much? Do you walk into the office with a self-assured and confident stride? Do you shake hands firmly? Do you make small talk easily, without being garrulous, or do you act formal and reserved, as though under attack? It's human nature to judge people by that first impression, so make sure it's a good one.

Arriving for the Interview

When you arrive for the interview, the first person you will probably meet is the receptionist or secretary. Let this person know you are here. Remember to be polite and respectful. Secretaries and receptionists often report their impressions of job candidates to their bosses.

If you are asked to, take a seat in the waiting area. If you are offered coffee politely turn it down. You don't want to have to balance a cup of coffee and your briefcase or portfolio while trying to shake hands with the interviewer when she greets you.

You may be asked to fill out an application while you wait. This is one reason you should have brought a pen. If you didn't, ask the receptionist if you can borrow one. It's not a bad idea to have a cheat sheet with you listing all pertinent dates, in case the application asks for that information.

Meeting the Interviewer

When the interviewer greets you he will likely extend his hand to you. Give a firm handshake. If you aren't used to shaking hands, practice a lot before the interview. A firm handshake—not a crushing one—indicates self-confidence.

Wait for the interviewer to offer you a seat before taking one. If she doesn't offer you a seat, follow her lead. When she sits down, you should as well.

Setting the Right Tone

The interviewer's decision about whether you'll be invited back for an additional interview will probably be influenced by your attitude and personality as much as your qualifications. So don't concentrate too much on trying to project the perfect image. Just try to relax and visualize yourself as smooth and confident.

Also remember that some things are beyond your control—some interviews go well without any effort on your part (and you still may not get the job), and others go awry no matter how poised you are (and sometimes you're offered the job anyway).

Generally, you should try to stress the following characteristics:

- Capability
- Confidence
- Dependability
- Easygoing manner
- Enthusiasm
- Flexibility
- Resourcefulness
- Strong work ethic

Often the interviewer will begin, after the small talk, by telling you about the company, the division, the department, and the position. Because of your detailed research, the information about the company should be repetitive for you, and the interviewer would probably like nothing better than to avoid this regurgitation of the company biography. So if you can do so tactfully, indicate that you're familiar with the firm. If the interviewer seems intent on providing you with background information despite your hints, then acquiesce. If you can manage to generate a brief discussion of the company or the industry at this point without being forceful, that would be great. It will help build rapport, underscore your interest, and increase your impact.

During the Interview

When you go on a job interview your goal, of course, is to make a good impression on the interviewer. Sometimes your nerves may interfere with your ability to do that. If you're a veteran interviewee, at least you know what to expect. If you're a novice, however, the whole interview process is a mystery to you. Once you become familiar with it, your anxiety may subside a little, thus allowing you to present yourself well.

Interview Formats

Interviews fall into one of two categories: structured and unstructured. In a structured interview, the recruiter asks a prescribed set of questions, seeking relatively brief answers. In an unstructured interview, the recruiter asks more open-ended questions, to prod you into giving longer responses and revealing as much as possible about yourself, your background, and your aspirations. Some recruiters mix both styles, typically beginning with more objective questions and asking more open-ended questions as the interview progresses.

Try to determine as soon as possible if the recruiter is conducting a structured or unstructured interview, and respond to the questions accordingly. As you answer, watch for signals from the recruiter as to whether your responses are too short or too long. For example, if the recruiter is nodding or looking away, wrap up your answer as quickly as possible.

Make an Impression

As the interview continues, the interviewer will probably mention some of the most important responsibilities of the position. If applicable, draw parallels between your experience and the demands of the position as detailed by the interviewer. Describe your experience the same way you do on your resume. When describing your activities at work, emphasize your results and achievements. Never exaggerate—be on the level about your abilities.

The first interview is often the toughest. It is where many candidates are screened out. If you're interviewing for a competitive position, you'll have to make an impression that will last. Focus on a few of your greatest strengths that are relevant to the position. Develop these points carefully and re-emphasize them where possible.

Remember to keep attuned to the interviewer and make the length of your answers appropriate to the situation. If you're really unsure as to how detailed a response the interviewer is seeking, ask.

Avoid the Negative and Emphasize the Positive

Try not to be negative about anything during the interview, particularly any past employer or previous job. Even if you detest your current or former job or manager, don't make disparaging comments. The interviewer may construe this as a sign of a potential attitude problem and not consider you a strong candidate.

Take some time to really think about how you'll convey your work history. Present "bad experiences" as "learning experiences." Instead of saying "I hated my position as a salesperson because I had to bother people on the phone," say "I realized cold-calling wasn't my strong suit. Though I love working with people, I decided my talents would be best used in a more face-to-face atmosphere." Always find some sort of lesson from previous jobs, as they all have one.

FACT

The interview isn't only about you making a good impression on the employer. The employer should also make a good impression on you. You should be observing the interviewer, especially if he is someone with whom you'll be working. If you don't like this person in the interview, you probably won't enjoy working with him either.

Don't Talk about Money

It's usually best to avoid talking finances until you receive the offer. Otherwise you'll look like you care more about money than putting your skills to work for the company. Your goals at an interview are simple: (1) to prove to the recruiter that you're well suited to the job as you understand it and (2) to make sure you feel comfortable with the prospect of actually doing the job and working in the environment the company offers. Even if you're unable to determine the salary range beforehand, don't ask about it during the first interview. You can always ask later. Don't ask about fringe benefits until you've been offered a position. Then be sure to get all the details.

If the interviewer presses you about your salary requirements during an interview and you feel you must name a figure, give a salary range instead of an absolute number. Naming a salary range gives you a chance to hook on to a figure that's also in the range the company has in mind. In fact, many companies base their offers on sliding salary scales. Therefore, if you name a range of, say, $25,000 to $30,000, it may be that the company was considering a range of $22,000 to $28,000. In this case, you'll be more likely to receive an offer in the middle to upper end of your range. Of course, your experience and qualifications also play a part here. If you're just starting out and have little experience, the recruiter may be more likely to stick to the lower end of the scale.

When discussing salary you should never talk about your needs or wants. For example, don't say "I have a lot of bills to pay, so I need more money." You are requesting a particular salary range because that is the going rate in your field (which you will discover through your research) and you will earn that much money because of your hard work, your experience, and what you will bring to the job.

In anticipation of the salary question, you must know what others in your field with your skills and experience are earning. You can use the Web to search for salary surveys. You can also learn about salaries through trade and professional associations, and by looking at government resources such as the *Occupational Outlook Handbook*, which is available online at *www.bls.gov/oco*.

Coping with Difficult and Inappropriate Questions

There are some questions you expect an interviewer to ask and even look forward to answering. After all, if you aren't asked those questions, how will you ever be able to let a potential employer know why you are the best person for the job? There are other questions that you hope never to be asked, some because they are so difficult you can't answer them and others because the interviewer's intention when asking those questions is never good.

Difficult Questions

One of the biggest fears candidates harbor about job interviews is the unknown question for which they have no answer. To make matters worse, some recruiters may ask a question knowing full well you can't answer it. They don't usually ask such questions because they enjoy seeing you squirm—they want to judge how you might respond to pressure or tension on the job. If you're asked a tough question you can't answer, think about it for a few seconds. Then, with a confident smile and without apology, simply say "I don't know" or "I can't answer that question."

Illegal or Inappropriate Questions

Some interviewers go beyond asking difficult questions. They ask questions that are considered "illegal." While asking the question isn't truly illegal, using your response to determine whether to hire you is illegal. For example, an interviewer asking someone what their nationality is, isn't illegal (although it is inappropriate). If you are asked that question on an interview and then aren't offered the job, you might assume it is because of your answer. That might be discrimination on the part of the interviewer, and that is illegal. When you are asked a question you feel is inappropriate, you can speak up and say so. Rather than being confrontational, you can say that you would rather not answer the question. You will be taking the risk that the interviewer won't like that answer and may choose not to offer you a job because of it. Given the tone of the question and what it says about the interviewer, though, would that really be a bad thing?

Asking Your Own Questions

As the interview winds down, the recruiter will probably say something like, "Are there any questions you'd like to ask?" It's essential to have a few questions to ask at this point—otherwise you won't seem serious about pursuing a career at that company. Some of your planned questions may already have been covered by the time you reach this stage of the interview, in which case you'll have to think on your feet.

ALERT!

When the interviewer asks if you have any questions, the worst thing you can say is "Nope. I'm all set." This response suggests that you are not that interested in the job and that you didn't take the interview very seriously. Quickly reflect on the conversation you've had and ask a thoughtful question. This small detail could make or break the interview for you.

Use the questions you ask to subtly demonstrate your knowledge of the firm and the industry and to underscore your interest in a long-term career position at the firm. But don't allow them to become an interrogation—pose only two or three thoughtful questions. Don't ask questions the recruiter will find difficult or awkward to answer. This is not the time to ask, for example, "Does your company use recycled paper for all its advertising brochures?" And, of course, avoid reading directly from your list of questions.

Following Up after the Interview

You've made it through the toughest part—but now what? First, breathe a sigh of relief! Then record the name and title of the person you interviewed with, as well as the names and titles of anyone else you may have met. Ideally, you'll have collected their business cards. Don't forget to write down what the next agreed-upon step will be. Find out when the employer will contact you. Then you have some things to attend to—and some waiting around.

Don't Forget to Write

Write a follow-up letter immediately, while the interview is still fresh in the interviewer's mind. Not only is this a thank-you, it also gives you the chance to provide the interviewer with any details you may have forgotten (as long as they can be added tactfully). If you lost any points during the interview, this letter can help you regain your footing. Be polite and make sure to stress your continued interest and competence to fill the position. Just don't forget to proofread it thoroughly. If you're unsure of the spelling of the interviewer's name, call the receptionist and ask.

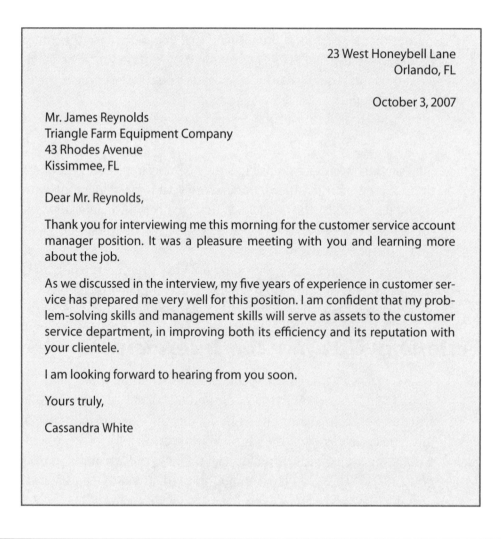

23 West Honeybell Lane
Orlando, FL

October 3, 2007

Mr. James Reynolds
Triangle Farm Equipment Company
43 Rhodes Avenue
Kissimmee, FL

Dear Mr. Reynolds,

Thank you for interviewing me this morning for the customer service account manager position. It was a pleasure meeting with you and learning more about the job.

As we discussed in the interview, my five years of experience in customer service has prepared me very well for this position. I am confident that my problem-solving skills and management skills will serve as assets to the customer service department, in improving both its efficiency and its reputation with your clientele.

I am looking forward to hearing from you soon.

Yours truly,

Cassandra White

Waiting for News about a Job Offer

Waiting to hear whether you got the job, or at least a second interview, can be excruciating. If the interviewer told you when you can expect to hear from her, then don't contact her until after that date. However, if she didn't provide that information, allow her five to ten business days to contact you after receiving your thank-you letter. If you haven't heard anything after that time, follow up with a phone call. Express your continued interest in the firm and the position and ask whether a decision has been made or when you'll be notified.

Don't be discouraged if you don't receive an immediate response from an employer. Most companies interview many applicants before making a final decision. Take advantage of this time to contact other firms and schedule more interviews, so that if a rejection does come, you have other options. Continuing to job search and interview is a good idea, even if you end up receiving the offer. Ultimately, you may have a number of opportunities to choose from, and you'll be in a better position to negotiate terms. So keep plugging away!

Handling Rejection

Rejection is inevitable, and it's bound to happen to you, just as it happens to all other job seekers. The key is to be prepared for it and not take it personally.

One way you can turn rejection around is by contacting each person who sends you a rejection letter. Thank your contact for considering you for the position and request that she keep you in mind for future openings. If you feel comfortable about it, you may want to ask her for suggestions to help you improve your chances of getting a job in that industry or for the names of people who might be looking for someone with your skills. You can ask something like "Do you have any suggestions about who else I might contact?"

Two cautions are in order: First, don't ask employers to tell you why they didn't hire you. Not only will this place a recruiter in an awkward position, you'll probably get a negative reaction. Second, keep in mind that if you contact employers solely for impartial feedback, not everyone will be willing to talk to you.

Send a well-written thank-you note, mailed within one or two days of receiving notice of rejection. This makes a positive statement. When Danny P. was turned down for a position as a publicity director, he wrote his interviewer a letter that expressed his disappointment at not being offered the job and also his thanks for the company's consideration of his qualifications. The interviewer was so impressed by Danny's initiative that she provided him with several contact names to assist in his continued search.

If, when talking to the employer about your rejection, you learn that your skills and background don't match the position the interviewer needed to fill, ask him if another division or subsidiary could perhaps profit from your talents. If the interviewer liked you, he may be willing to recommend you for a more suitable position in the company.

In your letter, emphasize an ongoing interest in being considered for openings. Also, be careful to use an upbeat tone. Although you may be disappointed, you don't want to put the employer on the defensive or imply that you don't respect his decision. Above all, don't give up! Stay positive and motivated, and learn from the process.

Strategies for Additional Interviews

When filling professional career positions, few companies make a job offer after only one interview. Usually the purpose of the first interview is to narrow the field to a small number of promising candidates. During the first meeting, therefore, the ideal strategy is to stand out from a large field of competitors in a positive way. The best way to do this is to emphasize subtly one or two of your key strengths as much as possible throughout the interview.

During later interviews, the competition for the position will drop off, and employers will look not for strengths but for weaknesses. At this point, focus on presenting yourself as a well-balanced choice for the position. Listen carefully to the interviewer's questions, so you can determine her underlying concerns and try to dispel them. On the other hand, if later interviews are primarily with people who are in a position to veto your hiring but not to push it forward, focus primarily on building rapport, as opposed to reiterating and developing your key strengths.

FACT

Usually you can count on attending at least two interviews for most professional positions, or three for high-level positions. Some firms are famous for conducting a minimum of six interviews for all professional positions. Though you should be more relaxed as you return for subsequent interviews, the pressure will still be on. The more prepared you are, the better.

Another way in which second interviews differ from first interviews is that the questions become much more specific and technical. The company must now test the depth of your knowledge of the field, including how well you're able to apply your education and work experience to the job at hand. At this stage, the interviewer isn't a recruiter. You may have one or more interviewers, each of whom has a job related to the one you're applying for. Typically, these interviewers will represent your potential boss, professional peer group, or executives who oversee the work group.

The second round of interviews can last one to two days, during which you might meet with as few as two or three people or as many as fifteen or more over the course of the visit. These interviews typically last longer than initial interviews. For many executive positions, you may also have meetings around breakfast, lunch, or dinner.

In all cases, remember—you're still in an interview. You may be having a dinner conversation about a recent topic of concern to the industry as a whole. Be ready with opinions and equally ready to listen and ask good questions. You may be asked to demonstrate how you'd go about performing some aspect of the job. Be ready in case you're presented with a tough problem and are asked to tackle it as though you'd already started your first day on the job. Use what you said in the screening interview as an outline (it's gotten you this far!), but be prepared to build on this outline in meaningful ways with more developed details, examples, and ideas.

Chapter 14

Practice Interview Questions

The more you do anything, the better you become at it. This is as true for job interviewing as it is for anything else. A great way to prepare for an interview is to practice answering possible interview questions. This chapter contains all different kinds of questions that might be posed to you during an interview, though there are certainly other possibilities as well. Use the suggestions that follow each question as a guide to help you formulate your best answer—the one that truly expresses who you are and convinces an employer that you are the best person for the job.

14

Personal Questions

If all that mattered were the skills you can bring to a job, a potential employer would need only to look at your resume and hire you based on what she sees there. However, there's so much more to finding the right person to fill a job opening. An interviewer is responsible for making sure the person she hires is a good fit. What that means is that the job candidate's personality must mesh well with others in the workplace. It also means that the candidate has what it takes to do the job effectively. Aside from tangible skills, that can mean energy, ambition, patience, and other things that make up who you are. That is why an interviewer will ask you questions that might seem to have little to do with your ability to do the job for which you are interviewing.

Tips for Answering Personal Questions

When answering personal questions you want to be honest, but you certainly don't want to reveal more about yourself than necessary. Keep your answers short and to the point. Only answer the question the interviewer is asking you. For example, if you have a short temper, but can manage to control it on the job, no one needs to know about that. You want to present yourself in the best possible light.

Make sure your answers highlight your professional character, including thoroughness, diligence, and accountability. Demonstrate how you gather resources, predict obstacles, and manage stress. Offer proof of your effectiveness, including your creativity, initiative, resourcefulness, and leadership. Think of examples you can provide for each.

Focus on how you overcome problems, how you take advantage of opportunities that might otherwise be overlooked, and how you rally the support of others to accomplish goals. Talk about the management style and the interpersonal skills you use with peer groups and leaders. Demonstrate the kind of boss, colleague, and employee you will be.

Sample Personal Questions

Tell me about yourself.

This seems like a very broad request—one that can go in many different directions. Your goal when answering this question is to provide the interviewer with information that reveals things about yourself that make you the perfect employee. Use this opportunity to talk about an accomplishment or something that sets you apart from every other job candidate. Did you win a special award? Did you complete an important project? The employer doesn't want to know how many siblings you have, if you have children, or if you are married. He wants to know what you can bring to his company.

What is your biggest weakness?

This is where you can really mess up. The trick here is to pick a weakness that can be seen as a strength, or one that you have turned into a strength. For example, you can say you are a perfectionist, but that may be a problem since perfectionists sometimes can't get their work done quickly enough. So you can say you were a perfectionist, but have learned to do an excellent job quickly and efficiently. Alternatively, you can talk about a weakness that is fairly innocent. For example you can say, "My weakness is chocolate."

Questions about Your Skills and Abilities

There are two categories into which skills fall: hard skills and soft skills. Hard skills are the technical or tangible skills you use to do your job. Generally they are the ones you've learned through your education and training. Soft skills aren't specific to any type of work. They are skills one can use to do any job well. Soft skills can include problem-solving, decision-making, multitasking, and delegating. When an employer asks about your skills, she wants to know that you have the ability to do the job if she hires you. It is likely that she is only interviewing people whose resumes indicate they have the proper technical skills. She is looking for the person who can do the best job, using both their hard and soft skills.

Tips for Answering Questions about Your Skills and Abilities

Answer questions about your skills and abilities by giving examples of when you've used them. For example if the interviewer asks you if you are a good problem-solver, don't just say "yes." Talk about a situation you were in when you had to solve a problem. Explain the situation and talk about the steps you took to solve it. Then discuss the results of your actions.

ALERT!

If you don't have a particular skill, don't say you do have it. The truth will come out. However, if you think it's a skill you can master fairly quickly, then you could say that you don't have that skill yet but you would be willing to learn it. Then explain how you can go about doing that.

We learn skills both on the job and in our lives outside of work. If you attained a skill outside of paid employment, say so. Again be specific about where you learned that skill and how you used it. Your goal on a job interview is to let the employer know what you will do for his company. When he asks you about a particular skill, take the opportunity to let him know how you will use it to his company's benefit.

A job interview isn't the time to be modest. Brag about yourself. No one will do it for you. Saying you have particular skills is not enough. As long as you're being honest about your skill level, talk it up! Let the employer know how great you are at this particular thing.

Sample Questions about Skills and Abilities

We use the ERE system for scheduling appointments. Are you familiar with that program?

If you, the job candidate, have used this system, of course your answer will be yes. You will go on to talk about where you used the system and your success with it. If you haven't used that particular system, what should you do? First of all, don't lie and say you've used it. You will be found out, maybe sooner than you expect, since the interviewer's next question may require you to talk about this program. If you used a similar program, talk about your skill in using that program. Then stress your willingness and ability to learn this one. You may not get the job if the employer won't consider someone without that skill, but you'll be in a better place than you'd be if you claimed to have a skill you don't have.

This is a very fast-paced office. Do you mind dealing with multiple projects and tight deadlines?

By asking this question the interviewer wants to know how skilled the job candidate is at managing her time and how she works under pressure. He also wants to know how good she is at multitasking. The job candidate, by giving specific examples of how she uses these skills, will demonstrate her success in that type of environment.

Questions about Your Education

When you've been out in the work force for a while, your experience will carry more weight than your education when an employer is considering you for a job. However, if you are a recent graduate, a prospective employer will want to know a lot about your education, and in general, the time you spent in school. So the interviewer will ask you about your course work, your extracurricular activities, your grades, and even about how you chose your college and your major.

Tips for Answering Questions about Your Education

Be prepared to not only talk about the courses you took in college, but also what you gained from them. What skills did you develop in the classroom? Were there any projects that were particularly helpful in cultivating some of those skills? For example, if you had a project that required you to work as part of a team, discuss what you learned from that experience.

The interviewer is interested in how you make decisions and may ask you how you chose your college and your major. Be prepared to discuss the process you went through when making your choices. It will put you in a better light if your choices were deliberate rather than random. For example, it probably isn't a great idea to say you chose your college because the campus looked nice.

If your college major is different than the field in which you are now seeking employment, the interviewer will probably ask you about this. Explain how you made your decision to change fields, again being sure to seem deliberate in your choice. Also talk about how your major helped prepare you for your current field.

When you talk about your extracurricular activities, try to think of them as jobs. Highlight the work you did for campus clubs and organization. Talk about leadership positions you may have held.

People change careers somewhere between three and seven times in their lives. Clearly it is not that unusual for someone to look for a job in a field other than her college major. The employer may not be daunted by the fact that you changed careers as long as you put serious thought into your decision.

Sample Questions about Education

Why did you choose to major in . . . ?

Don't forget that your choice was deliberate. You explored your options and decided based on your research that this was the right one for you. You want the interviewer to see you as someone who makes decisions carefully and not haphazardly. Even if you are seeking work in a field other than the one you majored in, you can explain what your thinking was at the time you made your decision and how you came to change your mind.

What extracurricular activities did you participate in?

You don't have to list every extracurricular club you joined. Choose those in which you had leadership roles and from which you gained important skills. If you participated in few activities outside the classroom, try to think of something (but be truthful). Extracurricular activities make you well rounded. It is in your best interests to show you did something other than schoolwork.

Questions about Your Accomplishments

A prospective employer is very interested in learning what, through your hard work, you have accomplished. By finding out what you have done, he can try to predict what you will do in the future—for his company. A person who has had many accomplishments is very likely to continue to have even more.

Tips for Answering Questions about Your Accomplishments

Most people find it difficult to think on the spot, so it is a good idea to prepare a list of your accomplishments prior to going on any job interviews. Of course, you can't refer to this list during the interview, but if you review it beforehand, you should be able to recall the information.

ESSENTIAL

While this may not help you in your current job search, here is something to think about for the future: Keep a journal or diary of your workplace accomplishments. When you do something of which you are proud, or when your boss commends you for a job well done, write it down in your journal. When you are asked to talk about your accomplishments in the future, you will be able to refer to what you wrote down.

Your list of accomplishments should include anything that came about because of your hard work and your skills. Don't include things that came about by chance—just because you were in the right place at the right time. You did something to make your accomplishments happen. They didn't just happen to you.

When preparing your list of accomplishments, choose ones that are relevant to the job for which you are applying. It will give the interviewer a chance to take a sneak peek at what you can do for his company.

If you can quantify your accomplishments, try to do so. For example, when saying you increased sales or cut expenses, talk in terms of actual amounts. Your accomplishment then becomes more than your own opinion of how well you did. It becomes something verifiable.

If you accomplished something that required the help of other people, include that on your list. Employers want to know that you can work as part of a team. By discussing this, you will be calling attention to a desirable skill.

Sample Questions about Your Accomplishments

What was your greatest accomplishment at work?

While you may think that getting a big raise and promotion was your greatest accomplishment at work, it isn't something that shows how your employer benefited. You can talk about the things you did to warrant being rewarded in such a way. In preparing your list, you should think of the reasons your boss gave you for your raise and promotion. Those reasons—increasing sales or getting new clients—are your accomplishments. You must also discuss the efforts you made to achieve your accomplishments and quantify them if you can.

What accomplishment are you proudest of?

Choose something that truly took a lot of effort to achieve. You want to show that you are proud when your hard work pays off. As you should always do, choose an accomplishment that greatly benefited your employer.

Questions about Your Work History

We can learn a lot about the future from the past. So can your potential employers. An employer wants to know about your work history so she can make projections about your future success—or failure.

Your answers about your work history provide, in a way, a narrative to your resume. While your resume gave little tidbits of information to whet the employer's appetite, your discussion of your work history on a job interview will flesh out this information. Hopefully it will give him a reason to want you in his employ.

The interviewer will not merely want to know what you did in your past jobs. He will want to know your thoughts about those activities, the outcomes of your efforts, how you got along with your boss and your coworkers, and what you learned from your experience.

Tips for Answering Questions about Your Work History

Every answer you provide about your work history gives the interviewer insight into your potential as an employee. Your answers should impart information about your positive characteristics—ambitious, logical, smart, detail-oriented, team player. Every answer is important. If the interviewer weren't interested in what you had to say, she wouldn't have asked the question in the first place. Take time to figure out what the interviewer wants to know before you begin answering her question.

When the interviewer asks you a question about a previous job, she doesn't want "yes or no" answers. She wants details about your work history that will help her learn something about you and therefore form an opinion. One note of caution, though—give only enough details to illustrate your answer. You don't want to say more than the interviewer needs to, or wants to, know.

The interviewer will use your resume to come up with questions to ask you about your work history. Carefully review your resume as you prepare your answers to possible questions. Be familiar with all the details on your resume since you don't want anything you say to differ from what you have written on it.

The interviewer doesn't just want a laundry list of your daily activities when she asks you to discuss a previous job. She wants to know about those activities: what you liked about them, what you didn't like (keep that to a minimum), how your boss and coworkers regarded you, and what motivated you.

Avoid talking about negatives if possible. If you have to talk about negative things, talk about the actions you took to correct bad situations. Whatever you do, don't badmouth prior employers. Employers tend to stick together, or at least empathize with one another. If you say you didn't get along with your boss, a prospective employer will wonder what you did to cause that to happen. You may know the situation was entirely beyond your control, but she won't know that.

Sample Questions about Your Work History

Can you tell me about your least favorite boss?

Here is someplace the job candidate can really mess up. He can talk about how much his boss hated him and how unfair that was. The job candidate may be entirely correct in his assessment, but that doesn't matter. He will look bad if he says any of that. Even though it is best to avoid negatives, the interviewer asked the question and expects an answer. Don't get personal when you answer this question. It has nothing to do with your relationship with your boss, but instead has to do with how he did his job. You can say that he had bad time management skills, for example. You shouldn't say that he made you work long hours.

How has your last job prepared you for the job opening we have here?

This is the time to highlight all your skills and abilities. Get specific. Talk about each skill and how you used it in your work. Talk about what you accomplished by using it and how it benefited your employer.

Difficult Questions

Almost everyone experiences some anxiety when it comes to job interviewing. They may be afraid of the interviewer asking questions they will have trouble answering. Even an innocuous question can trigger that "uh-oh" feeling. Being prepared for the job interview questions you may have to answer can help alleviate some of that fear.

That strategy works very well for the easy questions like "What did you like best about your last job?" What do you do, then, if you have something in your employment background that is a sensitive issue? For example, do you have a lengthy gap between jobs somewhere in your work history? Did you stay at one of your jobs for only a short period of time? Is there something in your background that could be embarrassing? Is there anything you would simply rather not discuss? Unfortunately, you can't control what questions the interviewer will ask you. You do have power over your response to these questions. Since you can't avoid difficult questions, you might as well prepare for them. Your answers to these questions can change a potential employer's perception of the situation.

Tips for Answering Difficult Questions

Just like with all other questions the interviewer might ask, it helps to know your answer before you go on the interview. If you hesitate for more than a few seconds, or look distressed, you will project that you are unsure of how to answer. The interviewer will wonder why and may think you have something about which to be concerned.

ALERT! Saying "uh" or "um" while collecting your thoughts makes you sound nervous. Many people use these "filler words" while trying to think of something to say. It is better to pause for a second or two. If you hesitate only briefly, no one will notice.

Have you been looking for work for a while? It may not be your fault. The economy may be slow, or the job market in your field may be tight now. If either is the case, you should say so. You can't be blamed for a bad job market, nor should you take the blame for it. Use the opportunity to talk about how you have made yourself better able to compete in the current market. If you've been out of work for a while, and the economy and your field are healthy, you may not be able to explain why.

Be honest about your employment history. If an interviewer asks you why you left a prior job, it's okay to say you were let go. If it was due to your own actions, then say that. He's going to find out anyway when he does a background check. Take ownership of your actions. Just as you are responsible for your successes and achievements, you are also responsible for your failures and shortcomings. If your answer reveals something negative about you to a prospective employer, use the opportunity to explain what you learned from the situation and what you did to effect positive changes.

Explain gaps in employment honestly. If you took time off to stay home with your children, say so. Talk about what you did with your life during this hiatus. Discuss the classes you took to keep your skills up to date (only if it's true, of course). If you spent your time off doing nothing career-related, talk about how you have recently been preparing for your return to work.

If an interviewer brings up your lack of education or experience, explain how you are making amends for that now. Discuss what you are doing to compensate. If you are taking classes or if you have plans to, tell the interviewer about those plans. Express your desire to learn.

Examples of Difficult Questions

I see that you've moved from job to job. Why have you had four jobs in four years?

As always, be honest. If you moved from job to job because you weren't sure of what you wanted to do, say that. Many people, especially those coming right out of school, aren't sure what they want to do, so they move from job to job looking for satisfaction. Then go on to talk about the commitment you are now making to your career, which came about because of careful planning.

Why did you leave or why do you want to leave your job?

If you left your job because you were fired, you had better spit out the truth. The employer will find out anyway, so it's better if you are up front. You can chalk it up to a difference of opinion between you and your former boss.

If you're still at your job but you're actively looking to move on, explain your motives there, too. Stick to positive information, such as that you're looking for more of a challenge, or you would really like to gain more experience in a different area of your field. Don't bring up petty disagreements with coworkers or insufficient workspace for this question. This is your chance to show the interviewer that you're looking to improve yourself and contribute your skills to a company you admire.

Illegal or Inappropriate Questions

Generally, when you think of interview questions that involve race or religion, the first word that comes to mind is "illegal." In reality, it is the way an employer uses the information she gets from your answers in deciding whether or not to hire you that could be illegal. Employment discrimination based on race, color, sex, national origin, religion, age, and disability is illegal according to United States federal law. So, if an employer asks what your nationality is and then decides not to hire you based on that information, that is discrimination and is therefore illegal. The U.S. Equal Employment Opportunity Commission (EEOC) evaluates cases where discrimination is suspected. While most questions aren't illegal according to federal laws, they may be illegal according to state laws. Here are some areas that are off-limits on a job interview:

- An interviewer can't ask if you were ever arrested or if you ever committed a crime. He may ask if you were ever convicted of one.
- According to the Americans with Disabilities Act, an employer can't ask about a disability, even if it is an obvious one.
- An interviewer cannot ask if you are pregnant or if you plan to become pregnant.
- The National Labor Relations Act prohibits an employer from asking about your union affiliation.

Some questions may simply be inappropriate. For example, an interviewer shouldn't ask if you plan to have children. She shouldn't ask what your spouse does for a living. She shouldn't ask what your marital status is. These questions have nothing to do with your ability to do the job and should be off-limits on a job interview.

Tips for Answering Illegal or Inappropriate Questions

When faced with an illegal or inappropriate question, you may feel cornered. If you don't answer the question, you feel you may offend the interviewer. If you do answer it and the answer isn't what the interviewer wants to hear, you think you won't get the job.

Don't be defensive. The last thing you want to do is give the employer a justifiable reason to turn you down for the job. If you become nasty, he has his reason to not hire you and you may have trouble proving that it was discrimination. If you don't want to answer the question, you don't have to. Explain, as nicely as you can, that the question is irrelevant to your ability to do a good job. If it was truly an innocent question, the employer may apologize and move on.

FACT

The U.S. Equal Employment Opportunity Commission (EEOC) handles complaints about employment discrimination. If you think an employer discriminated against you when you applied for a job, you can file a complaint with that agency. Find out where your local EEOC office is by calling 1-800-669-4000 or 1-800-669-6820 (TTY). You can also get more information by visiting *www.eeoc.gov*.

You can try to skirt the question. For example, an employer trying to determine whether or not a woman is married, may ask if she prefers to be addressed as Miss or Mrs. The job candidate can just say she prefers to be addressed by her first name and reveal nothing about her marital status to the employer.

Examples of Illegal or Inappropriate Questions

You seem a little winded from that walk. Do you have a heart condition or something else we should know about?

The Americans with Disabilities Act makes it illegal for an employer to inquire about a job candidate's health. You do not have to answer that question and can nicely say that.

Do you see children in your future?

The employer may be concerned that starting a family may interfere with the candidate's career. However, this question is inappropriate. The candidate can simply reassure the employer of her dedication to her career without answering the question.

Questions to Ask the Interviewer

Up to this point you've been concerned with your performance on the job interview. You have worked hard to come up with the best answers possible to every question you might be asked. After all you want to give a good impression and increase your chances of getting a job offer.

Let's switch gears now. The interview actually serves two purposes . . . or, more accurately, two parties. It serves the employer, whose goal is to find the best candidate for the job. It also serves you, the job seeker, who want to find the best job you can. And how will you know which job is right for you? First you will make some observations about the work environment. You will also do some research about the company, which may include speaking to current and past employees or to people who know them. You will also ask questions of the interviewer, which you will usually be given the opportunity to do at the end of a job interview.

Before you go on the interview, prepare some questions to ask. You probably won't get to all of them, so prioritize them. Ask about the company's financial health and its plans for the future. Inquire about employee turnover and job satisfaction. Find out how people advance through the ranks and how employees are evaluated.

QUESTION?

Should I ask a question, for example about the company's financial health, if I already know the answer from my research?
You shouldn't ask the question if you know the answer, but you can use this opportunity to let the employer know that you have done your research. You can do this by revealing what you know and then asking for further clarification about it.

Your questions should show your interest in the company. They should indicate that you were listening throughout the interview. You shouldn't ask something that was already answered, but you can ask for clarification. Phrase your questions in a way that lets the interviewer picture you in the job. For example, "What opportunities for advancement will I have?"

Questions to Avoid

There are some questions that are inappropriate and should not be asked unless the employer has made an offer. Don't ask about salary or benefits. Stay away from questions about vacation time. Don't ask what can cause someone to get fired. You should also avoid asking any questions that will reveal any of your insecurities about being able to handle the job. Such questions will turn the interviewer's attention away from your skills and strengths, which is the opposite of what you want.

Sample Questions

The following list contains some questions you might consider asking the interviewer when you're presented with the opportunity at the end of the interview. Of course, not all of these questions will be appropriate to bring up in every situation. Play it by ear and choose what to ask based on what has been discussed in the interview.

- Who will I be reporting to?
- What will I need to do to advance in this company?
- Are there formal performance reviews?
- How often will I be evaluated?
- Why is this job open?
- What has the company's growth been over the last five years?
- Do you consider the company to be in good financial health?
- Do you promote from within?
- How long do most employees stay with the company?
- How long have you been with the company?
- How many of those in upper management began their careers at this company?

Chapter 15

Special Interview Situations

When imagining what an interview would be like, you may have pictured yourself sitting in an office opposite your interviewer. That is a typical setting for a job interview, but it is not the only option. For example, you may not meet with the employer in his office but in a restaurant. And instead of speaking with someone one-on-one, you may be interviewed by a group or panel of people, or you may be interviewed as part of a group of job candidates. Your interview may not even take place in person, but instead over the telephone or via videoconference. You may even have to travel to a foreign country for your job interview!

Interviewing over a Meal

If you are unfamiliar with mealtime etiquette, you may want to brush up on your skills—you may be invited to join your potential employer for breakfast, lunch, or dinner. Some employers choose to interview job candidates over a meal. This is a real possibility, particularly if you are interviewing for a job out of town.

While sharing a meal with someone may conjure up feelings of familiarity, don't be fooled into thinking the interview is going to take on a more casual tone than it would have if it were taking place in an office. In reality, you have more to think about than how to answer the questions the interviewer is asking. The interviewer will not only be listening to your answers, she will also be judging your behavior. Learning some simple rules of dining etiquette should put you at ease. Then you can concentrate on more important things—like giving answers that make you shine.

Arriving at the Restaurant and Getting Seated

One of the more awkward moments of a mealtime interview could happen at the very beginning—arriving at the restaurant. Of course you are going to be punctual and arrive at the designated time, but that means you may arrive before the interviewer. If you do arrive first, give the interviewer's name to the host or hostess who may have a reservation for him. It is okay to sit down at the table to wait, but don't order anything yet.

When the interviewer arrives at the table, stand up until he sits down. If both of you arrive at the table at the same time, wait for the interviewer and others in your party, if there are any, to be seated before you sit down.

Gender rules generally do not apply when you're in a business setting, such as a mealtime job interview. It makes no difference whether you are a man and the interviewer is a woman or vice versa. If you are seated when the interviewer gets to the table, you should stand until he or she is seated.

Perusing the Menu

You may love spaghetti and meatballs, but is that the smartest thing to order when on a job interview? It probably is not. You should stay away from anything that is difficult to eat neatly. You don't want to risk looking like a slob or having to think too much about the process of eating instead of answers to the questions the interviewer is asking you. Also avoid foods that might get stuck between your teeth, like anything with poppy seeds or spinach.

Stick a package of dental floss in your purse or jacket pocket. If you suspect that you might have something stuck between your teeth, you can slip into the restroom to remove it. You also might want to carry around some breath mints (not chewing gum).

Avoid consuming any alcoholic beverages even if you can hold your liquor quite well. Alcohol dulls your senses and makes you less inhibited. This is one situation when you want to be at your sharpest. You can order a soft drink or water instead. If wine is being served at the table, to be polite, allow the server to pour you a glass, but sip it very slowly.

Before you pour yourself water or take a roll from the breadbasket, offer the item to your fellow diners. Ask if you can pour water for anyone else or pass the breadbasket around the table. The same goes for the butter or any other condiment on the table. If there's only one serving of something left, such as the last roll in the breadbasket, offer it to your dining companions before you take it.

Don't order the most expensive thing on the menu. Order a moderately priced item. You don't want to take advantage of the employer's generosity, since it is likely she will be footing the bill. Order a dish that can be prepared as described on the menu. You don't want to have to give the waiter a lot of specifications ("Can I get that without onions, mushrooms, or peppers, please."). If you order that way you will look too fussy.

Eating

Don't begin eating until everyone at the table has been served. Don't cut up all your food at once—cut off one piece at a time and put your knife down on the edge of your plate between bites. Use your napkin to remove crumbs from your face, remembering to dab at the corners of your mouth, not wipe the napkin across your lips. Put your napkin down on the table neatly. Don't crumple it up.

Even if you try to eat neatly you may end up getting something on your clothes. You don't have to worry about walking around like that all day, especially if you are heading back to the employer's office. There are several products on the market that can instantly remove stains from clothing. These products come in packages that are the size and shape of a pen and can easily fit in your pocket or purse.

ESSENTIAL

Unless you've been to several formal dinners, you might be baffled by the number of utensils at your place setting. You may wonder which fork to use first, for example. It's really quite simple. Generally, your salad or appetizer fork is smaller than the other one. Sometimes, though, you end up with two forks that are the same size. A good rule of thumb is to use the fork farthest away from your plate first and work your way in.

Since the whole point of this lunch (or dinner or breakfast) is to conduct a job interview, it is likely that you will have to speak during the meal. It may be obvious to you as you read this that you shouldn't talk with your mouth full. However, you may forget this important rule as you try to answer questions the interviewer asks you without looking like you are hesitating. It is always good manners to chew first, swallow, and then speak. Finish answering the question before you continue eating.

Wondering when the meal is over? Follow the interviewer's lead. If she puts her napkin on the table it means the meal is over. Finish chewing, wipe your face, and place your napkin on the table to signal that you are done, too. Don't stand up and get ready to go until the interviewer does, though. She may still have more questions to ask you.

When the interview is done, shake the interviewer's hand. Then thank her for her time and for the meal. Ask when you can expect to hear any further news and reiterate your interest in the job, just as you would at an interview that takes place in an office.

Interviewing in a Foreign Country

Today's economy is a global one and it is possible that you might have to travel abroad for a job interview. The job you are pursuing may be located in another country, or a company's headquarters may be located overseas even if your job won't be. Even when an employer based in a foreign country interviews you locally, you should be aware of the rules of etiquette in his homeland. A breach of etiquette, even if it is only in someone else's eyes, can be considered rude and may jeopardize your chance of the employer hiring you. Here are some basic things you should be aware of before you jet off to your job interview.

There are entire books devoted to the subject of international etiquette. Many public libraries and bookstores carry these books. Try looking under the following subjects: International Etiquette, Travel Etiquette, and Business Etiquette. Some of these books discuss the rules for many countries, and others focus on a particular country.

Body Language

One's interpretation of someone's body language is influenced by his culture. You are expected in some cultures, for example, to make eye contact with whomever you are speaking to. In other cultures it is considered rude to do so. In many countries people greet one another with a handshake, while in others people bow. Learn what is customary in the country you are visiting and what is acceptable and unacceptable. Then train yourself accordingly.

Dining Abroad

If you are traveling to another country for a job interview, there is a good chance you will have to share at least a meal or two with your hosts. You may have faultless table manners by your home country's standards. However, in the eyes of those in the country you are visiting, your manners may be more suitable for a toddler. Learn about proper dining etiquette and, again, practice the rules before you leave home.

While we're on the subject of dining, another issue you may encounter is food with which you're unfamiliar. You may be served things that you never even considered eating. If you are willing to try new foods, then do so. If someone offers you something you find totally repulsive, politely turn it down. Don't make a face or say anything negative. Something you wouldn't touch with a ten-foot fork may be someone else's fantasy meal.

Laws in Foreign Lands

Since you know the laws in your home country, you can probably avoid doing anything that could get you into serious trouble. However, if you don't know the law in the country you are visiting, you may do something inadvertently that can create legal problems for you, perhaps even get you into jail. Nothing will make a potential employer reject you faster than a phone call asking him to bail you out of jail.

A must-read for Americans traveling abroad is the U.S. State Department Web site: *http://usembassy.state.gov*. Resources on that site include general tips for traveling abroad, tips for those traveling to specific regions, and a list of U.S. embassies around the world. The State Department advises travelers who get into trouble abroad to immediately contact the nearest U.S. embassy.

Often people think they can get away with doing something in a foreign country because they are under the (false) assumption that the laws are more lenient there. For example, you may think it's okay to carry around marijuana or use it openly. Don't take that chance. Not only could you get into serious trouble, you may be treated more harshly because you are a foreigner. Know the laws and obey them completely.

Gender Differences

Men and women may be treated as equals in your home country. However, in many countries women and men are treated very differently from one another. Often there is one set of rules that applies to men and another one that applies to women. If you are aware of what the cultural norms regarding gender are in the country you are visiting, then you won't be surprised, or offended, when you encounter something that seems odd to you. For example, a woman may be expected to walk a few paces behind a man in some cultures instead of alongside him. In other countries women and men who aren't married to one another may never touch, so a handshake between a man and woman would be entirely inappropriate (and very offensive).

Telephone Interview and Videoconference

In some cases your interview may not even take place in person. A potential employer may choose to interview you by telephone or via videoconference. An employer may choose one of these methods if you don't live locally. It is much less expensive than flying a job candidate across the country. If you pass through this first interview, you will eventually need to be interviewed in person. If you are offered a job based only on a telephone or videoconferencing interview, don't accept it without first visiting the office in which you will be working. You definitely will want to see the facilities and meet those with whom you'll be working in person before making your decision.

Telephone Interview

There is a positive side to a telephone interview. It eliminates two sources of worry: what to wear and body language. You do, however, rely on your voice to convey all your emotions, including enthusiasm. Many communications experts advise people to stand up when they are taking part in a telephone interview. It is also a good idea to smile. It will relax you and help make you sound enthusiastic. Although it may seem unnecessary, you should also dress for the interview. That doesn't mean you have to wear your best suit, but you should at least get out of your bathrobe and fuzzy slippers. This will allow you to feel, and therefore speak, more professionally.

ALERT!

If you have young children or a dog that likes to bark, the busy living room may not be the best place to have your phone interview. Get a babysitter and ask your neighbor to take your dog for a walk for a half hour. If you're worried that you'll be interrupted—or if you actually are interrupted—you'll lose your concentration and become nervous. Make sure you have a relatively quiet, calm atmosphere for your phone interview.

Interviewing via Videoconference

In an interview that takes place by videoconference, you will be at a videoconferencing center while your interviewer, or interviewers, are at another location. Once there, you will be facing a camera and talking into a microphone as you answer questions, just as you would on a traditional interview. For someone who isn't used to being on camera—and most people aren't—a videoconference can be a nerve-racking situation.

Body language is very important, so remember to sit up straight, place your hands on your lap, and look directly at the camera. More than for any other type of interview, it is essential that you practice for a videoconference interview. Videotape yourself, or ask a friend to videotape you so you become accustomed to "talking" to the camera.

Panel Interview

In a panel interview, a group of people, rather than an individual interviewer, will ask you questions. This group may include managers, human resources personnel, and possibly those with whom you would be working if you get the job. You may also hear this type of interview called a committee interview. Often all of the people participating in the interview will be making the hiring decision.

It is important to stay relaxed during the interview even though you may feel like you are sitting before a firing squad. Your job is to interact with each person on the panel. As you answer each question, make eye contact with the person who asked it. Give each interviewer equal attention, even if you know who is higher up in the company's chain of command and thus will have more say over whether you get the job. The person you snub, even if he is lower down on the corporate ladder, may have a big influence on the person who wields the most power. If you can remember who's who, try to address each person by name.

QUESTION?

What should I do if I forget an interviewer's name on a panel interview?

If you can't remember one of your interviewers' names, it is okay to ask her to tell it to you again. Make sure you remember it this time, though. One good way to remember a person's name when you meet her is to repeat the name aloud (as in "It's a pleasure to meet you, Ms. Baker") or to yourself. This will keep the name fresher in your mind.

Shake hands with all participants at the end of the interview. Send an individual thank-you note to each person on the panel in which, if your memory is good, you can bring up something regarding a question that person asked. If you forget the names of anyone on the panel after the interview, a quick call to the receptionist or secretary can help you get that information.

Group Interview

When an employer has a lot of applicants to interview they may begin the process of weeding out the less desirable ones by conducting group interviews. In a group interview you will be interviewed at the same time as other job candidates. The interviewer or interviewers will address questions to the group as a whole or to individuals within the group.

In all groups there are people who are leaders and people who are followers. Which candidates take on which roles will become evident as the interview progresses. In many instances that is exactly the information the employer needs to help him make his decision. He wants to know who is a leader and who is a follower and will decide who to hire based on this information. All you can do is be yourself. Remember, the job needs to match your personality for you to be successful and happy doing it. With that said, remember to speak up even if your natural tendency isn't to be a leader. You want your voice to be heard, since your goal is to let the employer know more about you.

Behavioral Interviews

An employer wants to know, before they hire you, how you will behave in certain situations that you could potentially face on the job. Everyone possesses attributes that allow her to cope with different situations. These attributes are called competencies. On a behavioral interview you are expected to prove (or disprove) that you have certain competencies by describing circumstances under which you had to use them in the past. The interviewer will use this information to help him determine whether you will be a good employee.

Preparing for a Behavioral Interview

You will need to do a great deal of preparation before a behavioral interview. Begin by trying to figure out what competencies the employer desires. Read the job description thoroughly and try to pick up clues. You can consult your network to see if any of your contacts are familiar with the company. Someone familiar with the company may know what competencies it values. If you can't find out what competencies you might need to demonstrate on a behavioral interview with a particular employer, don't panic. The competencies employers most desire, and therefore the ones they often ask you about on a behavioral interview, are problem-solving, decision-making, organization, time management, interpersonal skills, and the ability to multitask.

Once you have figured out which competencies you will have to demonstrate, it is time to come up with an anecdote for each one. Review all the jobs listed on your resume to refresh your memory. Think about the projects you worked on at each one and what actions you took in order to complete them successfully. You should also consider the problems you may have encountered and how you solved them. Which of your strengths did you draw upon to help you achieve positive results?

Don't make up stories or embellish real ones to make your point. First of all, it's too easy to get caught in a lie. Second of all, you want your stories to be plausible. Most people can spot a lie from a mile away—particularly an interviewer, who has probably heard them all.

You should start by writing down these anecdotes, making sure to include details. Next, you should practice telling your stories out loud. Find a friend who is willing to listen to you, preferably someone who works in a similar job. Find out what your friend thinks of the story and whether it demonstrates the competency and skill you intend it to demonstrate.

Sample Behavioral Interview Questions

Each of these questions asks the job candidate to demonstrate one or a few competencies. The competency or competencies the employer expects you to demonstrate in your answer is shown in parentheses following the question.

- How have you handled being assigned several projects at once? (prioritizing, time management, multitasking)
- Describe a situation where you had to critique someone's performance and offer suggestions to help him do better. (interpersonal)
- Discuss a project you had to complete on short notice. (time management)

- Talk about a time you had to motivate members of a team. (leadership)
- Describe how you dealt with an unforeseen problem. (problem-solving)
- How have you set goals for yourself and achieved them? (goal-setting)
- Talk about a presentation you had to make. (presentation)
- Discuss a time when you had to deal with an unhappy client. (interpersonal)

Of course, these are only a few of the questions you may be presented with during a behavioral interview. You will most likely need to think on your feet in order to come up with an appropriate example for each question. The main way to prepare is to practice, practice, practice. The more situations you prepare for, the better your chances of impressing the interviewer and getting the job.

Chapter 16

Looking for a Job under Difficult Circumstances

The job search is hard enough under normal circumstances, but what should you do if you have to look for a job under an unusually difficult or awkward circumstance? Let's say, for example, you're still working. You will have to schedule interviews around your work schedule and you will have to keep your job search from your current employer. Other difficult circumstances include a long-distance job search, returning to work after an absence from the job market, looking for a job when you don't have work experience, and coping with a long-term job search.

Job Hunting While You're Still Employed

Job searching while you're still employed is particularly tiring because it must be done in addition to your normal work responsibilities. Don't overwork yourself to the point where you show up to interviews looking exhausted or start to slip behind at your current job. On the other hand, don't be tempted to quit your present job! The long hours are worth it. Searching for a job while you have one puts you in a position of strength.

ALERT!

Do not use your work telephone for job-hunting purposes. You also shouldn't send e-mail from your work computer. Employers often monitor e-mail and phone calls. Use your cell phone during breaks and lunch hours to make any job-search-related calls. Send and receive e-mail from your home computer using a personal address, rather than your work address. Most potential employers will understand that there are times during the day when you can't be reached, and they will probably appreciate the fact that you don't want to job hunt on your current employer's time.

Making Contact

If you must be at your office during the business day, you have additional problems to deal with. How can you work interviews into the business day? And if you work in an open office, how can you even call to set up interviews? Obviously, you should keep up the effort and the appearances on your present job. Maximize your lunch hour, early mornings, and late afternoons for calling. If you keep trying, you'll be surprised how often you can reach the executive you're trying to contact during your out-of-office hours. You can frequently catch people as early as 8 A.M. and as late as 6 P.M.

Scheduling Interviews

Your inability to interview at any time other than lunch might work to your advantage. Set up as many interviews as possible for your lunch hour. This will go a long way toward creating a relaxed atmosphere, but be sure the interviews don't stray too far from the agenda at hand. Lunchtime interviews are easier to obtain, however, if you have substantial career experience, and these are usually not standard practice for filling entry-level positions.

Often, you will find no alternative to taking time off for interviews, especially when your interview is not in close proximity to where you currently work. If you have to do this, try to take the whole day off in order to avoid being blatantly obvious about your job search, and try to schedule two or three interviews for the same day. It's difficult to maintain an optimum energy level at more than three interviews in one day. Explain to the interviewer why you might have to juggle your interview schedule. He should honor the respect you're showing your current employer by minimizing your days off and will probably appreciate the fact that another prospective employer is interested in you.

QUESTION?

Should I drop everything to go on a job interview?
No, you shouldn't drop everything to go on a job interview. If you are currently working, you are responsible to your current employer. Your future employer will understand if you tell her you must schedule your interview around your current job and will take that as a sign that you take your work seriously.

References

What do you tell an interviewer who asks for references from your current employer? Just say that while you're happy to have former employers contacted, you're trying to keep your job search confidential and would rather your current employer not be contacted until you have a firm offer.

Then offer to provide a list of previous employers who can provide a reference for you.

You must let someone know if you have given her as a reference. You don't want a phone call from your potential employer to catch her off guard. While it may be that your reference simply isn't expecting the call, the employer may interpret it to mean she isn't confident providing a reference for you. Furthermore, once a potential employer has asked for your references, be sure to forewarn or remind those references that they may expect to receive a phone call soon.

Be Discreet

The days when employees dedicated their entire careers to a single employer are long gone. It's expected that people will change jobs several times during their careers, and it could be unwise to leave a position without having something else lined up. You shouldn't feel obligated to inform your current employer you're job searching until you're ready to give your notice. Revealing this information too soon could cost you your job. Remember, employers would rather lose you at their convenience than at yours.

To ensure that your job search is kept quiet, avoid telling any of your coworkers or colleagues of your plans. This may sound obvious, but it's a mistake that's too often made—at the expense of the job seeker. Gossip flows very freely in most workplaces, and before too long your news will reach your boss.

If You're Fired or Laid Off

Being fired or laid off is demoralizing. Your self-confidence may be very low at the moment. Remember that you're not the first person and won't be the last one to go through this traumatic experience. In today's changing economy, thousands of professionals lose their jobs every year. Even if you were terminated with just cause, don't lose heart. Try to keep your confidence up. Your positive attitude will be a key element in helping you get your next job.

Severance and Unemployment Compensation

A thorough job search could take months, so be sure to negotiate a reasonable severance package, if possible. Make sure you know what benefits, particularly health, you still have. Also, register for unemployment compensation immediately. Look in the government listings in your telephone directory to find out where your local unemployment office is. Don't be surprised to find other professionals collecting unemployment compensation—it's for everyone who has lost her job.

FACT

The Consolidated Omnibus Budget Reconciliation Act, better known as COBRA, allows you to continue to participate in your employer's group health insurance plan by paying for the policy out-of-pocket. Your company's human resources or benefits department should be able to provide you with the proper paperwork.

Follow a Plan

Don't start your job search with a flurry of unplanned activity. Start by choosing a strategy and working out a plan. Now is not the time for major changes in your life. If possible, remain in the same career and in the same geographical location, at least until you've been working again for a while. On the other hand, if there aren't jobs available in your field, you may consider making a change now. If you had planned to make a career change prior to losing your job, you could also consider doing it now. Don't, though, make a change in the heat of the moment.

Expect the Inevitable Question

Avoid mentioning you were fired when arranging interviews, but be prepared for the question "Why were you fired?" during an interview. Be honest, but try to detail the reason as favorably as possible and portray what you've learned from your mistakes. If you're confident one of your past managers will give you a good reference, tell the interviewer to contact that person. Don't speak negatively about your past employer. The person with whom you are interviewing is more likely to identify with him and doing this will reflect poorly on you. Try not to sound particularly worried about being unemployed. If you were laid off as a result of downsizing, briefly explain this, being sure to reinforce that your job loss was not due to performance.

Finally, don't spend too much time reflecting on why you were let go or how you might have avoided it. Do try to look at the situation honestly, and if you think you made some mistakes along the way, plan to find ways not to repeat them. Think positively, look to the future, and be sure to follow a careful plan during your job search.

Planning Your Finances

In addition to being stressful, looking for a new job can be costly. Expenses relating to your job search, in addition to everyday living expenses, can mount to a formidable sum in the face of a reduced income. Following are some guidelines to help you make this aspect of your job search somewhat smoother.

- Find out about your company's severance pay policy.
- File for unemployment benefits.
- Extend your health insurance.
- Find out if your company offers outplacement services.
- Assess your financial fitness.
- Make a detailed list of your income and assets, including income from part-time, temporary, and freelance work, unemployment insurance, severance pay, savings, investments, spouse's income, and alimony.
- If you can't meet your expenses, ask your creditors for a reduced payment schedule. Establish a realistic budget and monitor it regularly.

You may not think about your monthly expenses until you suffer a financial hit, like job loss. If you lose your job, make a detailed list of your expenses, separating them into three categories: priority one, priority two, and priority three. Priority one expenses should include the essentials: rent/ mortgage, utilities, groceries, car payments, and job-search expenses. Priority two and three expenses should include items that can be sacrificed temporarily. Total your estimated expenses in each category.

Long-Distance Job Hunting

As if finding a job isn't tough enough, long-distance job hunting can be even more difficult. The ideal way to apply for a job in another city is to move there first, although this is not a viable option for everyone. Many people can't move to a new city unless they already have a job lined up. Others are open to moving to several locations and will choose which one after they are hired. Job searching long-distance is possible, but you should explain to potential employers immediately that you are willing to relocate to that particular area.

There are several Web sites that can help you with relocating to a new city. For example, RealEstateJournal.com (*http://homes.wsj.com*), from the *Wall Street Journal*, links to several helpful resources including one that profiles over 300 metropolitan areas, another that provides statistical information about school districts, and a few that help you with financial matters related to relocating.

When planning to move, there are several steps you can take to make the transition as smooth as possible. First, call or write to the chamber of commerce in the city (or cities) to which you want to relocate. Subscribe to a local newspaper, check for job postings online (see Chapter 10), and sign up with local employment agencies. Inform your networking contacts of your plans and ask them for any leads or suggestions they can give you in this new location. Do they know of anyone who works in that area who can give you suggestions? Also, be sure to check with your national trade or professional association. Most large associations offer members access to a national network. Contact the national office for a list of chapters in your new city.

Compare Costs of Living

What may be considered a high salary in one part of the country may be considered low in another. You must know what the cost of living is for the city to which you want to move and what the comparable salary should be. If you move from an area of the country where the cost of living is high, the salaries in that area will be high as well. It's not like you'll have a lot of disposable income floating around—you will use what you earn to pay your expenses. Likewise, don't be taken aback by what may look like a low salary. Your expenses will probably be lower as well.

You can compare costs of living between two different cities using tools that are available online. Using the Salary Calculator at Homefair.com (*www.homefair.com*), input your salary and your location, and then the place to which you want to relocate. This tool will calculate how much you will need to earn in your new city. The Cost of Living Comparison Calculator on Bankrate.com (*www.bankrate.com/brm/movecalc.asp*) takes it one step further. In addition to comparing incomes, it also gives a detailed list comparing expenses.

Returning to Work After an Absence from the Job Market

Many people, usually women, make the decision to stay home for a few years while raising their children. Others take time off from work to care for an elderly parent. Most don't take this decision lightly because they know the effect it could have on their careers. Several years out of the work force can mean several more years trying to get one's career back up to where it was before they left.

Keep Up with the Field

Stay-at-home parents, or anyone who takes a hiatus from work for whatever reason, have an obligation to keep up with the field they plan to return to "someday." You can do this by maintaining membership in professional or trade associations, reading relevant literature including journals and newsletters, and keeping your network alive. Take continuing education courses to help you keep up with a changing set of requirements in your field. Don't discount the value of taking a part-time job in your field. It will allow you to keep your skills sharp and up-to-date.

FACT

Attend meetings of professional and trade associations. While it may be expensive to attend a national conference of one of these organizations, many have local chapters. Attending meetings of these chapters is generally quite affordable. It is a great way to make contacts with others in your field and will help you keep up with current trends.

Discussing Your Absence

When a potential employer looks at your resume, he will undoubtedly make note of an extended gap in employment and inquire about it on a job interview. You shouldn't make excuses for your time away. You made a decision that was right for you and your family and you should be proud of the fact that you did so. You can briefly state your decision to take time off, but don't dwell on it. What you should do is stress the fact that you kept up with things while you were gone. Be ready to talk about new trends in your field. Tell the employer how you've enhanced your skills while away from the workplace. Talk about any classes you took or professional meetings you attended.

Lack of Work Experience

Whether you are new to the job market or new to a particular field, you will have to deal with your lack of experience. You can't create a resume full of jobs in your field if you haven't had any! What you can do is make any experience—work and otherwise—count in your favor.

ESSENTIAL

> This is another time when a journal comes in handy. If you don't do so already, start keeping a record—a journal or just a book with jotted notes—of all the experiences you have that relate to your preferred career field. The act of cataloging these items will help you remember their details, and you'll always be able to review your notes before an interview to refresh your memory.

Be ready to let a potential employer know about the things you've done that are related to the skills he wants. If one of the requirements of the job for which you are interviewing is the ability to work on a team, talk about sitting on the board of directors of a campus organization, or about working on a team cleaning up your local park. If strong organizational skills are needed, discuss the time you were on the committee that planned the high school yearbook. Remember that experience doesn't only come from paid employment. It also doesn't only come from paid work in a particular field. Part-time jobs count, too. So if you worked closing shift at a fast-food joint, you were part of a team that was responsible for making sure everything was cleaned up at the end of the day.

Long-Term Job Search

When the job market is tough, finding work can take a very long time. It can take months or even a year or more to find employment. While you may have started off with a very positive attitude, you may not have one after spending a significant amount of time facing rejection. Unfortunately, your negative attitude may sabotage your job search. You may feel so unenthusiastic that you won't feel like putting forth your best effort. Your attitude will be visible to employers who may be reluctant to hire someone who doesn't look like she has enough energy to get the job done. Changing your attitude isn't easy though. Here are some tips to help you stay positive:

- Don't be so hard on yourself. Remember, you aren't the only one in this situation.
- Stay in shape. Exercise can be a great way to relieve stress, and you will look better, too.
- Eat well. It's easy to get into bad eating habits when under pressure.
- Set aside some time each day to do something that makes you feel good.
- Spend time with people who make you feel good about yourself.
- Volunteer. Not only will it be gratifying, it may give you some valuable experience.
- Learn a new skill.
- Be supportive of someone else going through a tough time.

Following these tips or doing anything you can think of to help you feel better about yourself will revitalize you. Your self-esteem will get a much-needed boost. This self-confidence will be evident to prospective employers when you go on job interviews. Best of all, you will also have more energy to put into your job search, and that can really pay off in the end.

Chapter 17
The Job Offer

One of the most nerve-racking steps on the trail to a new job is near the end of the path: deciding whether to accept an offer. If you have been looking for a job for an extended period of time, your instinct may be to accept the offer even if you feel it is lacking in some way. Some job seekers turn down offers because of compensation only, even though the offer may be suitable in other ways. Job seekers can make unnecessary, costly mistakes during this vitally important stage.

Do You Want This Job?

If you're going to consider a job offer seriously, first be sure that it is a job you really want. Are you willing to live and work in the area in question? Is the work schedule and way of life one you would enjoy? If you're just graduating, is the job in the field you'd like to pursue? These are all things you should consider before you make your final decision.

Considering the Work Environment

Another important factor to consider is the kind of environment in which you'll be working. Is the company's atmosphere comfortable, challenging, and exciting? You must look at specifics, including office or workstation setting, privacy, proximity to other staff, amount of space, noise level, and lighting.

QUESTION?

Should I turn down a job if I don't like the way the office looks?
Don't automatically reject a job offer if the office is small or run down. Take it into consideration along with all the other factors. The office may look undesirable, but do the people working in it seem lively? The positive may outweigh the negative.

What is the level of interaction among coworkers? Some organizations strongly encourage teamwork and dialogue among staff, while others emphasize individual accomplishment. You should think about which approach works better for you. If you have serious doubts about whether you will like the work environment before you accept the job, you may grow to hate it after you accept the job.

Corporate Culture

Corporate culture encompasses many things. It includes a company's values, practices, and goals and the way it goes about achieving them. If you work for a company, you should feel comfortable with its culture. If you are a staunch environmentalist, for example, and the company you are considering working for is a big land developer that supports deforestation, this may not be the place for you. If your prospective employer expects their staff to put work ahead of family, and if that is something with which you don't feel comfortable, think carefully about accepting a job offer. It is unlikely that the corporate culture will change, and either you will be uncomfortable working within it or you will go against it. Either way, you may soon be looking for another job.

Location

Most people would be thrilled to be able to walk to work, or at least have to deal with only a five-minute ride. Unfortunately many workers don't have such an easy commute to their jobs. Getting to work often involves sitting in traffic or enduring a long trip on public transportation.

FACT

Americans spend a lot of time commuting to work. This results in quite a bit of down time for many people—time they can spend doing something more productive. According to the 2000 United States Census, the average travel time to work was almost twenty-six minutes.

One thing you must ask yourself before you accept a job offer is "How long will it take me to get to and from work each day?" And then you must ask yourself whether that commute is too long. You may not mind leaving your house at 6:30 every morning, but how will you feel about getting home at 8 o'clock every night?

Can You Work with These People?

When you think about the fact that the majority of your waking hours will be spent on the job, the importance of working with people with whom you get along looms large. While you don't have to love everyone in your workplace, you do have to have decent relationships with your coworkers and your boss.

When you are interviewing for a job, take note of your prospective boss's demeanor. Does she seem like a reasonable person or does she seem like someone who can fly off the handle pretty easily? Listen to her interact with other people—for instance, the receptionist. Is she polite and friendly? As you walk through the office, look at the people there. Do they look content? Do they seem friendly? It's difficult to make these assessments through first impressions, but if something doesn't seem right to you, pay attention to your instincts.

ALERT!

If the boss speaks in a derogatory tone of voice to one of his employees in your presence, think of what he will do when you aren't there. After all, shouldn't he be on his best behavior when there's a guest in the office?

Career Helper or Career Killer

Whether or not a job will help your career progress is ultimately a much more important question than what your starting salary will be. In some organizations, you may be given a lot of responsibility right away but then find your progress blocked. Make sure you know whether you have opportunities for advancement. Find out if you will be able to grow your career with this employer or if you will end up in a dead-end job.

Ask about performance reviews and how often they are conducted. Then find out if excellent performance reviews lead to promotions.

After a lengthy job search, you may be tempted to take a job that doesn't fit well with your career goals. If your goals have truly changed based on your re-evaluating your career, then that might be okay. However, if your goals remain the same, consider the impact that going off course could have on your career.

The Money Questions

The questions of salary and benefits strike fear into the hearts of job seekers young and old. But handling the inevitable money questions doesn't have to be difficult, and the more you think about them in advance, the easier they'll be to answer.

First, never try to negotiate salary or benefits until you've gotten an offer. At that point, don't worry about the recruiter withdrawing her handshake and showing you the door if you dare ask about flexibility in the company's offer. The worst case might be that the salary is set by company policy and the recruiter or hiring manager has no power to negotiate. He may not be able to give you an immediate answer and will have to get back to you.

> To learn about the opportunities for advancement within a particular company, you can ask for some statistics. Inquire about which members of upper management came from the lower ranks of the company. Does the employer promote from within? Find out what happened to other people who held the position you've been offered. Have they moved up, or have they moved out?

Before You Get the Offer

When it comes to buying a car, you can pretty much bet that the price the salesman gives you is negotiable. You are going to have to bargain. The same can't be said of a job offer. Before you even get an offer, you should have some idea of what salary to expect. That way, when an employer makes an offer, you will know how to respond. You will only know that if you do your homework.

Learn about Salaries in Your Field and Industry

Before you decide to ask for a higher salary you must know what the going rate is in your field. Just how do you know how much you should expect? The answer is the same as in every other step of your job search: Do your homework. Read the trade journals for your industry. Read the newspaper help-wanted ads. If possible, talk to current employees.

ALERT!

Salaries vary by geographic region. For example, a teacher in Wisconsin may earn a lower salary than a teacher in California. In addition to finding out what the average earnings are in your field and industry, you must also find out what those jobs pay where you plan to work. There is generally a relationship between the local cost of living, the salary, and the supply of and demand for workers with a specific set of skills.

There are many salary surveys available on the Web. Using your favorite search engine, type in the term "salary survey." Use your network to find out how much others are earning at the same level. Talk to alumni of your college or university in similar positions (or employed by the same organization). They may be an excellent source of information. By doing this research, you will get an idea of the salary level you can realistically expect.

Know Your Own Worth

Setting realistic expectations is especially important for the entry-level job seeker or recent graduate. If you don't have a lot of professional experience, you don't leave the employer with much hard evidence on which to base a decision to offer you more money. Instead, you're asking her to take a leap of faith based on potential you've demonstrated in classes, internships, volunteering, or extracurricular activities. Without a track record of professional experience, your arsenal is missing a powerful weapon. Even so, that doesn't mean you can't give negotiating your salary a try.

On the other hand, if you have some experience under your belt and are looking for a midlevel or executive position, your negotiating power might be much greater. For a lucky (or unlucky) few at the top of the heap, salary and benefit negotiations can be as complex and painstakingly slow as watching the grass grow. Whatever your level of experience, your task is to try to figure out just how high the employer is likely to go.

Deciding to Negotiate

Once you have decided to negotiate salary, you can approach your prospective employer with the confidence of knowing you are presenting a reasonable request, or at least one with which you are comfortable. The idea is to first assure him of your interest. Then give reasons for your proposed increase rather than just saying you need it or want it. Your financial needs are not a good enough reason for an employer to negotiate with you. They have no reason to offer you more money just because you have bills to pay. Everyone has bills to pay. The employer should be willing to pay you more because you are worth it and because you are asking for a fair salary based on what others doing the same job are earning. An employer may simply tell you they can't negotiate the salary, and then you must either be willing to accept their offer or walk away.

FACT

Some salaries are truly non-negotiable due to contractual constraints. In union shops, for example, salaries are set through negotiations between the union and the employer. The employer cannot offer a higher salary to a new employee than he is paying his current workers.

If you can negotiate, this doesn't mean you name a figure and the employer either matches it or doesn't match it. It means you're ready to listen to what she has to offer and give it consideration. To succeed in negotiation, both parties have to reach an agreement with which they're happy. If you succeed at winning yourself a bigger paycheck but antagonize your future boss in doing so, trouble lies ahead. If, on the other hand, you set realistic expectations and realize that you may not get everything you want, you'll probably do just fine.

How to Negotiate

If, after listening politely to the specifics of the offer, you're left hoping for a higher salary, greater health coverage, or something else, it's okay to (calmly) say so. Find out if the offer is firm. If it seems there may be some room to negotiate, make sure you have a figure in mind, because if the recruiter does have the freedom to barter, she will probably ask you point-blank to supply a figure. When you're asked that question, rule number one is as follows: Don't tip your hand by giving the interviewer a specific number for which you're willing to settle. You don't want to take yourself out of the running by naming a figure that's absurdly optimistic, and you certainly don't want to risk naming a figure lower than what the employer is ready to offer. Instead of naming your price, say something like, "Based on my experience and skills and the demands of the position, I'd expect I'd earn an appropriate figure. Can you give me some idea what kind of range you have in mind?"

ALERT!

When considering compensation, don't forget to look at the entire package. That includes health insurance, vacation time, sick days, and personal days. If the actual dollar amount you are being offered seems somewhat low, is it being made up for with very generous vacation time or with a paid-in-full health insurance plan? Don't forget that these things are valuable, too.

Of course, the recruiter may come back with "Well, how much were you interested in?" There's a limit to how far you can take this without antagonizing the other person, so if you can't get her to name a range, give in graciously and name your own. Be sure not to make the bottom number too low (because you may be stuck with it) or the range too large, and give yourself enough room at the top without being unrealistic. If you name a range of, say, $25,000 to $30,000, it may be that the company was considering a range of $22,000 to $28,000. Therefore, you should receive an offer in the mid-to-upper end of your range, depending on your experience and qualifications.

When Negotiating May Not Be a Good Idea

Perhaps the salary the employer is offering is fair, based on going rates and your experience. Should you still ask for more money? Your answer depends on what you feel comfortable doing. If you ask for more money even though you think the initial offer is fair, are you willing to walk away from the job if your request isn't met? Worse, are you willing to possibly create tension between yourself and your future boss?

Get It in Writing

If you're somewhat content with the distribution of funds but haven't discussed health insurance and other benefits, like a 401(k) plan and vacation time, do so immediately. Then request everything be outlined in writing, especially if you'll be leaving a job to take the new position. You have rights, and if something looks amiss, it's time to go back to the bargaining table—that is, if you're still interested. Regard with suspicion an employer who won't give you confirmation of the position in writing.

It's about Job Satisfaction

The point of your job search is not salary negotiation; it's finding a job you'll be happy with, that you'll grow with, and that will allow you to be yourself. If your starting salary isn't the one you dreamed about but the job presents the right opportunity, think about how much easier it'll be once you've had a chance to make yourself invaluable to the organization.

ESSENTIAL

Generally, a high salary doesn't buy job satisfaction. It may seem like the person with the BMW parked in the employee lot has the best job, but she may actually be unhappy at work. If you truly feel like a job will give you a lot of satisfaction, and you will be able to live comfortably on the salary being offered even if it isn't as high a salary as you would like, you should consider accepting the offer.

On the other hand, if the salary or benefits fall far short of your realistic expectations, despite all your efforts to negotiate, nothing says you have to take the job. Don't make the mistake of accepting a position with which you're fundamentally unhappy. Trust your instincts—if you're dissatisfied with the employer before your start date, don't bet the situation will get better.

Accepting a Job Offer

After going through the decision-making process and negotiating a salary, you've decided to accept a job offer. Before you tell the employer of your decision, make sure you are one hundred percent committed to it. Ask yourself the following questions one last time before you give your final answer:

- Do I fully understand the job and am I happy with what it entails?
- Will I be comfortable with the corporate culture?
- Will I be, as far as I can tell right now, compatible with my future coworkers and boss?
- Is the work environment one in which I will be happy?
- Is the location of the workplace acceptable? Will I be able to handle my commute?
- Do I understand the employer's expectations and will I be able to meet them?
- Does the employer understand my expectations and will he be able to meet them?
- Does the salary and other compensation seem fair to me? If not, will I be able to live with that?
- Will I have the opportunity for growth in this job?
- Do I believe I will be treated fairly by my new employer?

Of course, no one can predict the future, but if by answering these questions you can assure yourself you are making the right decision, you will at least be getting off to the best start you can.

Letting Your New Employer Know You'll Be Coming On Board

Once you've made your decision, it's time to let your new employer know. You can first do this by calling him on the phone, or by e-mail if that has been your primary mode of communication. Then follow that up with a written letter that states your acceptance of his offer.

1245 West 45th Street
New York, NY 10032

June 23, 2007

Mr. Terry Braun
Mather, Miller, and Low, LLC
23-95 Queens Boulevard
Forest Hills, NY 12445

Dear Mr. Braun,

I am pleased to accept your job offer and I am looking forward to working as your assistant at Mather, Miller, and Low. I am enthusiastic about beginning work on the file reorganization project we talked about during our last interview. I have some ideas about how to implement this endeavor and look forward to getting started.

I will inform my current employer of my decision immediately and will be able to begin working for you in two weeks, as we discussed.

Thank you for your confidence in me.

Yours truly,

Sybil Soo

No Turning Back Now

Once you've accepted a job offer, you must stick with your decision. If you are having any doubts about it, if you think you may get a better offer from another employer, or if you think your current boss might make a counteroffer, then don't accept yet. Wait until you've heard from everyone involved in your decision before you tell your future boss of your acceptance. Think about how you would feel if she decided to interview one last candidate after offering you the job and decided that he was the better choice. If the fact that this is just "the right thing to do" doesn't give you enough of a reason not to first accept and then reject an offer, remember that you don't know who you will meet in the future. This person, who may harbor very negative feelings toward you, can end up your future coworker or boss!

Declining a Job Offer

Whatever your reason is for deciding not to take a job offer, you must inform the employer of it. It would be rude to keep her waiting for your answer, just as it would be rude for her to keep you waiting. This advice holds true even if you feel the employer treated you unfairly by not presenting a fair offer or being willing to negotiate. Again, you simply don't know who you will meet again at another point in your career. The cliché "Don't burn any bridges" is certainly true here.

Here's a sample letter declining a job offer:

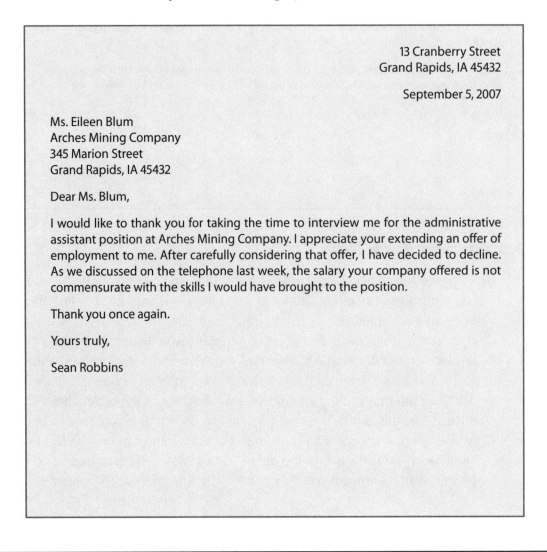

13 Cranberry Street
Grand Rapids, IA 45432

September 5, 2007

Ms. Eileen Blum
Arches Mining Company
345 Marion Street
Grand Rapids, IA 45432

Dear Ms. Blum,

I would like to thank you for taking the time to interview me for the administrative assistant position at Arches Mining Company. I appreciate your extending an offer of employment to me. After carefully considering that offer, I have decided to decline. As we discussed on the telephone last week, the salary your company offered is not commensurate with the skills I would have brought to the position.

Thank you once again.

Yours truly,

Sean Robbins

Chapter 18

How to Handle Roadblocks

Looking for a job is hard work. It is probably one of the most difficult things you will ever encounter. Most people will, unfortunately, have to embark on this task several times in their lives. Following the advice laid out in this book will greatly increase your chances of succeeding on your job search. However, even the most informed job seeker can meet with failure after failure. This can be extremely discouraging. Don't give up. You will find a job—it just may take longer than you expected when you started out.

What to Do When You Can't Find a Suitable Job

After searching through many job listings, applying for some jobs, and even going on a few interviews, you may still find yourself unemployed. There might be many reasons for this. Some reasons may be within your control and therefore fixable. Others may be outside your control, and your only solution may be making changes that may have a big impact on your life. Other reasons may require that you just keep doing what you're doing until something happens.

Here are possible reasons your job search has been unsuccessful:

- The economy is bad.
- Job opportunities in your field or industry are limited.
- You need more experience.
- Your resume doesn't represent you well.
- You don't represent yourself well on a job interview.

When the economy is bad, job seekers suffer. There's not much you can do about that. Keep looking at job listings. Use all available resources: newspapers, online job banks, your network, and employment agencies. Consider taking a temporary job until you find something you really want.

ESSENTIAL

Temporary jobs are a great way to get experience without committing to a full-time job. You can turn down assignments in order to go on job interviews or when you need to spend more time on your job search. Another big plus? Sometimes temporary assignments turn into permanent ones.

Some fields and industries experience downturns that are not tied to the current state of the economy. For example, American car manufacturers are losing business to foreign automobile makers. Many are laying off workers, causing a slump in the automotive industry. If job opportunities in your field or industry are limited, you may have to consider retraining for a different type of job. Later we will explore ways to find a new occupation. You may find it hard to think about retraining for a new career. After all, you've already made an investment in this one. You may not have a choice, though. Remember that some of the skills you have will be transferable, so you probably won't have to start entirely from scratch.

If you recently changed careers and you are lacking experience, you may have to lower your expectations of getting hired for the type of position you desire. You may have to consider an entry-level job in your field so that you can gain the necessary experience. Temporary work is one way to get more experience. You may consider doing an internship even if you are no longer a student. If you previously attended college, call or visit the career services office of your alma mater or contact the alumni association. You can also try to set up an internship by talking to members of your network.

Have you been slow to get job interviews? Perhaps you do have the experience and skills you need, but your resume doesn't show it. Consider revamping your resume (yes, again). Reread Chapters 4 and 5 to get some tips on how to write a resume that gets results.

If your resume is getting you calls for job interviews, it may not be the problem. Could it be the way you present yourself on the interview? Make sure your answers to interview questions highlight your skills. Don't try to be humble on a job interview. This is one time you want to brag about yourself. You may need more interview practice. Have a friend run through some interview questions with you. Make sure he knows that you are seeking criticism. After all, you do want to improve your interview skills.

Make a Career Change

As discussed earlier, some occupations experience downturns from which they have little chance of recovering. Unfortunately, many workers are caught in the crossfire, leaving them unable to find a job even though they may have years of experience and excellent skills. If you are having trouble finding work in your field, and you've eliminated possible causes like a poor resume or inadequate interview skills, then it may be time for a career change. Changing your career is not something you should do haphazardly.

It is a big decision and one that you should take very seriously. Take the time to find the best option for you.

Self-Assessment

Your first step should be to find the occupations that are suitable for you based on a variety of factors. You will learn about these factors—specifically, your personality, values, skills, and interests—while doing a *self-assessment*. You can use a variety of tools to help you learn about these factors. These tools are commonly referred to as career tests, but the word "test" is a misnomer. Tests generally have right and wrong answers. There are no right or wrong answers when you are doing a self-assessment. There is just the process of learning about yourself in order to figure out in what occupation you would be happiest and most successful.

ALERT!

It is important to be as honest as you can when doing a self-assessment. There are no right or wrong answers. You want your results to reflect your personality, skills, and values. You shouldn't go into it thinking that any answers are bad ones.

A career-planning professional can administer these self-assessment tests. This option will be discussed shortly. If money is an issue, you may want to try using a "career test" online. Many of them are available for free. You can find a few listed in Appendix A.

Exploring Your Possibilities

After completing the self-assessment, you should have a list of possible career choices. Now it's time to pare down your list so that it is more manageable. What do you know about some of the occupations on your list? Are there a few you've never heard of? Others you've never considered? Are there some you know only a little about?

It's time to do some research. You should try to gather information about as many of these occupations as you can. Often people discount a particular occupation because they either don't know anything about it or they are misinformed about it. You don't need to start off with in-depth research. Simply get a job description for each occupation on your list. You can use the Occupational Outlook Handbook, published by the Bureau of Labor Statistics of the U.S. Department of Labor. The print version is available in most libraries. It is also online at *www.bls.gov/oco*. The Occupational Outlook Handbook contains information about almost every occupation you can think of and is revised every other year.

FACT

While an occupation may be on an upward trend nationally, it could be on a downward slope where you live. You can find information on outlooks for various occupations in most states by visiting their labor offices' Web sites. The U.S. Department of Labor maintains a list of links to those sites at *www.dol.gov/esa/contacts/state_of.htm*.

Once you have narrowed down your choices based on job descriptions, you can begin to read more about the occupations that seem like good possibilities. Continue using the Occupational Outlook Handbook to find out about salaries, job duties, and educational requirements. There is one factor that should weigh heavily on your mind, especially if you are making a career change because job opportunities in your current field have dried up. You must look at the employment outlook for any occupations you are considering. This will help you figure out if you will have a good chance of finding work in the future. After all, changing careers every couple of years is probably not something you want to do.

Any occupation you are seriously considering deserves even further exploration. Talk to people in the field to learn more about it. You can conduct informational interviews, an informal way to learn about an occupation. Your network (see Chapter 3) will come in handy when you are looking for people to interview. Once you have made a decision, it is time to begin your job search if you already have the necessary skills. If not, you may have to look into getting some training.

Training for a New Career

When they choose a new career, some people pick one for which they don't need a lot of retraining. The skills they currently have can easily be transferred to this new occupation. Other people may pick a career in spite of the fact that they will have to acquire new skills. You may discover that your career change requires a return to school for an additional degree or you may find out that you just need to take a few classes. Since you are making this career change because opportunities in your prior field declined, you may be eligible for retraining provided by the federal government. The Employment and Training Administration of the U.S. Department of Labor provides job training to individuals through One-Stop Career Centers located around the country. America's Service Locator at *www.servicelocator.org* can help you find a local One-Stop Career Center.

ALERT!

You may be tempted to look at "top careers lists" that give you the expert's predictions of what jobs will have the best outlook in the future. While you should consider occupational outlook when choosing a career, you shouldn't make your decision based only on an occupation's appearance on such a list. You must take into consideration whether you will actually like the work.

Working with a Career Development Professional

Some people are at a loss as to what to do when their job search is failing. They aren't sure if their job-search strategy is at fault or if they need a career change. If that describes what you are thinking right now, don't feel you have to go through this alone. If you're having trouble figuring out what to do as far as your career is concerned, you should consider meeting with a career development professional.

These professionals come with many different titles. There are career counselors, career development facilitators, and job coaches. There are even social workers who specialize in career development. Whomever you choose to work with, make sure that person is properly licensed and has experience working with people with your particular issues. To find out if the person you want to work with has the proper license, check with your state's department of education. Interview him as well to make sure you will be able to work with this person.

FACT

Career counselors, to be licensed in most states, must have a master's degree in counseling. Many career counselors belong to the National Career Development Association. The NCDA has a state-by-state list of members on their Web site (*www.ncda.org*).

A career development professional can help you figure out what went wrong with your job search. She can assess your resume and your interviewing skills to find out if they are the problem. She can determine whether a career change is needed, and if so, can assist you in making the transition. A career counselor can administer a self-assessment to help you figure out what your options are and then can help you narrow down your choices. She can assist you in getting information about various occupations and can help you decide which one is best for you.

Of course, you will be the one making the final decision. Beware of any career development professional that tries to push you into a particular career. You should make your choice based on the professional's advice (after all that's why you're paying her), but ultimately it is your choice to make.

Career-planning help can be expensive. There are places you can get this service at a low cost, or even for free. Look into the career services provided by your alma mater. Many colleges offer free career counseling to alumni. Also check with your local college. They may provide these services to the community. Some public libraries even offer career-planning assistance, as do some community agencies.

Working with a Resume-Writing Professional

Your job search may be stalled simply because your resume isn't good. This may have nothing at all to do with your skills, experience, or education. Your resume may be poorly written and therefore it doesn't do you justice. If you've tried several times to put together a good resume but find yourself unable to do so, it may be time to hire a professional resume writer.

Many career development professionals, described in the prior section, provide resume-writing services. Other people working as resume writers have training provided by one of several organizations, including the National Resume Writer's Association.

ALERT!

Before engaging the services of a professional resume writer or any other career development professional, try to check out that business or individual with your local Better Business Bureau. Find out if they have any complaints on file. Visit the Better Business Bureau Web site (*www.bbb.org*) for a list of local affiliates.

Professional resume writers are not required to be licensed or certified, so when you hire one, you are really on your own. You should always ask to see samples of that person's work. You must also ask for references. Call those references to find out if they were successful in their job searches as a result of the resume writer's services.

Dealing with the Stress of a Lengthy Job Search

A job search that lasts for a long time can wear you down. You may have started out with a positive attitude, but if you've been looking for a job for a while, you may no longer be as upbeat. For one thing, rejection can really deflate one's ego. Then there's the frustration of plugging away at something that doesn't seem to be moving forward.

Remember, a job search, on average, takes several months. Depending on the economy, it may take even longer. The best thing you can do is to stay positive. A positive attitude will translate into self-confidence, something you surely need when you go out on job interviews. A negative attitude, in contrast, will make you look defeated. It will not bring you any closer to getting hired. And you certainly don't want to make your job search last any longer than it has to, do you?

If you are currently employed, continue to do your job well. You don't want the stress of job loss to be added to the stress of a job search. If your reason for looking for a new job is that you don't get along with your boss or coworkers, look for ways to improve these relationships. If you simply hate your work, remember that you're doing something proactive so that you will eventually not have to do it any longer. If money is the issue, remember that earning some money is better than earning none.

If you are unemployed and find yourself spending every waking moment on your job search, take a break. You need to set limits on the time you spend looking for a job. Try to stick to working only during business hours, let's say 9 A.M. to 5 P.M. Remember to take a lunch hour halfway through the day. You can even meet friends for lunch—perhaps catch up with your old work buddies. Or you may try doing something a little more productive, like scheduling lunches with your network contacts. Okay, that may feel a little more like work than a break, but you can always take a break at another time.

Get out of the house for a while. A change of scenery may revitalize you. If you have a laptop computer, work outdoors if the weather is cooperative. Some businesses, including coffee shops, have wireless Internet connectivity so you can pretty much work anywhere these days. If you don't have a laptop, find out if your local library has public computers.

If the stress of your job search is getting to you, consider taking a yoga class. It can help you relax while also keeping you in good physical condition. Eating a healthy diet is also very important when your body is under a lot of stress.

While you're in the library, borrow a book that isn't job-search-related. Reading a good novel after a long day working on your job search will be refreshing. If you can't concentrate on a book, take yourself to a movie. You may be trying to save money, so a matinee may be a better option. Remember, if you spend time away from your job search during the day, you can always make up for it in the evening. Just don't count on contacting any leads by phone after regular business hours.

Coping with Shyness

The job search can be torturous for someone who is extremely shy. We're not just talking about a person who is a little bashful, but instead one who has moderate to great difficulty interacting with others. If you find your shyness is acting as a barrier to your career success, keep reading.

Shyness can impact your job search in many ways. While you may be able to deal with it when interacting with people with whom you are familiar, talking to strangers can be very difficult. And what does the job search consist of more often than anything else? Talking to strangers including interviewers, recruiters, and even receptionists.

One way to combat your shyness is to keep a positive attitude about yourself. Try to refrain from negative self-talk, such as "I'm not good enough." You should be confident that you are worthy of getting hired. Focus on your skills and why they make you a desirable candidate.

FACT

If you consider yourself shy, you aren't alone. According to a study published in the mid-1990s by Lynne Henderson and Philip Zimbardo in the *Encyclopedia of Mental Health*, approximately 50 percent of people surveyed considered themselves to be shy. This represented an increase from those who said they were shy in a study published just twenty years before that one.

Practicing for the interview can also be helpful, but don't just practice your answers. You should also rehearse greeting the interviewer and shaking his hand. Become comfortable with making and maintaining eye contact. Ask someone to practice with you. Once you have these skills down, practice them on strangers. Go shopping and talk to salespeople. Talk to the teller at the bank or the clerk in the post office. The more you talk to people and the more often you make eye contact, the more comfortable you will become.

Networking can be a nightmare if you are shy. Not only do you have to talk to people you may not know well, you have to ask them for advice. As discussed in Chapter 3, networking is an ongoing process and not just something you have to do while you are job hunting. Hopefully you established your network long before you had to look for work. Remember, your contacts aren't total strangers. They may be people you don't know well, but at least you do know them. If someone in your network refers you to someone you don't know at all and you don't feel comfortable calling that person, send an e-mail instead. Once you've established a relationship via e-mail, it should be easier to make that first phone call.

Chapter 19

New and Recent Graduates

With your newly minted diploma in hand, you probably feel pretty confident. Relatives and friends told you your degree would open doors for you. And it will—eventually. First, you'll have to get your proverbial foot in one of those doors. That's not easy. Honestly, it can be downright difficult. You are lacking experience and skills, and since you are new to the job search, you may not present yourself well on interviews. Don't despair—you will get a job. This chapter will show how to make sure it happens sooner rather than later.

Dealing with Your Lack of Experience

Congratulations on your graduation! After approximately four years of burying your nose in books and endless hours of sitting in front of a computer screen writing paper after paper in order to earn your much-coveted college degree, now what? It's time to get a job, but you wonder who will hire you. You feel like you have nothing going for you! You have few skills and little experience. You have nothing!

Wait a minute. Stop being so hard on yourself. That's not true. You may not have as much experience as older job candidates, but you haven't been sitting around doing nothing for the last few years. There were summer jobs, part-time jobs during the school year, and extracurricular activities. And let's not forget that you have something many other people don't have—that piece of paper that tells the world you are ready to get your first real job.

FACT

If you are wondering if earning that college degree was worth it, the U.S. Bureau of Labor Statistics assures you that it was. An article published in the *Occupational Outlook Quarterly* states, "data consistently show that workers who have a bachelor's or graduate degree have higher earnings and lower unemployment than workers who have less education."

If someone would just give you a chance, you can prove yourself. Someone will give you a chance, but you must make potential employers look beyond the date on your final transcript. You must make them realize that you are much more than a twenty-one-year-old or twenty-two-year-old with a piece of paper emblazoned with the name of a college on it.

Talking about Your Experience

It seems that every job opening you come across requires that you have experience. Experience? What experience? You spent the last seventeen or so years of your life in school. How were you supposed to get work experience? It's truly frustrating.

Before you lose your mind or your motivation, let's take a step back and look at your situation. Yes, it's true that many employers won't hire you unless you have experience. It's also true that you may not have any full-time work experience in your field. Remember, though, it only takes one employer to give you your first full-time job and the opportunity to get that much-needed experience. You only have to impress one employer. Don't forget that there are some employers out there who don't care if you have experience. As long as you're willing to learn, they will hire you. Also keep in mind that not having worked full-time in your field doesn't mean you don't have any experience.

ALERT!

Beware of employers who have businesses that are primarily staffed by younger workers. Many consider this a cost-cutting measure since they don't have to pay inexperienced employees as much as seasoned ones. While you may get experience, you may find yourself out of work in a few years.

First of all, did you do any internships? If you did, you have hands-on experience in your field. That puts you at an advantage over your competitors who may have not done internships. Internships, in addition to providing work experience, also give you the opportunity to make connections in your field. You should contact your internship mentors or supervisors to find out if they can offer you any help with your job search.

Have you had any part-time jobs? If you worked part-time, even in jobs unrelated to the field you are now trying to enter, you do have some experience. Even if you consider the work you did uninspiring or simple, it is likely you had some responsibilities. After all, your employers weren't paying you to sit around and look pretty. They were actually paying you because they needed you to do something. Think about what you did at work. Make a list of all your duties at each job you had. Did you help customers, answer phones, supervise children, or even clear dishes from tables? All of this counts as work experience.

Your participation in extracurricular activities while you were in school can help you score points with potential employers, too. The experience you gained from being involved in campus clubs and organizations can set you apart from your competitors. Everyone who has a college degree attended classes. Not everyone went beyond that and really got involved in campus life. Potential employers look favorably upon new graduates who took on an active role in college activities by, for example, writing for a school newspaper, coordinating fundraisers, or organizing blood drives. If you held leadership positions, this puts you at an even greater advantage. Add this information to your list.

It's not too late to do an internship, even if you already have your degree. If you don't have any work experience in your field, an internship can be a great way to get some. Your college's career center should be able to help you find internships in your field. There are also Web sites on which internships are posted.

Also include any volunteer work on your list. Just because you weren't paid for your time, that doesn't mean the experience had no value. There's a good chance you got a lot out of what you did and picked up some useful skills in the process.

Talking about Your Skills

Take a look at your list of part-time work, extracurricular activities, and volunteer work. Consider each item on your list. Now try to figure out what skills you used in each one. You will be amazed to discover that you actually do have more skills than you first thought you did. If at this point you are thinking, "When will I ever use the skill of flipping burgers?" think about this: Were you simply flipping burgers or were you managing the grill? Were you trying to get the product (the burgers) to your customers in a timely fashion? Did you have to pay attention to what customers were ordering? There's more to every job than the actual job title might imply. You need to examine your job duties closely in order to discover what skills you used to carry them out. Next, you have to figure out how these skills are relevant to the career you are now pursuing. Skills gained in one job or activity can often be used in another. These are called transferable skills.

ALERT!

While you should look beyond your job titles to find out what skills you actually used, you must be careful not to exaggerate. If you say you have a particular skill, make sure you do. Be honest with yourself and with prospective employers about what you can bring to a job.

There are two types of skills: hard skills and soft skills. Hard skills are technical skills usually attained through your education and training, but sometimes acquired on the job. They may include your ability to use certain software or equipment or your proficiency in a foreign language. Soft skills aren't specific to any type of work, but instead can help you do your job well. Examples of soft skills are problem-solving and multi-tasking.

Here's how to figure out what your transferable skills are. Take a piece of paper and fold it in half to make two columns. Label the first column "Tasks" and the second column "Skills." In the Tasks column, list the different tasks you do or did at your jobs and activities. Next to each task, in the Skills column, list the skills you used to complete that task. Circle those skills you think potential employers will value. Here are some examples of transferable skills:

- Motivating others
- Knowledge of a specific software program
- Ability to use a certain piece of equipment
- Delegating responsibility to others
- Training others
- Problem-solving
- Multitasking
- Time management
- Resource management

- Budgeting money
- Evaluating the work of others
- Proficiency in a specific foreign language

Your Resume

By completing the exercise in the previous section of this chapter, you've laid the groundwork for writing your resume. Skills and experience are the foundation for any resume, but as a new graduate you may feel like you are sorely deficient in both. In spite of the fact that you are just now making your grand entrance into the work force, you have seen that you do have some experience and you are not as devoid of skills as you may have thought. Now you must transform all this information into a resume.

The first rule of thumb is "keep it real." Dishonesty is not allowed when writing your resume. Lying on your resume can do far more harm than good, even if it means that you might get a job faster than your fellow grads. You also may lose your job faster if your boss finds out you lied. You will be much better off if you focus on the skills and experience you do have rather than fretting about how much better your chances of getting hired would be if you had more experience or better skills.

The type of resume with which you may be most familiar is a chronological resume. A chronological resume lists all the jobs you've had, starting with the most recent and going backwards. It puts the spotlight on one's work history. Since you don't have much of a work history yet, that is probably something you don't want to do. You should write a resume that highlights your skills rather than your employment history. Using a skill-based resume allows you to put the spotlight on your skills and accomplishments. You can choose between a functional resume or a combination resume. If you use a functional resume, you will list your skills and accomplishments but not provide any information about past jobs. Alternatively, if you use a combination resume, you will briefly include information about your work history. This is the preferred option since it allows you to show that you have some experience, even if it appears to be unrelated to your current occupational pursuits. For more-detailed information about resume writing, see Chapter 4.

Networking

Networking, as defined in Chapter 3, is the utilization of your connections to improve your career and help others who want to improve their careers. Your network contacts can help you learn more about the field you are trying to enter. They can give you advice about work in general and about the process of job hunting. While you should not utilize your network for job-hunting purposes only, it can ultimately help you learn about job leads.

It is instrumental to your budding career to establish a network. When you are just starting out, though, you may ask yourself, "What connections could I possibly have?" It's unlikely that you have made many contacts yet, if any at all. You are going to have to build your network from the ground up.

When it comes to networking, your options are endless. Your parents' friends, your friends' parents, and your former professors can all be part of your network. Don't be afraid to ask for help, and be generous about offering it to others.

The alumni association of your college is a good place to start. Career centers in many colleges provide opportunities for new graduates to meet with those who have been out of school for a while. If you belong to a fraternity or sorority, the alumni of those organizations can prove to be very helpful. Read Chapter 3 for a wealth of information about establishing a viable network.

The Job Interview

There are probably few situations that make people more uncomfortable than job interviews do. After you have managed to put together a resume that takes what little experience you have and puts it into a very positive light, you now have to sit across the table from someone who will dissect it, bit by bit. You will be asked to prove why you are the best person for the job. Most people would find that quite intimidating. As a new graduate you not only have little work experience, you don't have a lot of experience with job interviews, either. This can put you at a disadvantage when competing with more savvy job seekers.

The best thing you can do to help improve your chance of succeeding on the job interview is to know your resume inside and out. With each question you answer on a job interview, you want to exude extreme confidence. You don't want to sound hesitant or unsure of yourself. You know what you're capable of doing, and you want the interviewer to know it too.

ALERT!

If an interviewer tries to offer you advice on your career, be careful how you respond. Interviewers sometimes try to take on the role of career counselor in order to determine how committed a candidate is to a particular field. If you are having doubts about being in a field, the job interview isn't the time for you to discuss them.

Leave any traces of college behind you when you go on a job interview. Backpacks are great for toting around your books on a college campus, but they scream "student," not "potential employee." Take a briefcase or even a small portfolio with you to a job interview. Wear a business suit, of course, and dress shoes. Make sure your nails are well manicured and your hair is neatly groomed. Wear simple jewelry. Unless you are interviewing in a creative field, cover up tattoos and piercings. Turn off your cell phone when you are on a job interview.

Learn to make eye contact. You should also speak clearly. You won't be able to convince the employer to hire you if the interviewer can't understand what you are saying. Refrain from using slang or obscene language: While it may be perfectly acceptable among your peers, it is not appropriate on a job interview. Learn how to shake hands properly. If your interview is taking place over a meal, become familiar with the rules of etiquette for dining. You can learn more about job interviews in Chapter 13.

Can I Find You on the Web?

You know what a wonderful tool the Internet can be. While you were a student, you used the Internet as a research tool for writing papers. You can't imagine life without e-mail. Right now, you are using it in your job search. The Web is truly an indispensable tool. However, it can also hinder your job search and potentially damage your career.

Many people, generally high school and college students, use social networking sites like MySpace.com and Facebook. Do you? These sites allow users to post profiles and photographs of themselves that others can easily access. "Others" include friends, strangers, relatives, potential employers . . . Potential employers? Well, of course, if strangers can find you online, why wouldn't an employer be able to? It turns out that employers are quite computer savvy—and quite nosy.

Is there a chance you may have forgotten something you put online a while ago? Do a Google search on your name to make sure there is nothing on the Web that can cause harm to your job hunt. Remember, some things stay online until you take them down. And since Google doesn't pick up everything, check some other search engines, like Yahoo! and Ask.com, as well.

When investigating job candidates, employers often turn to the Web, particularly sites like MySpace and Facebook, but they also look at blogs. If there's something you wouldn't want an employer to know about you or something you might find embarrassing, you should take it down now. You may argue that what you do outside of work is no one's business. Yes, you are entitled to a personal life, but if you open that personal life to the public, you may compromise your chances of getting hired.

Handling Rejection

While you were in school you were pretty much in charge of your own destiny. If you studied hard, your grades would usually reflect your efforts. When you are trying to get a job, however, you may feel like everything is out of your hands. You are partially right. Even those with excellent resumes sometimes find it difficult to get hired.

Because it's that much harder to get a job as a recent graduate, it's all the more important to make yourself stand out. Put in the extra work it takes to make yourself visible and appealing to employers. As a young, single person with no children, you have more freedom than an older parent or homeowner—and almost nothing to lose. Go for it! Think of every experience, including bad ones, as an opportunity to learn and grow.

Rejection hurts. It doesn't matter if you're a 22-year-old being turned down for a job because you don't have enough experience or a 45-year-old being told you have too much experience. The good part of being a younger job seeker is that you have fewer responsibilities at this point in your life, so spending a bit of extra time unemployed won't be too painful, at least not financially. Remember that your job search will be over someday. Someone will hire you. In the meantime, though, you must remain as positive as you can.

Chapter 20

The Mature Job Candidate

Older job candidates face special challenges when job searching. Although they usually have more experience than their younger competitors, mature job seekers often find that employers are reluctant to hire them. They are sometimes met with prejudice in the job market due to interviewers' preconceived notions about those over a certain age. In order to meet your goal—finding a job—you will have to learn how to combat this prejudice, as well as deal with overt age discrimination.

20

Who Are You Calling Mature?

When you think of a "mature person," you almost certainly think of someone much older than you are. No matter what your current age is, "mature" is always several years ahead of you. If you are in your forties, or fifties, or even in your sixties, you probably feel quite spry. And why shouldn't you? You are in the prime of your life. You are well past the awkwardness of young adulthood—okay, perhaps very well past it. You're settled down, have more than a few years of work experience under your belt, and you are ready to approach your job search with the self-confidence you didn't have when you were in your twenties or even in your thirties.

FACT

If you are worried about being the oldest one in the office, don't be. According to the U.S. Bureau of Labor Statistics, the number of people in the labor force who are 55 and older will increase by 49.1 percent through the year 2014.

Then you go on your first job interview and realize the interviewer is several years younger than you are—possibly even half your age. You find that she doesn't look at you and think of all the experience you would bring to the job. The interviewer instead looks at you, mentally calculates your age, and wonders how you will deal with all the "modern" technology in the office. This is in spite of the fact that you have been using computers for many years. She assumes you will resist learning new skills, regardless of your continually taking classes in order to improve your skills. She worries that you will be taking many days off for doctors' appointments although you haven't been healthier in your entire life.

Your interviewer, unfortunately, is afflicted with those prejudices and preconceived notions mentioned in the introduction to this chapter. Note the use of the word "afflicted." The interviewer's inability to recognize and reluctance to take advantage of the talents that mature workers possess can truly be detrimental to the employer, who may miss out on getting a highly qualified job candidate. Of course, it will make your job search difficult since you will have to work very hard to prove that you are the best applicant for the job.

Focus on Your Attributes

The word "experience" means different things to different people. You, as a mature job seeker, may think about the number of years you have spent working and feel confident that you are more qualified for a particular job than your much younger competitors. Alternatively, a potential employer may look at your lengthy work history and see red flags. He may think, because you are a mature candidate, that you are set in your ways and are unwilling to, or even unable to, adapt to a new job. A younger worker, the employer may reason, can more easily learn new skills. She can be molded into the type of worker he wants. This is untrue. Older workers are willing and able to learn new skills. It is your job to convince him that you are eager to do this. Also, as an experienced candidate, you will bring many attributes to the job that an inexperienced job seeker cannot. When on a job interview, use anecdotes from your work history to illustrate your attributes.

Skills Come from Experience

Focus on your skills. Your experience has allowed you to fine-tune those skills you acquired through formal training. After all, they say, "Practice makes perfect." You have also acquired skills through hands-on training over the years. In your resume and on job interviews, make sure you highlight all your skills.

Time Efficiency

Your years of experience have taught you how to get work done in a timely manner. You know the fastest routes to getting the best results you can get. After many years of trial and error, you now know which shortcuts result in success and which ones result in a subpar end product.

Workplace Savvy

As an experienced job candidate, you also have workplace savvy that can only be gained from age and experience. This is not something one can be taught, so there is no way your younger competitors can have it yet. You have the ability to deal with most situations that come along—there are few you haven't encountered over the years.

Don't Let Your Age Show

Age equals experience, but you don't want potential employers to automatically label you as an "older worker." You want all the attributes you've earned through your experience to jump out at them, not your age. However, it is impossible to hide your age, both in person and on your resume. For example, you will have to indicate the dates of employment on your resume. While you can choose how far back you want to go when listing prior jobs, you don't want to leave out a job that could set you apart from the other candidates.

ALERT!

Listing the years you attended school on your resume gives away your age. You should include your educational background on your resume, but leave out the dates. In addition, if you attended school more than five years ago, put your education at the bottom of your resume, not near the top.

Your job-search methods can also date you. A typewritten resume, for example, indicates that you may not have looked for a job in a while. Worse than that, it is a dead giveaway that you aren't up-to-date on the latest technology. Brush up on your computer skills if they are insufficient, and write your resume using word processing software. Get online if you aren't yet. You must be ready to send and receive e-mail since that is how most people communicate. If you don't have an e-mail account, you must get one. There are some services that offer free e-mail accounts. See Chapter 10 for more information. You should have an e-mail address included in the contact information on your resume.

You may have gotten every job you've ever had using traditional job-search methods like the help-wanted ads in the newspaper. Things have changed, and in order to improve your chances of finding a job, you must use current job-search methods. That means job searching online. Chapter 10 gives you all the facts on the latest online job-search tools.

Physically hiding your age would be a challenge for most people. Should you go out and get a face-lift if you are looking for a new job? No, of course not! However, try to avoid letting your appearance date you. If you've had the same hairstyle for the last twenty years, it's time to update your look. Buy a new suit if the only one you have is several years old (even if it looks brand new). If your briefcase was a graduation present (back in 1976) and is now "well-worn," don't bring it on a job interview.

Age Discrimination

Age discrimination is a real problem that comes up for current employees and in the hiring process. Older workers are sometimes denied opportunities employers give to their younger colleagues. When making hiring decisions, employers sometimes don't consider job candidates over a certain age. Refusing to hire someone because of his age is illegal in the United States. The Age Discrimination in Employment Act of 1967 (ADEA) protects individuals who are age 40 and above from employment discrimination, including discrimination in hiring. This means that an employer can't refuse to hire you because of your age (as long as you are 40 or older). An employer can't state an age preference in advertisements for most jobs. There are exceptions for jobs for which age is a real issue, such as a modeling or an acting job.

Responding to Age-Related Questions on Job Interviews

Even though an employer can't decide not to hire you because of your age, that might not stop her from inquiring about it on a job interview. And it won't keep you from feeling uncomfortable if the interviewer asks you how old you are. So what should you do if a prospective employer asks your age? You have some choices: You can answer the question honestly, you can lie, or you can refuse to answer it. Even if you normally are untruthful about your age, you are cautioned against lying about anything on a job interview. It will put you in a bad light with the employer—the employer can't discriminate against you because of your age, but he may decide to not hire you if he feels you are dishonest. You can either tell the truth or you can refuse to answer the question. If you refuse to answer the question, you should do so in a nonconfrontational manner. You might even consider joking about the question—for example, "A lady never reveals her age" (if, in fact, you are a lady).

It is a myth that it is illegal for an employer to ask your age on a job interview or on an employment application. In reality, it is not the question that is illegal. Rather, if the employer decides not to hire you because of your age, that is illegal.

What to Do about Age Discrimination

When you are turned down for a job, you will probably try to figure out the reason. It is often easy to jump to the one for which you bear no responsibility—your age. You may make the assumption that you weren't hired because the employer discriminated against you due to your age. Be careful before you take that accusation any further than your own mind. There could be other reasons you were rejected for a job. For example, although you have a lot of experience, it may not be the right experience.

Your formal training may not be appropriate. Maybe the interviewer just didn't like you or didn't think you would fit in well in his workplace.

QUESTION?

Does age discrimination happen often?
Age discrimination happens, but people don't always report it. There are also cases in which people claim they've been discriminated against because of age even though they haven't. They might have decided against hiring you for the job for entirely different reasons. In 2005 the U.S. Equal Employment Opportunity Commission (EEOC) received 16,585 claims of age discrimination. Of those claims, 63 percent were deemed nonreasonable.

Your suspicions could be right, though. Maybe the employer didn't hire you because of your age. Ask yourself these questions before you draw a conclusion:

- Did the interviewer ask overt questions about your age?
- Did he make derogatory comments about your age or the number of years you've been working?
- Did the employer turn you down for the job but hire someone a lot younger than you are?

If you do ultimately conclude that you were discriminated against because of your age, you can file a claim with the U.S. Equal Employment Opportunity Commission. You can file a claim by mail or phone with your nearest EEOC office. You can find a list of EEOC offices on the agency's Web site: *www.eeoc.gov/offices.html.* You can also look for a listing in the government pages of your telephone directory.

According to the EEOC Web site, you have 180 days from the date of the alleged violation to file your claim. You must provide the EEOC with your name, address, and telephone number, as well as the name, address, and telephone number of the employer who allegedly discriminated against you. You also have to include the date and a description of the violation.

Many states and localities also have age discrimination laws. Agencies within those states and localities are responsible for enforcing those laws. If you file a claim with one of those agencies (referred to as Fair Employment Practices Agencies—FEPAs—by the EEOC), that agency will dual-file your claim with the EEOC. Likewise, if you file your claim with the EEOC, it will dual-file it with your state or local FEPA.

ALERT!

If you think you have been a victim of age discrimination, as defined by the Age Discrimination in Employment Act of 1967, you can file a private lawsuit against the employer. You should be aware that you must file a claim with the EEOC before you file your private suit.

Returning to the Job Market

Out of choice or necessity, many people in midlife find themselves re-entering the job market after a lengthy absence. Their return to the work force may come about because of a change in life circumstances, including:

- "Empty Nest Syndrome"
- Divorce
- Death of a spouse
- Spouse's retirement / job loss

Regardless of one's reasons for returning to the job market, this can be a difficult endeavor, particularly if one is a mature worker. If you are re-entering the work force at any age, you must prove that you have kept up with changes in the field in which you want to work. You must show that your skills are up-to-date and that you are knowledgeable about the field.

If you are a mature job candidate who is returning to work, you will have a hard time making the argument that you have work experience that your younger competitors lack. You may in fact have work experience, but since there is a break in your work history, this may not count in your favor.

Make Your Non-Work Experience Count

Since you have spent a significant amount of time away from work, you will have to count on your non-work experience to help you prove you have the skills and other qualifications a potential employer desires. If you've been involved in volunteer work during your hiatus from work, you will definitely have an easier time doing this.

Begin by making a list of any volunteer work you've done since you've stopped working. Leadership positions you've held in various clubs and organizations should be at the top of your list. Also include any projects you've participated in, even if they were a one-time deal. For example, were you on the planning committee for a fundraiser or did you help organize a special luncheon? Don't forget to list committees you've sat on. Think about the skills you used in each of these situations. Were they skills you had from your previous jobs or were they new skills? Determine if a potential employer will find these skills valuable.

ALERT!

If you let your network die during your absence from the work force, you'll be at a disadvantage once you get started up again. It's best to begin to revive it as soon as you make the decision to return to work. Get in touch with some of your old contacts and begin to make new ones. For more information on networking, see Chapter 3.

Writing Your Resume

Since your work experience probably ranges from a few to many years old, depending on how long you've been away from the work force, you should not use a chronological resume if you are returning to work. A chronological resume focuses on your work history. The last thing you want to do is draw attention to the fact that you were last employed some time ago. You should instead use a functional resume. It will allow you to focus on your skills rather than on your work experience. When you write a functional resume, you list the skills that are relevant to the job for which you are applying. Beneath each skill, you then list accomplishments that are related to that skill. Since you don't have recent work experience, you can draw upon your unpaid or volunteer experience when you list your accomplishments.

Make sure you let your prospective employer know if you took any classes during your hiatus from work. This can show that you kept your mind active and your skills sharp.

Going on a Job Interview

When you're on a job interview, don't be surprised if a lot of the questions the interviewer asks you are about your lack of recent work experience. It is your goal to make him see that a lack of "paid experience" doesn't mean a lack of experience in general. Get the interviewer to think about the fact that you were productive during your time out of the work force. You improved your skills and gained new ones. As you did on your resume, focus on your unpaid or volunteer work. Discuss any classes you took. Make sure to do a lot of reading about your industry and profession so you can sound knowledgeable during the interview.

After Retirement: A New Career

When past generations retired from work, it usually meant the end of working for a paycheck. Most people spent their retirement years traveling or pursuing their hobbies, or maybe doing some volunteer work. These days, people enjoy better health and live much longer than they did in past decades. While some retirees look forward to not having to go to work every day, others use their retirement as an opportunity to pursue new careers. Sometimes this decision is precipitated by financial need. Other times it is a choice born of the desire to finally realize a dream career that, for various reasons, he could not chase after earlier.

If you want to have a post-retirement career, it is much easier to choose one for which you can use transferable skills. Transferable skills are skills obtained in one line of work or occupation that you can adapt to another. If you don't have to acquire new skills, you can begin looking for a job in your new field immediately. If you don't have these transferable skills, you will need to retrain for your new career. This can mean anything from completing a degree to simply taking one course.

QUESTION?

Will I still receive my Social Security retirement benefits if I'm working? According to the Social Security Administration, you can work while you are receiving Social Security benefits. Visit their Web site at *www. ssa.gov/retire2* for more information on planning for retirement.

Whether you are 26 or 66, you must have the necessary qualifications before an employer will hire you. Before you choose your new career, you must determine what skills you need and if you are willing to invest money, time, and energy to acquire them. Also take care to choose your career wisely, particularly if you must retrain in order to get hired. This will take extra time and money that you might not have originally planned for.

The bottom line is this: If you want to work in retirement, you absolutely can. Many people find that pursuing a long-lost dream in retirement revitalizes and inspires them. All it takes is a little extra thought and planning to do it right. The time and energy you put in now will contribute to a better experience down the road.

Appendix A

Glossary

This glossary contains job-search terms and definitions that you may need to reference at different points in your search for a new job or career.

Action words
Powerful verbs that describe the effort you used to complete a task.

Annual report
A report that publicly held companies must send to their shareholders each year.

Applicant-tracking systems
In-house resume banks that employers use to electronically store the resumes they receive.

Background check
See *pre-employment screening.*

Behavioral interview
An interview in which you are asked to prove your competencies by describing how you have acted in various situations.

Blogs
Short for weblogs or Web logs; online journals or diaries.

Career action plan
A written plan that takes you from choosing an occupation to your goal of finding a job within that field.

Chronological resume
A resume that focuses on one's work history, listing jobs and job descriptions in reverse chronological order.

Cold contact letter
A letter sent with an unsolicited resume.

Combination resume
A resume that combines the elements of a functional resume with those of a chronological resume.

Competitive intelligence
A corporation's gathering of information about its clients, competitors, and industry.

Contact list
A list of members of your network that includes information on how to reach them, such as phone numbers, e-mail addresses, and mailing addresses.

Corporate culture
A company's values, practices, and goals.

Cover letter
A letter that generally accompanies a resume.

Curriculum vitae
Also referred to as a vitae or CV, this is a document, more detailed than a resume, that describes your educational background and employment history. It is used outside the United States in place of a resume, as well as in academia.

CV
See *curriculum vitae*

Discussion group
A group of people that meets online to discuss a specific topic.

Electronic resume
A pared-down version of a resume that is suitable for posting to a resume database or sending through e-mail. Also called an ASCII resume, e-resume, or plain-text resume.

Functional resume
A resume that focuses on one's skills and accomplishments rather than one's work history.

Goal
Something you want to achieve. See *long-term goal* and *short-term goal*.

Informational interview
A meeting with an individual in order to get information about that person's occupation. Informational interviews are used by people considering entering a particular field.

Interest inventory
A self-assessment tool that is based on the theory that those with similar interests will enjoy similar occupations.

Job outlook
The number of opportunities that will be available in a particular field in the future.

Job search engine
A job-search site that lists jobs that were originally posted on other sites.

Long-term goal
A goal that may take three to five years to achieve.

Networking
Utilizing your connections to improve your career and to help others improve their careers.

News feed
Also called a news alert, this lets you know, by e-mail or through a news-feed reader, when there is breaking news on a topic you specify.

News-feed reader
Also referred to as a news-feed aggregator or RSS reader, this software collects news feeds to which you subscribe.

Niche job-search sites
Job-search sites that focus on a particular field or industry.

Online networking service
A Web-based service that allows people to develop networks through a Web site. Members are generally added through referrals from current members.

Personality inventory
A self-assessment tool that looks at aspects of one's personality, such as traits, motivations, and attitude.

Pre-employment screening
A hiring practice used by employers to help them learn about the background of potential employees.

Resume
A document that lists one's skills, education, and accomplishments. See also *chronological resume, combination resume,* and *functional resume.*

Resume bank
A database of resumes that employers may search when looking for job candidates. Job seekers post their resumes to these resume banks, which can often be found on Web-based job-search sites such as Monster.

Self-assessment
The step in the career-planning process during which you look at your skills, interests, values, and personality in order to find a suitable occupation.

Short-term goal
A goal that is achievable within a few months to a year.

Skills assessment
A self-assessment tool that is used to determine whether you have certain skills as well as whether you like using those skills.

Summary of qualifications
A synopsis of one's entire resume; this bulleted list immediately follows the objective, and contains four to five items.

Trade association
An organization in which those working in particular occupations or industries are members.

Transferable skills
Skills you have gained through one job or experience that you can use in another job.

Values inventory
A tool used in a self-assessment that asks you to rate different values according to how important they are to you.

Vitae
See *curriculum vitae.*

Appendix B
Additional Resources

The chapters you just read contain lots of great resources for your job search. If you're looking for even more, look no further. This appendix includes numerous Web site and book recommendations to help you in your search.

Internet Resources

Career Advice

About Career Planning

Dawn Rosenberg McKay, the About.com Guide to Career Planning and the author of *The Everything® Get-A-Job Book*, provides you with the help you need to get your career off the ground and moving forward.

✎ *http://careerplanning.about.com*

About Job Searching

About.com Guide to Job Searching Alison Doyle takes you through the process of finding a job that's right for you.

✎ *http://jobsearching.about.com*

CareerJournal.com

Job hunting and career advancement advice from America's leading business newspaper, the *Wall Street Journal.*

✎ *www.careerjournal.com*

The Riley Guide

The Riley Guide is a directory of career resources on the Web. Its author is Margaret F. Dikel, a librarian and private consultant.

✎ *www.rileyguide.com*

ThirdAge

ThirdAge is a Web site geared toward those over age 40. Their work section (click on Work at the top of the page) addresses such topics as workplace issues, job search, and retirement.

✎ *www.thirdage.com*

Career Information

Occupational Outlook Handbook

Also available in print at many public libraries, this publication from the U.S. Bureau of Labor Statistics gives detailed information about hundreds of types of jobs. Get job descriptions and learn about work conditions, educational requirements, compensation, and professional and trade associations.

✎ *www.bls.gov/oco*

Career Guide to Industries

Learn more about various industries and the occupations in each. This publication from the U.S. Bureau of Labor Statistics provides information about working conditions, training and advancement, employment outlook, and earnings.

✎ *www.bls.gov/oco/cg*

Career Tests

The Career Interests Game

The Career Interests Game, from the University of Missouri Career Center, is an exercise that lets you match your interests and skills with various careers.

✎ *http://career.missouri.edu/students/ explore/thecareerinterestsgame.php*

The Princeton Review Career Quiz

This quiz, which takes a few minutes to complete, asks questions about your interests and work style in order to come up with a list of suitable career options.

✎ *www.princetonreview.com/cte/quiz*

Professional Help

National Career Development Association

The NCDA, a division of the American Counseling Association, represents professionals who deliver career services. Use this site to search for a career counselor or other career development professional by state.

✎ *www.ncda.org*

National Resume Writers Association

The National Resume Writers Association represents professional resume writers. Search by location, company name, and keyword to find a member.

✎ *www.nrwa.com*

Job Listings

CareerBuilder

CareerBuilder lists help-wanted ads from newspapers around the country. It is owned jointly by Gannett Co., Inc., Knight Ridder, and Tribune Company.

✎ *www.careerbuilder.com*

CollegeGrad.com

College graduates can find entry-level positions listed on this site.

✎ *www.collegegrad.com*

Monster

Search for jobs on Monster and build an online resume.

✎ *www.monster.com*

Yahoo! HotJobs

Search Yahoo! HotJobs to find job openings posted directly on this site, as well as jobs posted on other sites across the Web.

✎ *http://hotjobs.yahoo.com*

SimplyHired

This site lists jobs from across the Web. It includes listings from company Web sites, job boards, and newspaper classified ads.

✎ *www.simplyhired.com*

Indeed

Like SimplyHired, Indeed is composed of job listings from company sites, major job boards, and newspapers.

✎ *www.indeed.com*

Jobster

Jobster, like Indeed and Simply Hired, compiles job listings from around the Web. It also lets you ask those you know for referrals to particular employers.

✎ *www.jobster.com*

6FigureJobs

Executives can use this site to search for jobs and post their resumes.

✎ *www.6figurejobs.com*

Government Jobs

USAJOBS

This is the official Web site of the U.S. Office of Personnel Management. Use it to search for a job with the federal government.

✎ *www.usajobs.opm.gov*

USPS Jobs

If you are looking for a job with the United States Postal Service, you will find it listed here.

✎ *www.usps.com/employment*

govtjobs.com

Use this site to search for jobs with local governments, including states, counties, cities, and towns.

✎ *www.govtjobs.com*

Salary Surveys

JobStar Profession-Specific Salary Surveys

Wondering how much money you can earn in a particular field? JobStar lists salary surveys for many different professions.

✎ *http://jobstar.org/tools/salary/sal-prof.php*

Salary.com

Use Salary.com to get basic salary reports for various job titles for free. You can purchase personalized salary reports if you need more information.

✎ *www.salary.com*

Blogs

Your HR Guy's Blog

This blogger, a human resources generalist, posts frequently about recruiting, interviewing, general HR, and employee performance.

✎ *www.yourhrguy.com*

The Monster Blog

The team responsible for the Career Advice section of Monster produces this blog about career-related issues.

✎ *http://monster.typepad.com/monsterblog*

Company Information

Corporate Research Resources from About Career Planning

The resources listed on this page include Securities and Exchange Commission filings, business directories, and news sources.

✎ *http://careerplanning.about.com/od/resources*

Discrimination in Employment

The Equal Employment Opportunity Commission

This U.S. government Web site can help you learn about discrimination issues and employment.

✐ *www.eeoc.gov*

Books

Baron, Renee. *What Type Am I: Discover Who You Really Are.* (NY: The Penguin Group, 1998.)

Bennett, Scott. *The Elements of Resume Style.* (NY: AMACOM, 2005.)

McKay, Dawn Rosenberg. *The Everything Practice Interview Book.* (Avon, MA: Adams Media, 2004.)

Nadler, Burton Jay. *The Everything® Cover Letter Book.* 2nd Edition. (Avon, MA: Adams Media, 2005.)

Nadler, Burton Jay. *The Everything® Resume Book.* 2nd Edition. (Avon, MA: Adams Media, 2005.)

Noble, David F., Ph.D. *Professional Resumes for Executives, Managers, and Other Administrators.* (Indianapolis: JIST Works, 1998.)

Parker, Yana. *The Resume Catalog: 200 Damn Good Examples.* (Berkeley, CA: Ten Speed Press, 1996.)

Tieger, Paul D. and Barbara. *Do What You Are: Discover the Perfect Career for You Through the Secrets of Personality Type.* (NY: Little, Brown & Company, 2001.)

Yates, John. *Knock 'em Dead: The Ultimate Job Seeker's Guide.* (Avon, MA: Adams Media, 2006.)

Before-and-After Resumes

This appendix contains several resumes in two different versions. Read the notes in the margins to get an idea of what the pros and cons are for each.

Advertising Account Executive (Before)

- ▶ Times New Roman font is professional and space efficient.

- ▶ Using two addresses for contact information is confusing.

- ▶ Objective is missing.

- ▶ Summary of qualifications is missing.

- ▶ Applicant uses a chronological resume, which doesn't do a good job of highlighting his skills.

- ▶ Descriptions presented in paragraph form are difficult to read.

CHRIS SMITH
csmith@comany.com

123 Main Street
Hometown, NY 00000
(555)555-1234

987 Centre Avenue
Hometown, NY 10001
(555)555-5678

Education

2004–2007   UNIVERSITY OF ROCHESTER, Rochester, NY
Bachelor of Arts, **French**, with a major GPA of 3.5, May 2007.
Bachelor of Arts, **Psychology**, with a major GPA of 3.3, May 2006.
Minor: **Economics**, with a minor GPA of 3.4
- **Management Studies Certificate**, for completion of courses taught by faculty of College and the William E. Simon School of Business Administration.
- Economics Council, Activity Board, and Campus Times Staff Writer.

2003–2004   HOBART AND WILLIAM SMITH COLLEGES, Geneva, NY

Experience

Fall 2006   THE FINANCIAL GROUP DISCOUNT BROKERAGE, Pittsford, NY
Intern/Assistant to Operations Manager: Used computerized financial transactions and market tracking systems. Updated customer databases using Excel. Interacted with completed administrative projects for licensed representatives and addressed client inquiries from throughout the United States.

Summer 2006   DAYS ADVERTISING, INC., Pittsford, NY
Intern/Assistant to Account Manager: Assisted with the design of television and radio ads and proposals for varied products and clients, including Wegmans and Bausch & Lomb. Developed customer database.

2005–2006   ADEFFECTS, Rochester, NY
Intern/Assistant to and Account Manager: Researched and developed promotional materials for local retail, manufacturing, and restaurant clients. Gained knowledge of small business marketing. Recommended changes in client advertising materials, consumer outreach strategies, and marketing literature.

Summer 2005   PEARLE VISION CENTER, Pittsford, NY
Sales Representative: Implement strategy targeting upscale markets

Summer 2004   IT HAPPENS, Antwerp, Belgium
Marketing Intern: Determined target markets and developed ad budget for concert, event planning, and entertainment agency. Conducted market penetration surveys. Assisted graphic artists producing ads, posters, brochures, and reports.

Advertising Account Executive (After)

CHRIS SMITH
123 Main Street • Hometown, NY 00000 • (555)555-1234 • csmith@company.com

Objective: Advertising Account Executive

Advertising Account Management Qualifications
- Marketing research, strategic planning, promotions, customer service, and sales talents nurtured by diverse advertising, promotions, and retail internships and employment.
- Skills gained via courses including: Marketing, Marketing Projects and Cases, Motivation, Public Relations Writing, Advertising, and Consumer Behavior.
- German, Dutch, French, and Farsi fluency, and conversational Spanish capabilities.
- UNIX, HTML, Word, WordPerfect, Excel, PageMaker, PhotoShop, and Internet skills.

Experience
Advertising and Marketing
Account Management Intern, Days Advertising, Inc., Pittsford, NY (Summer 2006)
- Assisted with design of TV and radio ads
- Assisted account executives with proposals for clients, including Wegmans and Bausch & Lomb
- Developed client database

Account Management Intern, Adeffects, Rochester, NY (2005–2006)
- Researched and developed promotional materials for retail, manufacturing, and restaurant clients, using knowledge of small business marketing.
- Recommended client changes in outreach strategies, advertising materials, and marketing literature

Sales Representative, Pearle Vision Center, Pittsford, NY (Summer 2005)
- Implemented strategy targeting upscale markets

Marketing Intern, It Happens, Antwerp, Belgium (Summer 2004)
- Determined target markets for concert, event planning, and entertainment agency
- Developed advertising budgets
- Conducted surveys to determine market penetration
- Assisted graphic artists with design of ads, posters, brochures, and reports

Finance
Intern/Assistant to Operations Manager, The Financial Group, Inc. Discount Brokerage Firm, Pittsford, NY
- Interacted with and completed administrative projects for licensed representatives
- Addresses client inquiries from throughout the United States

Education
University of Rochester, Rochester, NY
Bachelor of Arts, French, with a major GPA of 3.5, May 2007.
Bachelor of Arts, Psychology, with a major GPA of 3.3, May 2006.
Minor: Economics, with a minor GPA of 3.4.
William E. Simon School of Business Administration, Rochester, NY
Management Studies Certificate, Marketing and Finance/Accounting Tracks, May 2007.
Hobart and William Smith Colleges, Geneva, NY, 2003–2004

▶ A combination resume is used. This is the best choice for a recent graduate like Chris. Unlike a chronological resume that puts the focus on work history, a functional resume highlights skills while taking into account work history.

▶ The second address is removed since potential employers won't know which one to use.

▶ Use a cell phone number that will remain active after graduation.

▶ An objective is given as it should always be. This allows you to target your resume to certain jobs. If you are applying for jobs in other areas, use a different resume for each one and change the objective accordingly.

▶ A Summary of Qualifications highlights special skills and relevant coursework.

▶ Experience is presented before education.

▶ Within the Experience section, there are sub-categories for each of Chris's major skill areas.

▶ Job descriptions are presented as bulleted lists making them easier to read.

Day Care Worker (Before)

- ▶ Contact information is presented in a hard-to-read format.

- ▶ Objective and Summary of Qualifications are missing.

- ▶ Education is presented first and isn't clearly presented.

- ▶ Job titles are missing.

- ▶ Format, in general, is difficult to read.

- ▶ Courier font makes resume appear typewritten.

Jamie Brown

123 Main Street   Hometown, CO 00000
Home (555) 555-5555   Cell (555) 555-9999

EDUCATION
30 Education credits, with day care emphasis, and English minor.
Metropolitan State College, Denver, CO

EXPERIENCE
1999—Present   NANNY
Care for twin boys from the age of two months through two years.
Assist in selecting toys and equipment, provide environmental
stimulation, personal care, and play.
Private residence, Livermore, CO

1997—99   TEACHER
Taught infant, preschool, and after-school programs. Planned
curriculum, organized activities, communicated with parents and
staff regarding growth and development. Suggested equipment to
enrich children's experiences and helped create a stimulating
environment.
Baby Bear Preschool, Keystone, CO

1995—97   TEACHER
Planned and implemented curriculum for infants. Communicated with
parents and pother staff regarding daily progress of children.
This Little Piggy Daycare Center, Dove Creek, CO

1993—95   TEACHER
Planned and implemented curriculum for toddler program. Enriched
children's experiences through play, music, and art.
The Kid Corral, Wild Horse, CO

1991—93   CAREGIVER
Provided care in clients' homes, administering physical therapy
when necessary. Planned activities to stimulate and improve
children's skills and environment.
Residences, Dove Creek, and Keystone, CO

1995—Present   VOLUNTEER
Ivywild Coalition for Retarded Citizens, Ivywild, CO

SKILLS AND INTERESTS
Valid driver's license; perfect driving record. CPR/first aid certified. Skiing, reading, music, arts and crafts.

Day Care Worker (After)

Jamie Brown

123 Main Street • Hometown, CO 00000 • (555)555-1234 • Cell: (555) 555-9999

Objective: Day Care Worker

DAY CARE QUALIFICATIONS AND COMPETENCIES

- Over 9 years of diverse experience within home and school setting, teaching and caring for children ranging in ages from 2 months to 7 year.
- Commitment to the needs of infants, preschoolers, and kindergarteners.
- Academic background including courses in: Childhood Development, Early Childhood Education, Educational Psychology, and Assessments.

DAY CARE, TEACHING, AND CHILD CARE EXPERIENCE

1999–present　**Nanny**, Private Residence, Livermore, CO
- Provided environmental enrichment, personal care, and play supervision for twin boys from the age of two months through two years
- Accompanied family on trips
- Cared for children during illnesses

1997–1999　**Teacher**, Baby Bear Preschool, Keystone, CO
- Taught infant, preschool, and after-school programs
- Planned curriculum and organized activities
- Communicated with parents and staff regarding children's growth and development
- Responded to annual increase in students and move to new facility
- Worked collegially with owner on goal development
- Assisted with annual licensing documentation and visitation

1995–1997　**Teacher**, This Little Piggy Daycare Center, Dove Creek, CO
- Planned and implemented infant program, blending developmental and custodial needs
- Communicated with parents regarding student progress
- Enhanced skills development through interactive play and song

1993–1995　**Teacher**, The Kid Corral, Wild Horse, CO
- Planned and implemented curriculum for toddler program
- Enriched children's experiences through play, music and art

EDUCATION

1990–1993　Metropolitan State College, Denver, CO
- 30 credits in Education, with an emphasis on day care.

REFERENCES

William and Sarah Smither, (555) 555-4444, reference@company.com
Sue Bear, Owner, Baby Bear Preschool, (555) 555-1234, bbear@company.com

▶ Using the Garamond font helps make this resume look polished.

▶ Including an Objective and Qualifications and Competencies brings focus to the resume.

▶ Jamie's extensive experience in this field is served well by using a chronological format. It allows the employer to see the progress she has made in this field.

▶ Presenting job descriptions in bulleted lists allows potential employers to scan the resume to see if the candidate has the necessary skills.

▶ In a field where references are essential, this information is clearly presented on this resume.

Financial Planner (Before)

- Dana is an experienced financial service professional. She is not in active job-search mode, but because of her status she regularly is called upon to serve as spokesperson and seminar leader, so she updated her resume.

- Courier font makes resume look typewritten.

- Name (large and in bold) and e-mail address, flush left and phone number and e-mail address, flush right, makes top of resume look unbalanced.

- Summary of Qualifications is missing. Objective isn't needed since Dana isn't actively job hunting.

- Presenting the employer's name and location, and the dates of employment above the job title, takes the focus off the candidate's experience.

Dana Johnson

123 Main Street
Hometown, New Jersey 00000

(555) 555-1234
djohnson@company.com

Experience

ABC FINANCIAL CONSULTANTS, Princeton, NJ
July 1990—present
Financial Consultant/Financial Planner
· Developed $210 million clent base via prospecting.
· Built portfolio that includes stock, bonds, options, and insurance products for more than 450 clients.
· Implemented financial plans and operations through account development and growth.

October 1988—1990
Sales Associate
· Worked directly with firm's top producer, profiling high net worth individuals for future business.
· Generated $90,000 for top producer via new accounts.
· Analyzed portfolios to expand account performance.

September 1987—October 1988
Account Executive Trainee/Intern
· Supervised about 35,000 accounts in the area of trade settlement, NASD regulations, and customer inquiries.
· Reported recommendations to upper management.
· Acted as liaison with New York operations.

MAPLEWOOD INVESTMENTS, Maplewood, NJ
Summers 1986 and 1987
Prospecting Intern
· Planed, created documents for, and oversaw invitations and confirmations for 3 annual Summer Financial Seminars.
· Researched stock and updated transactions.

Related Training
Successfully completed ABC Financial Consultant Sales Training and Advanced Training program in Princeton, NJ, headquarters. Licensed in Series 6, 7, 63 and health and life insurance.

Education
IONA COLLEGE, Iona, New York
Bachelor of Arts degree in Economics, 1988

Financial Planner (After)

Dana Johnson

123 Main Street • Hometown, NJ 00000 • (555) 555-1234 • djohnson@company.com

Financial Planning Qualifications and Objectives

- Over a decade of progressively significant roles and achievements in planning, portfolio management, and client services.
- Personally managed $210 million in client assets.
- Recognized for asset-based performance and customer service.
- Developed curriculum for and trained junior-level planners.

Financial Planning Experience and Accomplishments

ABC Financial Consultants, Princeton, NJ

Financial Consultant / Financial Planner (1990–Present)

- Oversee individual and group portfolios
- As senior manager, supervisor and trainer within corporate headquarters, responsible for over $800 million in client assets
- Implemented financial plans and operations through account development and growth.
- Gained expertise associated with estate planning, asset allocation, and wealth succession.

Sales Associate (1988–1990)

- Worked directly with firm's top producer, profiling high net worth individuals for future business.
- Generated $90,000 through new account openings.
- Analyzed portfolios to expand account performance.

Account Executive Trainee/Intern (1987–1988)

- Completed about 35,000 account transactions annually
- Completed comprehensive training related to trade settlement, NASD regulations, and customer service.

Maplewood Investments, Maplewood, NJ, Summers 1986–87

Prospecting Intern

- Planned, created documents for, and oversaw invitations and confirmations for two annual summer financial seminars
- Researched stocks and updated transactions

Licenses and Credentials

Licensed in Series 6, 7, 63, and health and life insurance

Education and Training

ABC Financial Consultant Sales Training and Advanced Training Program, Princeton, NJ, 1995
Iona College, Iona, New York
Bachelor of Arts degree in Economics, 1988

▶ Use Arial. It is a professional looking and easy-to-read font.

▶ The "before" version appeared professional, but it lacked focus and didn't highlight achievements. The "after" version, introduced via a qualifications and credentials section, is achievement-oriented, and it highlights career growth.

▶ Used bold type for job titles to make them stand out.

▶ Placed dates in parentheses after job titles.

▶ Listed licenses and credentials separately so they can easily be spotted.

▶ Changed "Education" to "Education and Training" and included both Iona College and ABC Training program in that section.

Medical Product Sales (Before)

- ▶ Times font appears professional.

- ▶ Francis is relocating and therefore used two addresses in his contact information.

- ▶ This resume, because it is missing an objective and summary of qualifications, does not project focus or desired goal.

- ▶ Education is presented first.

- ▶ Francis used a chronological resume format which draws too much attention to his lack of experience and not enough attention to his related skills.

Francis Williams

123 Main Street
Hometown, NY 0000
(555) 555-1234 fwilliams@company.com

987 Centre Ave.
Homeville, NY 10001
(555) 555-5678

EDUCATION
UNIVERSITY OF ROCHESTER, Rochester, NY
Bachelor of Arts, Health and Society, anticipated May 2003
Management Certificate in Public Sector Analysis, anticipated May 2002
Completed Language and Cultural Studies in Rome, Italy Spring 2001

ACTIVITIES AND LEADERSHIP
SIGMA DELTA FRATERNITY
President, 2002–2003, *Secretary*, 2000–2001, and *Member*, 1999–Present

STUDENT HEALTH ADVISORY COMMITTEE
Member, 2002–2003

EXPERIENCE
CHECK YOUR PULSE AMERICA RESEARCH STUDY, Rochester, NY
Research Assistant: Helped design aspects of nationwide research tudy dealing with stoke prevention. Responsibilities included distribution of questionnaire, data entry, and report writing and editing. Fall 2001

NYS VETERANS NURSING HOME, Wood Cliff, NY
Human Resource Assistant: Supported various recruiting, payroll, and benefits activities. Collected, reviewed, and rated resumes. Communicated with candidates by phone and e-mail. Summer 2002

THE CARDIOLOY GROUP, Wood Cliff, NY
Administrative Assistant: Greeted and scheduled patients, maintained files, assisted with billing, communicated with insurance carriers and pharmacies, and completed special tasks as assigned. 1998–present

YOUR INSURANCE GROUP, White Plains, NY
Office Assistant, Summer 2001

COMPUTER AND OFFICE SKILLS
Word, Excel, PowerPoint, Access, and Internet capabilities.
Ability to serve in receptionist, billing, and human resource roles.

Medical Product Sales (After)

Francis Williams

123 Main Street • Hometown, NY 00000 • (555) 555-1234 • fwill@company.com

Objective: Medical Product Sales Representative

SUMMARY OF QUALIFICATIONS

- Knowledge of health care, business, and economics-related topics gained from courses including: Accounting, Microeconomics, Business Administration, Changing Concepts of Disease, Medical Sociology, Domestic Social Policy, Organizational Psychology, and Statistics.
- Confidence and experience communicating with physicians, health care practitioners, patients, and others associated with medical devices.
- Research, project management, time management, writing, and oral communication skills gained from employment, education, and activities.
- Capacities to conduct topic-specific research, identify trends or key issues, and document findings in reports as well as presentations.
- Persuasive communication style, required to educate regarding protocols and studies specific to medical products and treatment techniques.

HEALTH AND SOCIETY AND BUSINESS EDUCATION

University of Rochester, Rochester, NY

Bachelor of Arts, Health and Society, anticipated May 2003

- Health and Society Major focused on study of Community and Preventive Medicine, as well as history and economics of health care delivery.
- Sigma Delta Fraternity President, Secretary, and Member.
- Student Health Advisory Committee, Member, and Class of 2002 Senator.

William E. Simon School of Business Administration, Rochester, NY

Management Certificate in Public Sector Analysis, anticipated May 2003

- Certificate for completion of business, economics, and policy-focused courses taught by faculty of the College and of the Simon School.

Temple University Rome, Rome, Italy

- Completed Language and Cultural Studies, Spring Semester 2001

HEALTH CARE, BUSINESS, AND RESEARCH EXPERIENCE

Research Assistant

Check Your Pulse America Research Study, Rochester, NY

- Helped design aspects of nationwide research study dealing with stroke prevention. Fall 2001

Human Resource Assistant

NYS Veterans Nursing Home, Wood Cliff, NY

- Supported recruiting, payroll, and benefits activities. Summer 2002

Administrative Assistant

The Cardiology Group, Wood Cliff, NY

- Summer and Part-time 1998–present

Office Assistant

Your Insurance Group, White Plains, NY

Summer 2001

▶ Use of objectives and summary of qualifications immediately tells a prospective employer what job the candidate is interested in and what he can bring to it.

▶ The focus is on Francis' education since his experience and skills in this field are limited.

Paralegal (Before)

► Garamond font is professional.

► Identifying information does not contain e-mail.

► Experienced candidate with extensive post-college experience in one field.

► All types of experience, for example law, retail and administrative, are lumped together.

► Bullets used as effective highlighting technique.

COREY DAVIS
123 Main Street • Santa Fe, NM 00000 • (555) 555-5555

EXPERIENCE
BRENDAN ELLIS CIVIL LITIGATION SPECIALIST/OFFICE MANAGER
Santa Fe, NM 1998–present
- Manage office and staff of 3 secretaries, ensuring smooth operation of firm.
- Interview clients; prepare files and discovery.
- Request and review medical documentation; ascertain evidence information and process all with the appropriate parties.
- Negotiate and settle cases with defense attorney and insurance companies,
- Attend mediations and conciliations.
- Prepare clients for depositions and trials.
- Control and maintain law office accounts.

BROWNINGTON, INC. ADMINISTRATIVE ASSISTANT
Albuquerque, NM 1993–98
- Confirmed all manpower hours and prepared logs to bill various sites.
- Provided clerical support to 24 software engineers.
- Recognized for "Excellence in Customer Satisfaction Southwest Region."

WILD RAIN EXOTIC GIFTS MANGER/SALESPERSON
Silver City, NM 1990–93
- Sold art and memorabilia on consignment.
- Hired, trained, and supervised 8 sales pseronnel.
- Handled accounts, managed orders, and created promotions.

SANTA FE DISTRICT ATTORNEY'S DOMESTIC VIOLENCE WITNESS ADVOCATE
Santa Fe, NM Spring–Summer 1990
- Interviewed victims and witnesses, prepared documents, and organized information for court appearances.
- Assisted attorneys during trials.

NEW MEXICO PUBLIC DEFENDER'S LEGAL INTERN
Santa Fe, NM Summers 1988 and 1989
- Researched and drafted motions on criminal law and procedural issues.
- Interviewed clients at Illinois correctional institutions.
- Negotiated plea and bail agreements for defendants.

ATTORNEY DANIEL GALL LEGAL SECRETARY/LEGAL ASSISTANT
Santa Fe, NM 1986–90

EDUCATION
SAINT JOHN'S COLLEGE B.S., HUMAN RESOURCE MANAGEMENT
Santa Fe, NM 1990

Paralegal (After)

COREY DAVIS

123 Main St. • Hometown, NM 00000 • (prior to November 1, 2006)
987 Centre Avenue • Hometown, CA 00000 (after November 1, 2006)
(555) 555-1234 • cdavis@company.com

Objective: Paralegal

PARALEGAL QUALIFICATIONS AND ACHIEVEMENTS

- Case research, client relations, document management, and writing skills gained in progressively responsible positions over a 12-year period.
- Expertise as law office manager, compiling training manual, supervising support personnel, revamping accounting, debit, and credit systems.
- Trained and accomplished interviewer, negotiator, and mediator
- LexisNexis, WestLaw, Word, FileMaker, Excel, QuickBooks, and Internet skills.

PARALEGAL AND MANAGEMENT EXPERIENCE

1990–present: **Civil Litigation Specialist/Office Manager**, Law Offices of Brendan Ellis, Santa Fe, NM
- Manage office and staff of 3 secretaries, ensuring operation of firm with 3 attorneys and billings of $1.5 million and awards over $10 million annually.
- Interview clients; prepare files and discovery; handle multiple cases.
- Request and review medical documentation; ascertain evidence information and process all with the appropriate parties.
- Negotiate and settle cases with defense attorneys and insurance companies.
- Attend mediations and conciliations.
- Prepare clients for depositions and trials.
- Control and maintain office accounts, using accounting software.

Spring 1990: **Witness Advocate**, Santa Fe District Attorney's Domestic Violence Unit, Santa Fe, NM
- Interviewed victims and witnesses
- Prepared documents and organized information for court appearances
- Assisted attorneys during trials by taking notes and facilitating access to evidentiary documents

Summer 1988 **Legal Intern**, New Mexico Public Defender's Office, Santa Fe, NM
- Researched and drafted motions on criminal law and procedural issues
- Interviewed clients at New Mexico correctional institutions
- Negotiated bail agreements for defendants accused of misdemeanors
- Attended criminal trials and depositions

Related Legal Experience
1986–1990: **Legal Secretary/Legal Assistant**, Attorney Daniel Gall, Santa Fe, NM

EDUCATION

Saint John's College, Santa Fe, NM
B.S., Human Resource Management, with Honors, 1990
Completed degree part-time while employed.

▶ Corey is an experienced paralegal who is relocating to the San Francisco Bay area. Although it is confusing to use two addresses, in this case it is necessary in order to explain why he is looking for a job in California. He indicates the dates before and after which he can be reached at each address in parentheses.

▶ Instead of providing a different phone number, one for each location, Corey uses his cell phone number, which won't change.

▶ Added "Objective" and "Qualifications and Achievements" to add focus to this resume.

▶ Experience is split into two sections: "Paralegal and Management Experience" and "Related Legal Experience."

▶ Job titles are in bold type so they stand out.

Index

THE EVERYTHING SERIES!

BUSINESS & PERSONAL FINANCE

Everything® Accounting Book
Everything® Budgeting Book
Everything® Business Planning Book
Everything® Coaching and Mentoring Book
Everything® Fundraising Book
Everything® Get Out of Debt Book
Everything® Grant Writing Book
Everything® Home-Based Business Book, 2nd Ed.
Everything® Homebuying Book, 2nd Ed.
Everything® Homeselling Book, 2nd Ed.
Everything® Investing Book, 2nd Ed.
Everything® Landlording Book
Everything® Leadership Book
Everything® Managing People Book, 2nd Ed.
Everything® Negotiating Book
Everything® Online Auctions Book
Everything® Online Business Book
Everything® Personal Finance Book
Everything® Personal Finance in Your 20s and 30s Book
Everything® Project Management Book
Everything® Real Estate Investing Book
Everything® Robert's Rules Book, $7.95
Everything® Selling Book
Everything® Start Your Own Business Book, 2nd Ed.
Everything® Wills & Estate Planning Book

COOKING

Everything® Barbecue Cookbook
Everything® Bartender's Book, $9.95
Everything® Chinese Cookbook
Everything® Classic Recipes Book
Everything® Cocktail Parties and Drinks Book
Everything® College Cookbook
Everything® Cooking for Baby and Toddler Book
Everything® Cooking for Two Cookbook
Everything® Diabetes Cookbook
Everything® Easy Gourmet Cookbook
Everything® Fondue Cookbook
Everything® Fondue Party Book
Everything® Gluten-Free Cookbook
Everything® Glycemic Index Cookbook
Everything® Grilling Cookbook

Everything® Healthy Meals in Minutes Cookbook
Everything® Holiday Cookbook
Everything® Indian Cookbook
Everything® Italian Cookbook
Everything® Low-Carb Cookbook
Everything® Low-Fat High-Flavor Cookbook
Everything® Low-Salt Cookbook
Everything® Meals for a Month Cookbook
Everything® Mediterranean Cookbook
Everything® Mexican Cookbook
Everything® One-Pot Cookbook
Everything® Quick and Easy 30-Minute, 5-Ingredient Cookbook
Everything® Quick Meals Cookbook
Everything® Slow Cooker Cookbook
Everything® Slow Cooking for a Crowd Cookbook
Everything® Soup Cookbook
Everything® Tex-Mex Cookbook
Everything® Thai Cookbook
Everything® Vegetarian Cookbook
Everything® Wild Game Cookbook
Everything® Wine Book, 2nd Ed.

GAMES

Everything® 15-Minute Sudoku Book, $9.95
Everything® 30-Minute Sudoku Book, $9.95
Everything® Blackjack Strategy Book
Everything® Brain Strain Book, $9.95
Everything® Bridge Book
Everything® Card Games Book
Everything® Card Tricks Book, $9.95
Everything® Casino Gambling Book, 2nd Ed.
Everything® Chess Basics Book
Everything® Craps Strategy Book
Everything® Crossword and Puzzle Book
Everything® Crossword Challenge Book
Everything® Cryptograms Book, $9.95
Everything® Easy Crosswords Book
Everything® Easy Kakuro Book, $9.95
Everything® Games Book, 2nd Ed.
Everything® Giant Sudoku Book, $9.95
Everything® Kakuro Challenge Book, $9.95
Everything® Large-Print Crossword Challenge Book
Everything® Large-Print Crosswords Book
Everything® Lateral Thinking Puzzles Book, $9.95
Everything® Mazes Book

Everything® Pencil Puzzles Book, $9.95
Everything® Poker Strategy Book
Everything® Pool & Billiards Book
Everything® Test Your IQ Book, $9.95
Everything® Texas Hold 'Em Book, $9.95
Everything® Travel Crosswords Book, $9.95
Everything® Word Games Challenge Book
Everything® Word Search Book

HEALTH

Everything® Alzheimer's Book
Everything® Diabetes Book
Everything® Health Guide to Adult Bipolar Disorder
Everything® Health Guide to Controlling Anxiety
Everything® Health Guide to Fibromyalgia
Everything® Health Guide to Thyroid Disease
Everything® Hypnosis Book
Everything® Low Cholesterol Book
Everything® Massage Book
Everything® Menopause Book
Everything® Nutrition Book
Everything® Reflexology Book
Everything® Stress Management Book

HISTORY

Everything® American Government Book
Everything® American History Book
Everything® Civil War Book
Everything® Freemasons Book
Everything® Irish History & Heritage Book
Everything® Middle East Book

HOBBIES

Everything® Candlemaking Book
Everything® Cartooning Book
Everything® Coin Collecting Book
Everything® Drawing Book
Everything® Family Tree Book, 2nd Ed.
Everything® Knitting Book
Everything® Knots Book
Everything® Photography Book
Everything® Quilting Book
Everything® Scrapbooking Book
Everything® Sewing Book
Everything® Woodworking Book

Bolded titles are new additions to the series.
All Everything® books are priced at $12.95 or $14.95, unless otherwise stated. Prices subject to change without notice.

HOME IMPROVEMENT

Everything® Feng Shui Book
Everything® Feng Shui Decluttering Book, $9.95
Everything® Fix-It Book
Everything® Home Decorating Book
Everything® Home Storage Solutions Book
Everything® Homebuilding Book
Everything® Lawn Care Book
Everything® Organize Your Home Book

KIDS' BOOKS

All titles are $7.95

Everything® Kids' Animal Puzzle & Activity Book
Everything® Kids' Baseball Book, 4th Ed.
Everything® Kids' Bible Trivia Book
Everything® Kids' Bugs Book
Everything® Kids' Cars and Trucks Puzzle & Activity Book
Everything® Kids' Christmas Puzzle & Activity Book
Everything® Kids' Cookbook
Everything® Kids' Crazy Puzzles Book
Everything® Kids' Dinosaurs Book
Everything® Kids' First Spanish Puzzle and Activity Book
Everything® Kids' Gross Hidden Pictures Book
Everything® Kids' Gross Jokes Book
Everything® Kids' Gross Mazes Book
Everything® Kids' Gross Puzzle and Activity Book
Everything® Kids' Halloween Puzzle & Activity Book
Everything® Kids' Hidden Pictures Book
Everything® Kids' Horses Book
Everything® Kids' Joke Book
Everything® Kids' Knock Knock Book
Everything® Kids' Learning Spanish Book
Everything® Kids' Math Puzzles Book
Everything® Kids' Mazes Book
Everything® Kids' Money Book
Everything® Kids' Nature Book
Everything® Kids' Pirates Puzzle and Activity Book
Everything® Kids' Princess Puzzle and Activity Book
Everything® Kids' Puzzle Book
Everything® Kids' Riddles & Brain Teasers Book
Everything® Kids' Science Experiments Book
Everything® Kids' Sharks Book
Everything® Kids' Soccer Book
Everything® Kids' Travel Activity Book

KIDS' STORY BOOKS

Everything® Fairy Tales Book

LANGUAGE

Everything® Conversational Chinese Book with CD, $19.95
Everything® Conversational Japanese Book with CD, $19.95
Everything® French Grammar Book
Everything® French Phrase Book, $9.95
Everything® French Verb Book, $9.95
Everything® German Practice Book with CD, $19.95
Everything® Inglés Book
Everything® Learning French Book
Everything® Learning German Book
Everything® Learning Italian Book
Everything® Learning Latin Book
Everything® Learning Spanish Book
Everything® Russian Practice Book with CD, $19.95
Everything® Sign Language Book
Everything® Spanish Grammar Book
Everything® Spanish Phrase Book, $9.95
Everything® Spanish Practice Book with CD, $19.95
Everything® Spanish Verb Book, $9.95

MUSIC

Everything® Drums Book with CD, $19.95
Everything® Guitar Book
Everything® Guitar Chords Book with CD, $19.95
Everything® Home Recording Book
Everything® Music Theory Book with CD, $19.95
Everything® Reading Music Book with CD, $19.95
Everything® Rock & Blues Guitar Book (with CD), $19.95
Everything® Songwriting Book

NEW AGE

Everything® Astrology Book, 2nd Ed.
Everything® Birthday Personology Book
Everything® Dreams Book, 2nd Ed.
Everything® Love Signs Book, $9.95
Everything® Numerology Book
Everything® Paganism Book
Everything® Palmistry Book
Everything® Psychic Book
Everything® Reiki Book
Everything® Sex Signs Book, $9.95
Everything® Tarot Book, 2nd Ed.
Everything® Wicca and Witchcraft Book

PARENTING

Everything® Baby Names Book, 2nd Ed.
Everything® Baby Shower Book
Everything® Baby's First Food Book
Everything® Baby's First Year Book
Everything® Birthing Book
Everything® Breastfeeding Book
Everything® Father-to-Be Book
Everything® Father's First Year Book
Everything® Get Ready for Baby Book
Everything® Get Your Baby to Sleep Book, $9.95
Everything® Getting Pregnant Book
Everything® Guide to Raising a One-Year-Old
Everything® Guide to Raising a Two-Year-Old
Everything® Homeschooling Book
Everything® Mother's First Year Book
Everything® Parent's Guide to Children and Divorce
Everything® Parent's Guide to Children with ADD/ADHD
Everything® Parent's Guide to Children with Asperger's Syndrome
Everything® Parent's Guide to Children with Autism
Everything® Parent's Guide to Children with Bipolar Disorder
Everything® Parent's Guide to Children with Dyslexia
Everything® Parent's Guide to Positive Discipline
Everything® Parent's Guide to Raising a Successful Child
Everything® Parent's Guide to Raising Boys
Everything® Parent's Guide to Raising Siblings
Everything® Parent's Guide to Sensory Integration Disorder
Everything® Parent's Guide to Tantrums
Everything® Parent's Guide to the Overweight Child
Everything® Parent's Guide to the Strong-Willed Child
Everything® Parenting a Teenager Book
Everything® Potty Training Book, $9.95
Everything® Pregnancy Book, 2nd Ed.
Everything® Pregnancy Fitness Book
Everything® Pregnancy Nutrition Book
Everything® Pregnancy Organizer, 2nd Ed., $16.95
Everything® Toddler Activities Book
Everything® Toddler Book
Everything® Tween Book
Everything® Twins, Triplets, and More Book

PETS

Everything® **Aquarium Book**
Everything® Boxer Book
Everything® Cat Book, 2nd Ed.
Everything® Chihuahua Book
Everything® Dachshund Book
Everything® Dog Book
Everything® Dog Health Book
Everything® **Dog Owner's Organizer,**
    $16.95
Everything® Dog Training and Tricks Book
Everything® German Shepherd Book
Everything® Golden Retriever Book
Everything® Horse Book
Everything® Horse Care Book
Everything® Horseback Riding Book
Everything® Labrador Retriever Book
Everything® Poodle Book
Everything® Pug Book
Everything® Puppy Book
Everything® Rottweiler Book
Everything® Small Dogs Book
Everything® Tropical Fish Book
Everything® Yorkshire Terrier Book

REFERENCE

Everything® Blogging Book
Everything® **Build Your Vocabulary Book**
Everything® Car Care Book
Everything® Classical Mythology Book
Everything® Da Vinci Book
Everything® Divorce Book
Everything® Einstein Book
Everything® Etiquette Book, 2nd Ed.
Everything® Inventions and Patents Book
Everything® Mafia Book
Everything® Philosophy Book
Everything® Psychology Book
Everything® Shakespeare Book

RELIGION

Everything® Angels Book
Everything® Bible Book
Everything® Buddhism Book
Everything® Catholicism Book
Everything® Christianity Book
Everything® History of the Bible Book
Everything® **Jesus Book**
Everything® Jewish History & Heritage Book
Everything® Judaism Book
Everything® Kabbalah Book
Everything® Koran Book
Everything® **Mary Book**

Everything® Mary Magdalene Book
Everything® Prayer Book
Everything® Saints Book
Everything® Torah Book
Everything® Understanding Islam Book
Everything® World's Religions Book
Everything® Zen Book

SCHOOL & CAREERS

Everything® Alternative Careers Book
Everything® **Career Tests Book**
Everything® College Major Test Book
Everything® College Survival Book, 2nd Ed.
Everything® Cover Letter Book, 2nd Ed.
Everything® **Filmmaking Book**
Everything® Get-a-Job Book
Everything® Guide to Being a Paralegal
Everything® Guide to Being a Real Estate
    Agent
Everything® **Guide to Being a Sales Rep**
Everything® **Guide to Careers in Health**
    Care
Everything® **Guide to Careers in Law**
    Enforcement
Everything® **Guide to Government Jobs**
Everything® Guide to Starting and Running
    a Restaurant
Everything® Job Interview Book
Everything® New Nurse Book
Everything® New Teacher Book
Everything® Paying for College Book
Everything® Practice Interview Book
Everything® Resume Book, 2nd Ed.
Everything® Study Book

SELF-HELP

Everything® Dating Book, 2nd Ed.
Everything® Great Sex Book
Everything® Kama Sutra Book
Everything® Self-Esteem Book

SPORTS & FITNESS

Everything® **Easy Fitness Book**
Everything® Fishing Book
Everything® Golf Instruction Book
Everything® Pilates Book
Everything® Running Book
Everything® Weight Training Book
Everything® Yoga Book

TRAVEL

Everything® Family Guide to Cruise Vacations
Everything® Family Guide to Hawaii

Everything® Family Guide to Las Vegas,
    2nd Ed.
Everything® **Family Guide to Mexico**
Everything® Family Guide to New York City,
    2nd Ed.
Everything® Family Guide to RV Travel &
    Campgrounds
Everything® Family Guide to the Caribbean
Everything® Family Guide to the Walt Disney
    World Resort®, Universal Studios®,
    and Greater Orlando, 4th Ed.
Everything® **Family Guide to Timeshares**
Everything® Family Guide to Washington
    D.C., 2nd Ed.
Everything® Guide to New England

WEDDINGS

Everything® Bachelorette Party Book, $9.95
Everything® Bridesmaid Book, $9.95
Everything® **Destination Wedding Book**
Everything® Elopement Book, $9.95
Everything® Father of the Bride Book, $9.95
Everything® Groom Book, $9.95
Everything® Mother of the Bride Book, $9.95
Everything® Outdoor Wedding Book
Everything® Wedding Book, 3rd Ed.
Everything® Wedding Checklist, $9.95
Everything® Wedding Etiquette Book, $9.95
Everything® **Wedding Organizer, 2nd Ed.,**
    $16.95
Everything® Wedding Shower Book, $9.95
Everything® Wedding Vows Book, $9.95
Everything® **Wedding Workout Book**
Everything® Weddings on a Budget Book,
    $9.95

WRITING

Everything® Creative Writing Book
Everything® Get Published Book, 2nd Ed.
Everything® Grammar and Style Book
Everything® Guide to Writing a Book
    Proposal
Everything® Guide to Writing a Novel
Everything® Guide to Writing Children's
    Books
Everything® Guide to Writing Research
    Papers
Everything® Screenwriting Book
Everything® Writing Poetry Book
Everything® Writing Well Book

Available wherever books are sold!
To order, call 800-258-0929, or visit us at *www.everything.com*
Everything® and everything.com® are registered trademarks of F+W Publications, Inc.